A Survey of Chinese-American Manpower and Employment

Betty Lee Sung

The Praeger Special Studies program—utilizing the most modern and efficient book production techniques and a selective worldwide distribution network—makes available to the academic, government, and business communities significant, timely research in U.S. and international economic, social, and political development.

A Survey of Chinese-American Manpower and Employment

PRAEGER SPECIAL STUDIES IN U.S. ECONOMIC, SOCIAL, AND POLITICAL ISSUES

Praeger Publishers   New York   Washington   London

Library of Congress Cataloging in Publication Data

Sung, Betty Lee.
    A survey of Chinese-American manpower and employment.

    (Praeger special studies in U.S. economic, social, and
political issues)
    Bibliography: p.
    Includes index.
    1. Chinese Americans—Employment. 2. Chinese
Americans. I. Title.
HD8081.C5S9   331.6'3'951073   76-14435
ISBN 0-275-23090-2

PRAEGER PUBLISHERS
111 Fourth Avenue, New York, N.Y. 10003, U.S.A.

Published in the United States of America in 1976
by Praeger Publishers, Inc.

© 1976 by Betty Lee Sung

Printed in the United States of America

To my husband

Charles Chia Mou Chung

For the purpose of focusing on racial inequality in employment the Manpower Administration of the U.S. Department of Labor awarded me a grant to undertake a study of the economic characteristics and occupational status of the Chinese in the United States. The intent was to obtain a demographic profile of the Chinese and to determine where the Chinese stand both occupationally and economically. It was suggested that I utilize the findings of the 1970 census instead of undertaking my own survey. This was an excellent suggestion; however, in the past the Census Bureau had tabulated and published very little detailed information about the Chinese. The information was there—all gathered during the taking of the census—but in racial breakdown the Chinese usually were lumped under the indistinguishable heading, "Others." The grant afforded me the opportunity to take the Public Use Sample Tapes and do a special tabulation pertaining to the Chinese.

There are drawbacks to sole reliance upon the 1970 census data. The most obvious one, of course, is that the information is already out-of-date. Rapid increase in the Chinese population over recent years has radically changed the makeup of this ethnic group. Like water that is soaked up by parched land after a drought, the Chinese have been flocking here since 1965 to be reunited with their families. Approximately one-fourth of the Chinese now living in the United States have come in since 1970. Consequently, the census of that year reflected the situation of the settled Chinese, who had been in the United States a bit longer, more than it did the situation of recent immigrants.

Without question, there has been underenumeration of the Chinese, and the excluded population may be sizable. We shall see that the Chinese are heavily concentrated in urban areas and especially in the coastal Chinatowns. Almost half of the population is foreign-born. The native-born are the younger generations, but it is the parents or the foreign-born who fill out the questionnaires. Censuses are definitely not a part of their tradition or background.

The Chinese are highly suspicious of government officials. They had experienced 61 years of stringent exclusion (1882-1943) and 22 more years of restricted immigration (a 105 quota until 1965), so that the ghosts of illegal or extralegal entry still haunt them. These people tend to avoid the census taker.

Chinatowns today are not secure neighborhoods, and people do not readily open their doors to strangers. Even when the door is opened and an interviewer is introduced by a mutual acquaintance, the suspicions are there. A wall of silence greets the census taker.

Fully cognizant of the difficulties that would be encountered, New York's Chinatown carried out an extensive campaign to educate the people and whip up enthusiasm so that everybody would be counted. At the last moment, the New York City Council even voted monies to print the census forms in Chinese. A group of dedicated young people, concerned about underenumeration, worked very hard as census takers, but they would be the first to admit that many Chinese chose not to be counted or were left out inadvertently.

The Chinese who filled out the questionnaires, or who responded to the census takers, tended to be native-born, English-speaking, better educated, and non-Chinatown residents. If we take into account the fact that the data are slanted in these directions, the census is not without its worth. After all, the census attempts a 100 percent head-count and a 20 percent sampling of social and economic characteristics. In interpreting the census data, therefore, one must constantly keep in mind these biases.

In 1970 the Census Bureau devoted a special report to the Japanese, Chinese, and Filipinos for the first time, and this volume, PC(2)1G, provided a wealth of statistics never before tabulated or published. As the data presented in this volume came from the basic records made from the original census questionnaires and were based upon a 20 percent sample, I utilized the data from this volume wherever possible. But my study called for many cross tabulations or other information not found in the special report. Since the basic census records are confidential and not available to the public, I utilized the Public Use Sample Tapes, which had been carefully constructed to reflect as closely as possible an accurate cross section of the demographic characteristics of the American population.

The Public Use Sample Tapes draw upon a 1 percent sample. In comparing the computer print-outs from the tables I constructed with the available 20 percent data from the Census Bureau, I found that the figures for the larger categories were fairly close. In the finer categories and minute breakdowns, there were discrepancies. In those cases, I discounted the data or omitted those tabulations entirely. All data used have been carefully studied and analyzed.

This study was prepared for the Manpower Administration, U.S. Department of Labor, under research and development grant No. 21-36-73-13. Since grantees conducting research and development projects under government sponsorship are encouraged to express their own judgment freely, this study does not necessarily represent the official opinion or policy of the Department of Labor. The grantee is solely responsible for the contents of this book.

A great deal of attention was devoted to scrutiny of the census questionnaire and the Public Use Sample Tapes to see what information could be gleaned and what cross tabulations were possible. For invaluable assistance in this phase of my research, I am indebted to Ms. Tobia Bressler and Nampeo McKenny and their wonderful staff at the Ethnic Origins Division of the Census Bureau.

When the tables were set up and formulated, they were sent to Walter Postle of the Region IX Manpower Administration in San Francisco, who had generously offered me the use of his computer facilities at the Lawrence Radiation Laboratories.

Sylvia Sorrell was assigned to program my tabulations. I cannot stress enough the importance of her expertise in deciphering and translating my needs into meaningful print-outs.

I did not rely upon the census data alone. I searched the bibliographies and indexes for private research materials, as well as other governmental sources. Luckily, the Equal Employment Opportunity Commission (EEOC) reports generated much information on the ethnic makeup of work forces. State and municipal government statistics were combed for comparative purposes. Annual publications, such as Vital Statistics of the United States and the Immigration and Naturalization Service Annual Reports, were goldmine sources.

I tried to corroborate my findings or test them by talking to Chinese people, young and old, from all walks of life and from different regions of the country. I studied the listings pasted on the employment offices in the Chinatowns of San Francisco and New York. I interviewed successful men and women in their fields. I had long talks with my graduating seniors to find out how they went about applying for jobs and what their attitude was toward work and the future. My research assistants were sent out to ascertain the pay scale for certain occupations by asking people on the job.

I would like to acknowledge the contributions of a few of my student assistants. They are Wai Ting Leung, Anita Yue, Chor Lee, Ellen Lau, and Yuk Wah Mui. The voluminous tables in this report were typed by Lillian Ling and Cynthia Sung.

Most important, I was in the midst of where things were happening. New York City has become the focal point of Chinese-American awareness. Ethnic consciousness is most acute with the young and rising generations of Chinese-American youth who are in colleges and universities. At City College, New York, there is an Asian-American student enrollment of approximately 1,400. Its Department of Asian Studies stresses the Asian-American aspect, and it can claim to be the East Coast birthplace of the Asian-American movement.

I needed the activity, the pace, the strong sentiments expressed by my students to cull from their attitudes and to validate my findings. I am also grateful for the strong support given by the college administration that enabled me to undertake this research.

Before and after I embarked on my project, I consulted Dr. Eli Ginzberg of the Graduate School of Business, Columbia University, and recently appointed chairman of President Ford's National Commission for Manpower Policy. In spite of his tremendous commitments to teaching, writing, research, and civic undertakings, he took time out to point me in the right direction and to read my manuscript.

Alan Wong of San Francisco and Danny Yung, both of whom are involved in research on Chinese-Americans, also graciously consented to look over my findings and recommendations.

Of course, none of this research would have been possible were it not for the grant awarded me by the Manpower Administration. At Manpower, ten thousand thanks go to Howard Rosen, Herman Travis, Stuart Garfinkel, Frank Mott, and Karen Greene. Ms. Greene supervised my grant, and she was a Houdini when it came to unraveling red tape.

At the Research Foundation of City College, it was Morton Pavane who hounded me relentlessly until I handed in my proposal, which started the ball rolling, and it was he and his staff who kept a fiscal eye on the grant expenditures.

Credit for editing the manuscript goes to Muriam Hurewitz and Barbara Kelman-Burgower, who helped me tie the report together and who polished those rough edges.

As I have already recounted, this was a massive endeavor involving many groups and many people, all of whom played essential roles in the structuring of this study and report. To each and every one, I again acknowledge my debt and proffer my thanks. One more expression of gratitude remains, and that one goes to my family: To my husband, Charles Chia Mou Chung, for his moral support and understanding, to my daughter, Cynthia Sung, who typed the final report, and to all eight of our children, who shared and spared their mother during these past two and a half years.

CONTENTS

LIST OF TABLES AND MAPS

Here at long last we have a mine of information on the Chinese-American, particularly on manpower and employment characteristics. The subjects include patterns of Chinese immigration, geographical dispersion, demographic characteristics, educational level, occupational pattern, working women, unions, income, unemployment and underemployment, cultural differences, as well as a general discussion on racism in the United States.

Professor Betty Lee Sung is to be commended for not only generating a basic statistical body of data but also for her capacity to select important issues, to ask good questions, to think about them deeply, and to write clearly free of technical jargons. As one reviewer wrote, "she excels in an area where many academics fall down, namely in picking good themes, in knowing how to tackle them, and most importantly in communicating her scholarly findings."

In addition, Professor Sung has made many concrete policy recommendations to expand the occupational opportunities of Chinese-Americans and to include this ethnic group of Americans in the provisions and benefits of minority programs. However, Professor Sung is not a Chinese-American chauvinist; she has argued for a universal approach. For example, she demanded a special commission to review the curriculum and the content of our educational curriculum in order to eliminate "intentional ethnic slurs and stereotyping, not just for Chinese-Americans, but for all ethnic groups."

Winberg Chai

Professor and Chairman
Department of Asian Studies
The City College of New York

PATTERNS OF CHINESE
IMMIGRATION

The history of this nation spans but a few hundred years, and for more than a century and a quarter the Chinese have been a part of it. The Chinese were among the "Forty-niners" who flocked to California during the Gold Rush. These Chinese came from the southern Chinese province of Kwangtung, near the mouth of the Pearl River. They left their homes, braving the unknown, pulling up firmly embedded roots, risking the executioner's ax, and journeying 7,000 miles across the Pacific in sail-driven vessels to seek their fortunes in a new land they called the "Mountain of Gold." They were referring to the hills of San Francisco during the days of the Gold Rush. The pull was the prospect of gold, but the push was the impoverished soil of China, which would yield not even a marginal livelihood—made poorer by civil strife and political unrest.

Hardly two years after the first cry of gold went out, 25,000 stalwarts from Cathay were found in California. The virgin lands and undeveloped country needed hands, and the Chinese willingly provided the manpower to work the mines, drain the ditches, till the soil, harvest the seas, and build the net of railroads that would bind the nation together. When their work was done, their ungrateful beneficiaries said, "America is for whites. Go back to where you came from."

CHINESE EXCLUDED

Thus was set in motion a racist campaign that resulted in a continuing series of legislative maneuvers designed to keep the Chinese out and to make life intolerable for those who remained.

Chinese immigrants dropped from 40,000 in 1882 (prior to exclusion) to 10 persons in the year 1887. During the following 61 years, 14 separate pieces of legislation were enacted by the U.S. Congress that virtually sealed the doors of the United States against Chinese immigration. These laws were repealed in 1943, when a gesture of goodwill was made toward China, but repeal was little more than that —a gesture.

Beginning in 1943, the Chinese were given a quota of 105 immigrants per year, and this quota included anyone of Chinese blood, regardless of his country of birth or residence or allegiance. For the next 22 years, until 1965, a mere 6,055 Chinese were admitted to the United States. This figure included persons admitted under a number of refugee relief acts.

To preserve themselves against complete extinction, the Chinese resorted to inconspicuous circumvention of the immigration laws so that, for a half century before repeal, the Chinese population for the entire country hovered around 60,000 to 80,000 and was almost all adult male, with few females and few children. It was the express intent of the U.S. government to keep it that way.

Governmental policy was directed not only against the Chinese but also against any people of darker shades of skin (the most desirable were the Northern European types). This intent was spelled out in the immigration laws by the national origins quotas; Great Britain, Germany, Ireland, and the Scandinavian countries had claim to about 120,000 quota slots out of the 150,000 total available annually. By 1965, this racist viewpoint was no longer in vogue and was absolutely indefensible. The national origins quotas were amended and an entirely different premise substituted for U.S. immigration policy.

China and most other Asiatic countries were prime beneficiaries of this change in the immigration laws. With the exception of Japan, with a quota of 185, Turkey, with a quota of 225, and, of course, the Chinese with 105, no other Asian country had had a quota of more than 100. The Immigration Act of 1965 extended the upper limit of any one country to 20,000. Consequently, it was inevitable that a spurt in Asian immigration would result.

IMMIGRATION LAWS RELAXED

Since 1965 and the liberalization of quotas, Chinese immigration in particular has been spectacular. Table 1.1 shows the rate by sex at which Chinese aliens were admitted to the United States for 31 years following repeal of the exclusion acts. If admittance had depended solely upon the 105 quota allotted to Chinese persons, the total numbers would have remained in the hundreds. But in 1946 some re-

TABLE 1.1

Chinese Immigrants Admitted, by Sex, 1944–74

Year	Male	Per-cent	Female	Per-cent	Annual Total
1944	10	29	24	71	34
1945	20	41	64	59	109
1946	71	31	162	69	233
1947	142	13	986	87	1,128
1948	257	8	3,317	92	3,574
1949	242	10	2,248	90	2,490
1950	110	8	1,179	92	1,289
1951	126	11	957	89	1,083
1952	118	10	1,034	90	1,152
1953	203	19	890	81	1,093
1954	1,511	55	1,236	45	2,747
1955	1,261	48	1,367	52	2,628
1956	2,007	45	2,443	55	4,450
1957	2,487	49	2,636	51	5,123
1958	1,396	44	1,799	56	3,195
1959	2,846	47	3,185	53	6,031
1960	1,873	51	1,799	49	3,672
1961	1,565	41	2,273	59	3,838
1962	1,916	42	2,753	58	4,669
1963	2,297	43	3,073	57	5,370
1964	2,597	46	3,051	54	5,648
1965	2,242	47	2,527	53	4,769
1966	8,613	49	8,995	51	17,608
1967	12,811	51	12,285	49	25,096
1968	7,862	48	8,572	52	16,434
1969	10,001	48	10,892	52	20,893
1970	8,586	48	9,370	52	17,956
1971	8,287	47	9,335	53	17,622
1972	10,437	48	11,293	52	21,730
1973	9,937	46	11,719	54	21,656
1974	10,724	47	11,961	53	22,685

Source: U.S. Department of Justice, Immigration and Naturalization Service, Annual Reports (Washington, D.C., 1944–74).

3

lief was given by a proviso permitting Chinese male citizens to bring their wives and children into the country without charge to the national quota. That same year the War Brides Act was passed, allowing GI wives to join their husbands in the United States, again without charge to the quotas. Consequently, Chinese immigration slowly climbed up to 6,000 until President John Kennedy, by executive order, permitted the admission of a number of refugees. This took Chinese immigration into a higher plateau, but it was not until the full force of the Immigration Act of 1965 took effect that immigration really soared, increasing by as much as 400 percent to 500 percent.

This percentage increase can be exploited by sensationalism and it has been. Scaremongers are already headlining their articles with captions like "Growing Surge of Immigrants from Asia" and "Trickle Turns to Flood." Few take note of the fact that the base was so small for so long and that, consequently, a comparable increase in numbers for other countries with larger immigration bases would yield smaller percentage increases.

Nonetheless, the spurt in immigration has made a tremendous impact upon the Chinese communities in the United States and has completely altered the demographic characteristics of this ethnic group. The immigrants of yesteryear were able-bodied males whose purpose in coming was to earn and save enough to go back to China. They brought no family, and they lived the lives of rootless transients. They filled the gap in the lower occupational strata, working at jobs that others disdained. They clustered in Chinatowns for the familiarity and security in numbers. They were poorly educated and made little or no attempt to learn the English language.

Before 1943, Chinese immigrants were not permitted to become citizens no matter how long they had resided in this country, so they had no political backing and little use for American customs or ways. They were made scapegoats for the ills of the times and were used as a political football to be booted and booed at even when their numbers had dwindled to the point of insignificance. They were forbidden by the Alien Land Acts to own land. Denied a normal family life by a court ruling that all Asians were aliens ineligible to citizenship and hence not permitted the benefits of the family reunification aims under the immigration laws, they were also denied the right to intermarry in many western states.

Thus oppressed by the weight of institutionalized discrimination, the Chinese worked hard within his circumscribed confines, looking only to the day when he could be free to return to his homeland. The Chinese was not an immigrant, but a transient, a sojourner. Each generation departed these shores leaving no roots that reached into American soil. In spite of the long history of the Chinese in this country, each successive generation had to start anew without the benefit of a foundation built by those before him.

The picture began to change after World War II. The impetus
was not the repeal of the entire body of Chinese exclusion acts in 1943
—the 105 quota was tantamount to exclusion and was so intended. It
was the War Brides Act of 1946 that wedged open the door for wives
of Chinese who had served in the Armed Forces of the United States.
The spurt in Chinese immigration after 1946 (see Table 1.1) reveals
that almost 90 percent of the immigrants were females taking the first
opportunity they could to join their husbands in this country.

Almost every year since that time, female immigrants have exceeded males. The tremendous disparity of the sexes seems to exert
a magnetic pull that is still evident among Chinese immigrants today.
The proportion of females to males hovered around 9:1 for many years.
It has declined, but as late as 1973 females still made up 54 percent
of the total Chinese immigrants (see Tables 1.2 and 1.3).

The predominance of the female in the Chinese immigration
pattern has great implications for the Chinese population in this country. For one, the genocidal policy of cutting off a future native-born
Chinese generation was arrested. Children born of the reunions made
possible by the War Brides Act are the emerging leaders of their people, and their outlook is entirely different from that of past generations.
The communities are now better established by the presence of women
and children, young and old, thus bringing about a restructuring of
Chinese society into families rather than communal organizations.

AGE GROUPS

An outstanding feature of the Chinese female immigrants is that
generally one-fourth to one-third are concentrated in the 20- to 29-
year age group. This one factor has held constant for more than a
decade (see Table 1.3). It probably indicates that females are generally taken as brides in China and then are brought to the United States
by husbands at least ten years older than they, for the largest age
group for male immigrants is the 30- to 39-year one.

The fact that Chinese immigrants consist overwhelmingly of
grown adults has several implications. First, these people are already
set in their ways and outlook. In other words, adjustment takes longer
than for the younger ones, and most likely there will be a gravitation
toward Chinatowns. Second, these immigrants will need to seek a
livelihood immediately. Third, they are producers rather than de-
pendents; instead of adding to the taxpayers' expense for schooling,
they will join the labor force directly.

Immigration below the ten-year age bracket is insignificant.
The future young of the Chinese-American population will be the offspring of the heavy influx of young women and will be native-born. At

TABLE 1.2

Chinese Immigrants Admitted, by Sex and Age Group, 1962-73

	1962		1963		1964		1965		1966		1967	
	Male	Female	Male	Female	Male	Female	Male	Female	Male	Female	Male	Female
Under 5 years	92	160	98	110	102	137	78	103	548	520	734	646
5-9 years	104	85	115	117	135	165	117	115	953	828	1,125	1,006
10-19 years	335	335	389	483	419	448	439	430	1,888	1,739	2,309	2,187
20-29 years	319	885	411	992	316	939	338	704	1,376	1,649	2,221	2,913
30-39 years	232	409	407	509	554	611	438	398	1,817	1,480	3,310	2,329
40-49 years	210	306	256	315	355	312	293	294	998	912	1,528	1,223
50-59 years	278	311	262	302	288	277	226	274	532	904	879	955
60-69 years	279	192	276	193	327	128	221	165	355	630	514	683
70-79 years	61	54	77	51	86	32	82	41	130	289	160	288
80 years and over	6	15	6	1	15	2	10	3	16	44	31	55
Total	1,916	2,752	2,297	3,073	2,597	3,051	2,242	2,527	8,613	8,995	12,811	12,285
Total immigrants	4,669		5,370		5,648		4,769		17,608		25,096	

	1968		1969		1970		1971		1972		1973	
	Male	Female	Male	Female	Male	Female	Male	Female	Male	Female	Male	Female
Under 5 years	399	450	686	622	437	438	396	390	617	531	571	539
5-9 years	639	518	989	891	685	636	561	509	755	734	750	660
10-19 years	1,412	1,523	1,964	2,037	1,427	1,428	1,153	1,245	1,506	1,548	1,445	1,583
20-29 years	1,436	2,409	1,588	2,756	1,776	3,249	2,106	3,679	2,610	4,264	2,537	4,058
30-39 years	1,996	1,478	2,337	1,823	2,258	1,602	2,345	1,606	2,622	1,797	1,981	1,630
40-49 years	904	789	1,277	1,182	1,028	862	901	767	1,234	965	1,164	1,045
50-59 years	530	645	709	744	551	557	484	556	629	688	765	1,119
60-69 years	379	478	311	545	285	374	246	367	323	467	526	743
70-79 years	151	223	117	239	117	177	87	171	112	239	174	277
80 years and over	16	59	23	53	22	47	8	45	29	60	24	65
Total	7,862	8,572	10,001	10,892	8,586	9,370	8,287	9,335	10,437	11,293	9,937	11,719
Total immigrants	16,434		20,893		17,956		17,622		21,730		21,656	

Source: U.S. Department of Justice, Immigration and Naturalization Service, Annual Reports (Washington, D.C., 1962-73), Table 9.

6

TABLE 1.3

Percentage of Chinese Immigrants Admitted, by Sex and Age Group, 1962–73

	1962		1963		1964		1965		1966		1967	
	Male	Female	Male	Female	Male	Female	Male	Female	Male	Female	Male	Female
Under 5 years	4.8	5.8	4.3	3.6	3.9	4.5	3.5	4.1	6.4	5.8	5.7	5.3
5–9 years	5.4	3.1	5.0	3.8	5.2	5.4	5.2	4.6	11.1	9.2	8.8	8.2
10–19 years	17.5	12.2	16.9	15.7	16.1	14.7	19.6	17.0	21.9	19.3	18.0	17.8
20–29 years	16.6	32.1	17.9	32.3	12.2	30.8	15.1	27.9	16.0	18.3	17.3	23.7
30–39 years	12.1	14.9	17.7	16.6	21.3	20.0	19.5	15.7	21.1	16.5	25.8	19.0
40–49 years	11.0	11.1	11.1	10.3	13.7	10.2	13.1	11.6	11.6	10.1	11.9	10.0
50–59 years	14.5	11.3	11.4	9.8	11.1	9.1	10.1	10.8	6.2	10.1	6.9	7.8
60–69 years	14.6	7.0	12.0	6.3	12.6	4.2	9.9	6.5	4.1	7.0	4.0	5.6
70–79 years	3.2	2.0	3.4	1.7	3.3	1.0	3.7	1.6	1.5	3.2	1.2	2.3
80 and over	0.3	0.5	0.3	0.0	0.6	0.1	0.4	0.1	0.2	0.5	0.2	0.4
Total	100.0	100.0	100.0	100.0	100.0	100.0	100.0	100.0	100.0	100.0	100.0	100.0

	1968		1969		1970		1971		1972		1973	
	Male	Female	Male	Female	Male	Female	Male	Female	Male	Female	Male	Female
Under 5 years	5.1	5.2	6.9	5.7	5.1	4.7	4.8	4.2	5.9	4.7	5.8	4.6
5–9 years	8.1	6.0	9.9	8.2	8.0	6.8	6.8	5.5	7.2	6.5	7.6	5.6
10–19 years	18.0	17.5	19.6	18.7	16.6	15.2	13.9	13.3	14.4	13.7	14.5	13.5
20–29 years	18.3	28.1	15.9	25.3	20.7	34.7	25.4	39.4	25.0	37.8	25.5	34.6
30–39 years	25.4	17.2	23.4	16.7	26.3	17.1	28.3	17.2	25.1	15.9	19.9	13.9
40–49 years	11.5	9.2	12.8	10.9	12.0	9.2	10.9	8.2	11.8	8.5	11.7	8.9
50–59 years	6.7	7.5	7.1	6.8	6.4	5.9	5.8	6.0	6.0	6.1	7.7	9.6
60–69 years	4.8	5.6	3.1	5.0	3.3	4.0	3.0	3.9	3.1	4.1	5.3	6.3
70–79 years	1.9	2.6	1.2	2.2	1.4	1.9	1.0	1.8	1.1	2.1	1.8	2.4
80 and over	0.2	0.7	0.2	0.5	0.3	0.5	0.1	0.5	0.3	0.5	0.2	0.6
Total	100.0	100.0	100.0	100.0	100.0	100.0	100.0	100.0	100.0	100.0	100.0	100.0

Source: Table 1.2.

7

the same time, it is unusual to see men and women in their 80s immigrating to the United States. This is a definite departure from the past, when the old invariably returned to China to enjoy their latter years and be buried in the motherland; traffic now seems to be heading the other way. These elderly are not all sitting in their rocking chairs, smiling benignly at their large brood of grandchildren. In fact, one-fourth of the Chinese males over 65 are still in the labor force, as are one-eighth of the females in the same age bracket (see Table 5.1).

INTENDED RESIDENCE IN THE UNITED STATES

In 1960 the census showed that three states contained almost three-fourths of all the Chinese in the United States. California held the lead with 40 percent; New York and Hawaii trailed with 16 percent each. By 1970 a shift had taken place. California maintained its position, but New York pulled ahead of Hawaii and more than doubled its Chinese population. By looking at Table 1.4 one can readily see why. Immigrants heading for New York outnumbered by a wide margin those who indicated that their future home would be in San Francisco/Oakland, Honolulu, Los Angeles, or Chicago. California's population increase is coming from births, but New York's increase is coming from immigration. Consequently, the native-born/foreign-born ratio for the three states varies widely:

	Percent Native-Born	Percent Foreign-Born
California	54.4	45.6
New York	35.6	64.4
Hawaii	88.9	11.1

What significance do these figures have? A trans-Pacific leap means major readjustment for the new immigrants, who must deal with a new environment, new culture, new language, and new social alignments all at once. The experience at times is overwhelming and bewildering. The Chinese community of New York, therefore, will experience greater difficulties than that of Hawaii or California because of its larger percentage of newcomers, especially in view of the fact that cities like New York are losing jobs rapidly to the suburban areas or, more likely, to other areas of the country.

TABLE 1.4

Intended City of Residence of Chinese Immigrants, Years Ending June 30, 1962–72

	1962	1963	1964	1965	1966	1967	1968	1969	1970	1971	1972
San Francisco and Oakland	831	853	764	799	3,621	3,233	1,827	2,502	1,845	968	1,696
New York City and New Jersey	999	1,010	957	817	3,336	4,624	3,029	3,304	2,776	3,263	4,839
Honolulu	93	113	89	90	303	294	220	369	385	242	334
Los Angeles and Long Beach	210	257	241	262	865	1,300	772	938	743	802	930
Sacramento	76	76	77	87	402	353	146	223	163	107	146
Seattle	66	88	122	55	207	301	224	251	158	150	199
Chicago	88	161	206	104	306	754	386	407	367	402	661
Boston and Cambridge	75	104	110	100	337	418	308	252	206	223	241
Philadelphia	33	34	47	22	82	167	119	136	99	135	184
Houston	42	44	37	34	124	175	121	155	184	106	177

Source: U.S. Department of Justice, Immigration and Naturalization Service, Annual Reports (Washington, D.C., 1962–72), Table 12B.

ORIGINS

In the past, Chinese immigrants generally have originated from the area within a small radius of the mouth of the Pearl River near the city of Canton. The district of Toishan and four districts adjoining it are the fountainhead. To ascertain whether Chinese immigrants are more diverse in their places of origin now or whether these places are still the main sources of immigration to the United States, a count was taken from the data of a study now under way by the China Institute. Of those indicating their home town, 48 percent of those surveyed in 1972 were from Sze Yup, or the four districts, and 30 percent were from Toishan itself—12 percent were from the city of Canton. Chinese immigrants are still predominantly Toishanese, but those from other areas and provinces are increasing.

The immigrants hail from the abovementioned districts in mainland China, but they embark from Hong Kong because an exit visa is difficult to obtain from the Chinese government. An exit visa is also required to leave Taiwan, and immigrants to the United States from this island constitute a growing proportion, though not as great as that from the Pearl River Delta. These two groups speak a different dialect, and their backgrounds are quite dissimilar.

OCCUPATIONS

Because of such past immigration barriers to this country as exclusion, circumvention of the laws, and detention in quasi-prisons like Ellis Island or Angel's Island, only the laboring classes subjected themselves to the indignities of trying to gain admission to the United States. What Chinese of any wealth, position, background, or educational attainment would come to the United States? Not until the 1950s was there any shift in the emphasis from brawn to brains.

The very early immigrants were miners, farmers, and railroad laborers. Then followed the service workers and operatives, who perpetuated themselves in the laundry and restaurant businesses until recent times. Today, of those who indicate their occupation in their application for immigration, the largest percentage are professionals and technicians. This can be verified by the figures put out by the Immigration and Naturalization Service, by a direct tabulation of applications from the Hong Kong Consulate and by a special tabulation of the 1970 census. This preponderance of professionals also holds true for immigrants from other nations.

Since 1966 especially, the professional and technical category exceeded the other occupational groups by a wide margin. To a large measure this is dictated by the preference system of the Immigration

Act of 1965, which gives priority to those with needed skills and training. On the other hand, it is also a reflection of the flight of the intel-
ligentsia and monied classes from China, Taiwan, and Hong Kong following the overthrow of the Nationalist government and the takeover
by Mao Tse-tung in 1949. An elite corps of former officials and experienced personnel in business, technology, and education sought political refuge in this country, and this group has contributed immeasur-
ably to the advancement of science, medicine, art, and the understanding of China. Thousands of these refugees now teach in the American
colleges and universities, and thousands more are in private industry
and enterprises. Since 1949, over 20,000 Chinese have entered the
country under the various refugee relief acts (see Table 1.5).

STUDENTS AND INTELLECTUALS

From the American point of view, the high caliber of recent
Chinese immigrants is a positive factor because the human resources
of a nation are its most valuable asset. But from the point of view of
the emigrating nation, it is an incalculable loss and what is popularly
termed a "brain drain."

The anomaly of the situation is that the brain drain is not always
reflected in the official immigration figures. Many Chinese are admitted under nonimmigrant classifications as officials or students or
visitors. Afterward, their status is adjusted to permit them to remain
in this country.

As shown in Table 1.6, the number of students from China and
Hong Kong admitted to this country over the past ten years has increased from 2,045 in 1963 to 9,189 in 1974 (Taiwanese students are
included in the figures). These students must be college graduates,
over 22 years old, and, if male, have completed their military service.
Most must qualify by highly competitive examinations before they are
permitted to go abroad for higher study. These students are the cream
of the crop. Their family circumstances also must be above average
to enable their parents to support sons and daughters abroad. The
students are more likely to be males because of the traditional emphasis placed upon giving males in the family better educational opportunities.

Students of Chinese descent originating from Southeast Asia,
Canada, or Latin America are tabulated separately under their country
of origin. In the United States, these students tend to identify more
closely with the Chinese population than with the country that issued
them a passport, but they are not counted in the totals of Chinese students.

TABLE 1.5

Immigrant Aliens Admitted from China or Hong Kong as Region of Birth, by Major Occupational Group, 1950–72

	1950	1951	1952	1953	1954	1955	1956	1957	1958	1958	1959	1959	1960	1960	1961	1961
Number admitted	1,494	1,821	1,421	1,536	2,770	2,705	4,450	5,425	3,213	342	5,722	844	3,681	475	3,213	625
Professional, technical, and kindred workers	83	106	70	66	95	118	551	1,029	589	52	787	63	279	40	182	22
Farmers and farm managers	1	2	4	—	—	3	32	12	4	—	12	1	12	—	4	—
Managers, officials, and proprietors	9	21	16	15	33	43	119	250	108	6	231	9	251	6	198	6
Clerical and kindred workers	39	99	35	17	35	52	214	392	101	50	233	60	155	26	94	51
Sales workers	7	47	3	5	2	17	44	67	29	5	65	4	33	2	15	3
Craftsmen, foremen, and kindred workers	11	58	14	3	12	7	60	60	25	2	68	2	63	1	36	—
Operatives and kindred workers	2	13	9	16	24	16	64	74	38	1	196	2	245	2	152	3
Private household workers	1	1	6	2	4	6	44	49	22	1	26	1	37	—	18	4
Service workers, except private household	3	18	4	5	18	36	110	321	235	3	388	6	386	6	255	4
Farm laborers and foremen	—	2	7	—	—	1	22	12	10	—	20	—	9	—	10	—
Laborers, except farm and mine	2	3	2	—	—	1	27	14	9	—	16	—	34	—	18	—
No occupation	1,336	1,451	1,251	1,407	2,547	2,405	3,163	3,145	2,043	224	3,680	696	2,177	392	2,231	532

	1962	1963	1964	1965	1966	1967	1968	1969	1970	1971	1972
Number admitted	4,017 652	4,658 712	5,009 639	4,057 712	13,736 3,872	19,741 5,355	12,738 3,676	15,440 5,453	14,093 3,868	14,417 3,205	17,339 4,391
Professional, technical, and kindred workers	270 44	712 96	1,014 53	281 79	1,142 139	3,924 403	2,536 344	2,688 194	3,715 209	4,108 184	4,060 203
Farmers and farm managers	3 —	5 —	6 —	27 —	30 —	23 3	18 1	15 —	18 —	4 1	1 —
Managers, officials, and proprietors	239 10	223 7	307 13	307 9	573 15	851 58	539 69	569 48	544 36	458 24	672 46
Clerical and kindred workers	168 39	160 48	157 42	143 37	585 42	739 141	481 103	640 82	603 97	541 106	746 117
Sales workers	26 4	38 8	42 19	37 5	213 13	184 33	107 26	199 17	137 18	132 23	196 21
Craftsmen, foremen, and kindred workers	62 2	43 2	40 5	59 1	251 9	349 16	221 19	445 19	325 22	349 12	464 16
Operatives and kindred workers	233 2	254 6	207 —	287 7	1,386 29	1,298 52	603 28	706 29	575 44	610 62	971 94
Private household workers	66 1	57 4	12 1	20 3	133 4	251 15	345 13	519 23	218 5	127 2	229 4
Service workers, except private household	332 7	336 7	382 8	473 11	1,884 37	2,023 84	1,091 48	1,253 37	980 47	1,145 44	1,513 65
Farm laborers and foremen	5 —	9 —	14 —	14 1	34 —	27 3	23 4	17 1	13 3	16 3	22 —
Laborers, except farm and mine	27 —	24 —	13 —	12 —	88 1	155 7	105 5	300 16	164 15	55 2	145 6
No occupation	2,586 543	2,797 534	2,838 517	2,372 559	7,417 3,583	9,917 4,540	6,669 3,036	8,089 4,987	6,801 3,367	6,872 2,745	8,320 3,819

Note: Beginning with 1958, top figure refers to China, including Taiwan, and bottom figure refers to Hong Kong.

Source: U.S. Department of Justice, Immigration and Naturalization Service, Annual Reports (Washington, D.C., 1950–72).

13

TABLE 1.6

Students Admitted to the United States from Hong Kong and China,
1963-74

Year	Hong Kong	China	Total
1963	831	1,214	2,045
1964	854	1,674	2,528
1965	895	1,995	2,890
1966	1,202	2,713	3,915
1967	1,287	2,127	3,414
1968	1,673	2,306	3,979
1969	2,412	3,082	5,494
1970	3,336	3,400	6,736
1971	3,954	3,014	6,968
1972	4,633	3,561	8;194
1973	3,645	4,161	7,806
1974	4,550	4,639	9,189

Note: China includes Taiwan.

Source: U.S. Department of Justice, Immigration and Naturalization Service, Annual Reports (Washington, D.C., 1963-72).

Of those who leave Hong Kong, mainland China, and Taiwan, how many remain in this country? The information here is taken from two separate studies by Tai K. Oh,[1] and Shu Yuan Chang.[2] Oh based his deductions on a survey of Asian students on the campuses of the Universities of Wisconsin and Minnesota. His estimate of those who did not plan to leave the United States immediately upon completion of their studies was approximately 80 percent at the highest and 46 percent at the lowest. Chang's study included intellectuals as well as students. When queried whether they would like to remain permanently in the United States, only half said yes, 10 percent were undecided, and 40 percent said no. Yet Chang found that only 2 percent to 6 percent of the Chinese students from Taiwan actually went back during the years 1962-69.

This discrepancy is quite revealing. Many do not intend or desire to remain, but they stay anyway, hoping that political conditions in their homeland will improve so that they can go home. These students or intellectuals have tasted freedom and want to live under a more democratic form of government. This is one of the main reasons why they prefer the United States to their motherland.[3]

OBJECTIVE: FAMILY REUNIFICATION

In Table 1.5 the column on the far right, labeled "No Occupation," is consistently the largest proportion of the Chinese immigrants. Taking the year 1970 as an example, of the 17,961 persons admitted, 10,168 said they had no occupation. Of these, 5,051 were under 19 years of age and 742 said they were over 60 (see Table 1.2). Of the remainder, no doubt most are women—wives and mothers who keep a home for their families. From these figures it is obvious that well over half of the immigrants from China and Hong Kong are not immediate contenders in the labor market. But they lend stability to the Chinese community by immigrating as part of a family unit or to be reunited with family members already in the United States. Immediate family members such as spouse and children are entitled to enter the country without charge to the quota. Table 1.7 shows Chinese immigration by quota and nonquota. One can see a steady and consistent decline in the nonquota column, indicating that the objective of family reunification may soon be achieved and that most future Chinese immigrants will be coming in under the numerical limitations and preference categories of the quota.

In essence, then, Chinese immigration consists of two major groups, both of which directly reflect the immigration policy of the U.S. government. At one extreme, we have highly qualified profes-

TABLE 1.7

Quota and Nonquota Immigrants from China and Hong Kong, 1963-72

Year	Quota		Nonquota	
	Number	Percent	Number	Percent
1963	367	6.8	5,003	93.2
1964	333	5.9	5,315	94.1
1965	1,152	24.2	3,617	75.8
1966	12,900	73.3	4,708	26.7
1967	19,712	78.5	5,384	21.5
1968	12,386	75.4	4,048	24.7
1969	17,258	82.6	3,635	17.4
1970	14,699	81.9	3,257	18.1
1971	14,598	82.8	3,024	17.2
1972	16,546	85.2	2,881	14.8

Source: U.S. Department of Justice, Immigration and Naturalization Service, Annual Reports (Washington, D.C., 1963-72).

sionals, screened under the third preference of the Immigration Law of 1965, who, in all probability, are somewhat conversant in English. The other extreme mirrors the family reunification goal. This latter group consists of relatives of former immigrants. In general, the latter group has a lower educational and socioeconomic background. By and large, they do not speak English and will have greater difficulty accommodating themselves to life in the United States.

WORK AND PAY

Among the conditions upon which a visa is issued to an immigrant are that he have a sponsor and can demonstrate that he will not be a public charge. In other words, he must have an offer of employment from an employer and certification from the U.S. Department of Labor that his line of work does not compete unduly with jobs of U.S. citizens. The Department of Labor also requires that his skills or training be in short supply or in demand in this country. Consequently, most immigrants will not be unemployed. Their primary problem is underemployment. For instance, a former official in the Chinese government with years of technical experience to his credit accepted a draftsman's job, primarily because that firm offered to sponsor him. There are innumerable other instances of former doctors, teachers, accountants, engineers, and the like who take jobs as janitors and waiters when they first arrive. Some stay in the rut because of language problems or because they are afraid to venture out and compete vigorously in the job market. For others, it is a matter of time before they can utilize their knowledge and skills in the profession in which they were educated.

David S. North found that upper occupational level immigrants generally moved lower and the lower occupational level immigrants generally moved upward right after arrival in this country. The crucial factor in job success was command of the English language. [4]

In the case of the Chinese, although a concentration toward the lower pay scale can be seen for recent immigrants, an isolated few have already penetrated the $20,000 plus level.

ILLEGAL ENTRY

In the past, illegal entry was fairly commonplace because that was practically the only way to gain admission to this country. The fear of detection was so great that the Chinese refrained from any publicity or visibility. Illegal entry is not as widespread today. The Chinese can enter as bonafide immigrants and these make up the larger

TABLE 1.8

Chinese Found Deportable by Violation of Status,
1963-72

Year	Visitor	Student	Crewmen
1963	238	282	1,979
1964	265	293	2,182
1965	339	431	3,068
1966	388	618	2,855
1967	507	779	1,963
1968	588	992	3,232
1969	554	953	5,263
1970	550	705	3,519
1971	534	828	2,910
1972	605	456	4,692

Source: U.S. Department of Justice, Immigration and Naturalization Service, Annual Reports (Washington, D.C., 1963-72), Table
27B.

numbers. Violators of the immigration laws generally fall into the
categories of visitors, students, and crewmen. These people are admitted to the United States as nonimmigrants. In other words, they
enter the country for a specific purpose, and they are required to
leave after that purpose is fulfilled. There is an increase in the number of illegal nonimmigrants.

In 1972, 64,000 visitors from China came in as tourists or for
a brief visit, and most departed. Table 1.8 shows us that approximately 600 who were apprehended overstayed their visit. This may
have been intentional or inadvertent, but the numbers who violated
their status are small in relation to the numbers who came. Students
who stay on after they have finished school are more numerous. By
and large, these students file quickly to readjust their status to permanent resident so that they will not be in violation of the immigration laws. Since 1973, when a new immigration ruling went into effect,
students from Hong Kong have found it more difficult to adjust their
status. "Jumping ship" is the popular term used for the failure of a
crewman to leave the country when his shore leave is up. For some,
the overstay is unintentional: they cannot find another vessel to ship
out on before their leave expires. Technically, they are in violation
of their immigration status and are subject to deportation.

Austin T. Fragomen asserts that approximately 2,900 Chinese who entered the country without inspection were deported in 1973.[5] Presumably, these people were smuggled in. How this was accomplished and how they were apprehended as entering without inspection are not known. Nonetheless, the rate of apprehension is quite high.

HERE TO STAY

Unlike the Chinese immigrant in bygone years, today's immigrant is here to stay. This fact can be ascertained by the increasing numbers who apply for citizenship. The jump from 2,800 naturalized immigrants in 1971 to 9,056 in 1973 attests to the eagerness with which the Chinese are becoming citizens as soon as they fulfill the requirements (see Table 2.4). The reason why the numbers are not greater than they are is that there is a waiting period of five years before citizenship can be conferred. Large-scale Chinese immigration was not possible before 1965. The bureaucratic process and red tape add to the interval between setting foot on American soil and the issuance of naturalization papers.

SUMMARY OF FINDINGS

1. The first wave of Chinese immigrants were pioneers of the American West.

2. In spite of its long history, the Chinese-American population has continually been a first-generation one made up predominantly of adult males. This distorted population picture was brought about by 61 years of Chinese exclusion and 22 more years of restricted immigration.

3. The impact of the Immigration Act of 1965 on the Chinese-American community has been tremendous. The Chinese are the fourth largest immigrant group in the United States today. They are fully utilizing their annual quota of 20,000.

4. Since 1946, Chinese immigrants have been predominantly female. About one-fourth of the females fall within the 20- to 29-year age group and one-half within the 20- to 39-year age group. Male immigrants are older. The largest age group is 30-39 years old.

5. Whereas former immigrants were from the lower socioeconomic classes, today's immigrants are gradually shifting toward the professional and technical classes.

6. Approximately one-half of the immigrants do not indicate an occupation. In all likelihood, these are housewives who did not work outside the home in China.

7. The Chinese immigrants are still a fairly homogeneous group hailing primarily from the Canton area, but this homogeneity is being diluted.

8. By the shifting of the proportion between quota and nonquota immigrants, the effects of governmental policy toward family reunification may be leveling off and the upper limits of Chinese immigration may stabilize around the 20,000 annual national quota.

9. Crewmen are the most common violators of the immigration laws, according to the Immigration and Naturalization Service, but the rate of apprehension is high.

10. Today's Chinese immigrant is no longer a sojourner. He intends to put down roots in this country and to make it his home.

RECOMMENDATIONS

Congress should reexamine its immigration policy and laws with respect to its third and sixth preference quotas, which have brought about a drastic change in the type of men and women coming into the United States.

As presently set up, the law favors those with better education, skills, and money. Is the United States to be a haven only for the privileged and the rich? Is it fair to the world's developing countries to siphon off the cream of their sons and daughters? The law should be revised for a more equitable mix of rich and poor, male and female, young and old, and not be restricted primarily to the highly skilled and educated and to those who can show that they have at least $10,000 in the bank to bring into the United States.

Another reason for the reexamination of our immigration policy is the manpower anomaly that it creates. The immigrant of yesteryear was expected to come in at the bottom and work his way up. Today's immigrant is screened for his education and skills, and he cannot be expected to start at the lowest rung in the economic ladder. Yet, at the same time, he may be denied the choicer occupations.

The federal government should allocate some resources to an immigrant aid program for the Chinese. Since 1949, 216,000 Chinese have been admitted to this country. This large and sudden influx has taxed the facilities of the Chinese-American communities that used to take care of their own. These Chinese, by and large, are no less refugees than the Cubans who were aided by a massive government program. The success of the Cuban Refugee Program has been hailed as a prime example of how government seed money can be utilized to advantage, for in aiding these people in their transition the economy of those places where the Cubans have resettled has benefited considerably.

The Chinese are no less deserving of a helping hand. They have suffered nearly a century of discriminatory immigration practices against them. In this period of transition and readjustment, cognizance must be taken of the immigration difficulties that some Chinese communities are now facing.

NOTES

1. Tai K. Oh, "A New Estimate of the Student Brain Drain from Asia," International Migration Review 7 (1972): 449–56.

2. Shu Yuan Chang, "China or Taiwan: The Political Crisis of the Chinese Intellectual," Amerasia Journal 2 (Fall 1973): 47–81.

3. Ibid.

4. David S. North, "Immigrants and the American Labor Market," 31 (Washington, D.C.: U.S. Department of Labor, 1974).

5. Austin T. Fragomen, "The Illegal Alien: Criminal or Economic Refugee?" (New York: Center for Migration Studies, 1973).

2

**FOREIGN-BORN
AND ALIEN**

The very fact that the Chinese population in the United States is by and large an immigrant group creates for them special problems of employment. To be foreign-born, alien, and non-English speaking are decided disadvantages that are not easily overcome.

NATIVITY

Each decade since 1900 has seen an increase in the percentage of native-born Chinese in America and a corresponding decrease in the percentage of foreign-born. The year 1970 was an exception to this trend (see Table 2.1).

It is this author's belief that the 1980 decennial census will show a greater percentage of foreign-born Chinese for two basic reasons. The Chinese birthrate is 1.5—less than the replacement rate of 2.1. Each year from 6,000 to 7,000 Chinese babies are born (see Table 2.2), whereas annual immigration from China runs close to 20,000. There is no question that the Chinese population in the United States will be sustained by immigration and not by native births.

The native-born/foreign-born proportions vary greatly from state to state. In New York, the percentage of foreign-born runs as high as 64; in Hawaii, it is 11 percent; in California, 46 percent.

In actuality, the proportion of foreign-born is greater than it seems because of the definition of "native-born" as held by the U.S. Census Bureau. It includes in the category of native-born people born abroad who have at least one parent who is a U.S. citizen. In other words, if a person were born in China but his father claimed U.S. citizenship, he would be classified as native-born. This derivative

TABLE 2.1

Nativity of Chinese in the United States, 1900–70
(in percent)

Year	Native–Born	Foreign–Born
1900	10	90
1910	21	79
1920	30	70
1930	41	59
1940	52	48
1950	53	47
1960	61	39
1970	53	47

Source: U.S. Census Bureau, Decennial Census (1900–70).

citizenship was the channel whereby most Chinese effected entry into this country despite the exclusion laws. Until the late 1940s there were only a few Chinese women here, so Chinese born on American soil are a fairly recent occurrence. Since Native–born cannot be taken literally to mean U.S.-born, we must make allowance for this definition and reduce the numbers considerably.

How does the Chinese native–born/foreign–born ratio compare with other ethnic groups? In 1900 approximately 15 percent of the American population was foreign–born. By 1970 the percentage had shrunk to less than 5 percent (see Table 2.3). The United States is now producing her own sons and daughters. The percentage of foreign–born Japanese–Americans in the United States is considerably smaller than that for Chinese–Americans—about 21 percent, or one in five. Again, the variation between states is great—10 percent in Hawaii versus 57 percent in New York. For the Chinese, the nativity ratio is approximately 1:1; but if we revise the census definition of native–born to exclude those not born in the United States, the foreign–born proportion would be greater.

CITIZENSHIP

Place of birth is a major, but by no means the sole, determinant of citizenship. The United States confers citizenship by two means: by birth and by naturalization. Birth means being born on

TABLE 2.2

Comparison of Live Births with Deaths of the Chinese in the United States, by Sex, 1946-69

Year	Live Births			Deaths		
	Male	Female	Total	Male	Female	Total
1946	796	738	1,534	1,139	140	1,279
1947	1,093	1,077	2,170	977	146	1,123
1948	2,218	1,992	4,210	1,004	158	1,162
1949	2,581	2,481	5,062	978	184	1,162
1950	2,562	2,467	5,029	888	169	1,057
1951	2,560	2,310	4,870	1,046	142	1,188
1952	2,504	2,238	4,742	1,038	168	1,206
1953	2,408	2,184	4,592	1,031	164	1,195
1954	2,256	2,140	4,396	1,102	191	1,293
1955	2,252	2,177	4,429	989	176	1,165
1956	2,364	2,326	4,690	1,088	195	1,283
1957	2,364	2,302	4,666	1,150	206	1,356
1958	2,424	2,282	4,706	1,114	221	1,335
1959	2,614	2,410	5,024	1,134	209	1,343
1960	2,966	2,880	5,846	1,328	292	1,620
1961	3,160	3,012	6,172	1,376	301	1,677
1962	2,990	2,790	5,780	1,355	319	1,674
1963	3,198	2,850	6,048	1,427	302	1,729
1964	2,378	2,120	4,498	986	319	1,305
1965	3,032	2,776	5,808	1,337	334	1,671
1966	2,864	2,804	5,668	1,331	390	1,721
1967	n.a.	n.a.	5,798	1,401	414	1,815
1968	3,232	3,038	6,270	1,450	461	1,911
1969	n.a.	n.a.	n.a.	1,458	487	1,945

n.a. = not available

Source: U.S. Department of Health, Education and Welfare, National Center for Health Statistics.

TABLE 2.3

Comparison of Native-Born with Foreign-Born, Chinese, Japanese, and Filipino, 1970

	United States (in thousands)		Chinese		Japanese		Filipino	
	Native-Born	Foreign-Born	Native-Born	Foreign-Born	Native-Born	Foreign-Born	Native-Born	Foreign-Born
United States	193,591	9,679	229,237	204,232	464,175	122,500	157,853	178,970
Percent	95.2	4.8	52.9	47.1	79.1	20.9	46.9	53.1
California	18,199	1,758	92,663	77,711	167,438	44,683	56,583	79,058
Percent	91.2	8.8	54.4	45.6	78.9	21.1	41.7	58.3
New York	16,127	2,110	29,586	53,595	8,551	11,254	4,166	9,391
Percent	88.4	11.6	35.6	64.4	43.2	56.8	30.7	69.3
Hawaii	693	76	46,566	5,809	196,848	20,821	61,731	33,623
Percent	90.1	9.9	88.9	11.1	90.0	10.0	64.8	35.3

Sources: U.S. Department of Commerce, Bureau of the Census, U.S. Summary, PC(1)C1, Table 143; and Subject Report, PC(2)1G, Tables 3, 18, 33.

24

American soil or born to at least one parent who is a U.S. citizen. To become a naturalized citizen, one must meet certain requirements and make application.

Before 1943 Chinese in the United States were not eligible to apply for naturalization no matter how long they had resided in the country, how fluently they spoke English, or how ardently they subscribed to the ideals of American democracy and its form of government. As far back as 1870, the Chinese had been declared "aliens ineligible to citizenship." The logic for this was that the constitution granted the free white man the right to be naturalized; the Fourteenth Amendment certainly extended this right to the black man, but, since the yellow man was neither white nor black he was adjudged ineligible. Only after repeal of the exclusion acts was the right of naturalization given to the Chinese.

The requirements for citizenship are more stringent than is ordinarily presumed. To enter the United States, one needs an immigration visa. To obtain such a visa, the applicant must prove that he will not become a public charge, that he is not taking a job away from anyone else, that his training or skills are in short supply, and that he will have a place to live when he gets here. Furthermore, a visa is issued only if there is a quota number available to him. These requirements must be fulfilled if the applicant does not have a parent or spouse who is already a citizen or permanent resident to sponsor him.

Labor certification is the most difficult hurdle. In effect, the U.S. Department of Labor must approve of the person's entry into the United States. After certification, permission to remain in this country is obtained when the Immigration and Naturalization Service issues a little green card granting the applicant permanent resident status. Getting a green card is the first step on the road toward citizenship.

Citizenship regulations require that the applicant be 18 years of age, that he have lived in this country continuously for at least five years (with a few exceptions), * that he be able to read and write the English language and know basic facts of U.S. history, and that he be of good moral character. For Chinese persons, the most difficult stipulation to fulfill is the language requirement.

Table 2.4 shows the number of Chinese who became naturalized citizens in the decade 1963-73. Prior to 1971, only 2,000 to 4,000 Chinese changed their allegiance each year. What caused the sharp spurt in 1972 and 1973 of 9,000 and more? It is important to remember that there is a lag from five to seven years between the time immigrants enter this country and when they are eligible to apply for citi-

---

*The most common exception is three years residence instead of five for persons married to U.S. citizens.

TABLE 2.4

Chinese Who Became Naturalized Citizens, 1963–73

Year	Number
1963	4,268
1964	4,045
1965	3,692
1966	3,111
1967	2,924
1968	3,186
1969	3,399
1970	3,099
1971	2,880
1972	9,434
1973	9,056
Total	49,094

Source: U.S. Department of Justice, Immigration and Natural-ization Service, Annual Reports (Washington, D.C., 1963–73), Table 39.

TABLE 2.5

Citizenship of Chinese in Seven Selected States, by Percent, 1970

	Citizen	Alien
Total United States	72.6	27.4
California	72.7	27.3
New York	62.5	37.5
Hawaii	96.1	3.9
Illinois	70.9	29.1
Massachusetts	58.8	41.2
Washington	78.8	21.2
Texas	53.3	46.7

Source: U.S. Department of Commerce, Bureau of the Census, Special Tabulation, Public Use Sample Data, 1970.

zenship, and it seems that a large percentage did so immediately following the liberalization of the immigration laws in 1965. The sharp
increase in naturalization certainly indicates that the Chinese do want
to apply for citizenship.

Table 2.5 shows that 73 percent, or approximately three-fourths,
of the Chinese in the United States are American citizens. Almost
all the Chinese in Hawaii have citizenship; but of the Chinese in New
York, only 63 percent are citizens.

What is the relationship between citizenship and employment
opportunity? The entire federal government service is closed to noncitizens. Defense-related industries like aerospace will not employ
them. At one time, most scientific and technological industries were
closed doors to the noncitizen because many companies held government contracts related to military supplies. Before 1970 all local,
municipal, and state governments banned noncitizens from their payrolls. Since then, local governments have relaxed this ban, but the
federal government has not. For many professionals, such as doctors
and teachers, citizenship is required before one can practice or teach.

Naturalization requirements call for at least five years of continuous residence in this country. Several months of red tape and
several more months of processing time often stretches the waiting
period to nearly seven years. (For example, most of the people who
got their citizenship papers in 1973 arrived in this country in 1966 or
1967.) During these six or seven years, the noncitizen is severely
restricted in his options. He has few alternatives except to take any
job available at any pay offered.

MOTHER TONGUE

To what extent is language a problem among the Chinese in the
United States? The census data reveals that it is a greater problem
than is generally presumed, although the Census Bureau tends to feel
that the mother tongue data is overstated. According to Table 2.6,
at least three out of four Chinese persons listed Chinese as their
mother tongue. In the state of New York, only 4 percent of the Chinese listed English as their mother tongue; in California, 12 percent;
and in Hawaii, 44 percent. These figures also point out the places
where English language classes are needed. The Chinese in the
United States are still very much a Chinese-speaking group. To what
extent they are bilingual or also fluent in English, we do not know.
From personal observation, it would appear that a very large proportion have problems with the English language—even college graduates
or postgraduate students. A number of the author's acquaintances
have no difficulty reading or writing, but they have a heavy accent

TABLE 2.6

Mother Tongue of Chinese in the United States, by Percent, 1970

	English	Chinese	Other or Not Reported
United States	14	74	12
California	12	78	11
New York	4	83	13
Hawaii	44	45	11
Illinois	14	72	14
Massachusetts	4	85	11

Note: Based on 1 percent sampling.

Source: U.S. Department of Commerce, Bureau of the Census, Special Tabulation, Public Use Sample Data, 1970.

that is difficult to understand. As a result, these people are extremely self-conscious about their speech and tend to gravitate toward occupations where they will not have to deal with the public, preferring instead to closet themselves with numbers or machines.

But at least these persons can still resort to the written language. The people most in need of help are those who can neither speak nor read nor write English. The most handicapped, of course, are those who are illiterate in any language. Learning builds on learning and, without learning techniques carried over from childhood, an illiterate starts far below ground zero.

SUMMARY OF FINDINGS

1. There are more Chinese-Americans born abroad than are born in the United States. The foreign-born ratio will become greater because immigration exceeds native births. The Chinese-American population is largely a first- or immigrant-generation one.

2. Not having citizenship in this country is a definite handicap. Many industries will not or cannot hire noncitizens; professionals may not practice. A large area of the job market, therefore, is forbidden ground to those without citizenship papers.

3. The Chinese do apply for naturalization as soon as they fulfill the length of residence requirement. The law says five years; the usual wait is six to seven years before papers are issued. There is no recourse except to wait.

4. Lack of knowledge of the English language places the Chinese in a most unfavorable competitive position when it comes to looking for a job. In most instances it puts the Chinese out of the job market, except in occupations owned and operated by other Chinese or catering to the Chinese.

RECOMMENDATIONS

Immigrants

In August 1973, U.S. Representative Patsy Mink introduced a bill (H.R. 9895) in the Ninety-Third Congress to provide federal programs in education, employment, and other forms of assistance to areas with heavy concentrations of foreign-born persons. The bill declared that whereas:

1. many foreign-born persons in the United States lack sufficient education to function adequately in our technological society;

2. the lack of adequate education prevents many such persons from having satisfactory employment opportunities;

3. newly arrived foreign-born Americans also experience difficulty in such areas as food, housing, and health;

4. the needs of newly arrived foreign-born Americans may place heavy financial strains on communities in which they reside;

5. a number of "gateway cities" exist where such persons reside in great numbers, thereby placing disproportionate burdens on particular areas of the country;

6. the policies under which persons move to the United States are set and determined by the federal government;

7. the federal government therefore has a responsibility to assist those states and cities having concentrations of foreign-born populations in meeting the special needs thereby thrust upon such communities.

Congresswoman Mink called for federal aid to states where more than 5 percent of the population are immigrants. The aid would go toward programs of education, health, housing, and job training. In addition, travel grants of up to $250 per immigrant would be provided for travel from a "gateway city" to another state for purposes of employment. Mink recognized that most immigrants tend to concentrate in seaboard cities, placing the burden of adapting the immigrant to his new homeland upon a limited number of such cities. The travel allowance would induce immigrants to disperse and relocate to other states.

It is hoped that Representative Mink's bill will be enacted. If such funds are available to the states, the following administrative recommendations should be considered:

1. A multiservice center should be set up where immigrants can go for help if the need should arise.

2. The center must have multilingual personnel if it is to be able to effectively help the new immigrant.

3. The existence of the center must be publicized so that the immigrant knows that there is a place to which he can turn if he needs help. A brochure describing the center and its services might accompany the issuance of the immigration visa.

4. More incentives should be offered to encourage dispersion of the immigrants inland or to cities other than those designated as "gateway cities."

5. Subsidiary grants should be offered to community institutions or organizations if these organizations can provide a more personal touch in dispensing services.

6. Social service agency directories directing the new immigrant to other places where he might seek assistance or guidance should be compiled.

7. A simple language or phrase book, like the Berlitz language booklets for travelers, should be made available to enable the immigrants to look up essential phrases they will use daily.

Citizenship

In January 1970, the Equal Employment Opportunity Commission issued guidelines on discrimination because of national origin. The following is taken from The Federal Register (January 13, 1970), Chapter XIV, Part 1606.1:

> (c) Title VII of the Civil Rights Act of 1964 protects all individuals, both citizens and noncitizens, domiciled or residing in the United States, against

discrimination on the basis of race, color, religion,
sex, or national origin.

(d) Because discrimination on the basis of citizenship has the effect of discriminating on the basis of
national origin, a lawfully immigrated alien who is
domiciled or residing in this country may not be
discriminated against on the basis of his citizenship,
except that it is not an unlawful employment practice for an employer, pursuant to section 703(g), to
refuse to employ any person who does not fulfill the
requirements imposed in the interests of national
security pursuant to any statute of the United States
or any Executive Order of the President respecting
the particular position or the particular premises in
question.

(e) In addition, some States have enacted laws pro-
hibiting the employment of noncitizens. For the reasons stated above, such laws are in conflict with and
are, therefore, superseded by Title VII of the Civil
Rights Act of 1964.

This guideline is effective upon publication.

State and local governments have removed their ban upon noncitizens for civil service jobs, but the federal government has not.
In February 1974, the Ninth Circuit Court of Appeals in San Francisco
handed down a unanimous decision calling upon the federal government
to permit resident aliens to apply for federal employment. The ruling
came as a result of a lawsuit filed more than three years previously
by five San Franciscan Chinese aliens.[1] As of this writing, the ruling
is being appealed by the federal government and more than 3 million
civil service jobs are still closed to noncitizens. It is ironic that the
government that is asking for enforcement of the Civil Rights Act
should try to circumvent the guidelines of its own laws, especially
since exemption has already been provided for those jobs that might
jeopardize national security. Besides, most of the jobs in the national
bureaucracy are not defense-related.

Language

English language classes for adults will equip them to step beyond the boundaries of Chinatown and enable them to expand their occupational horizons. Of all programs, this should be given top priority. Adults are emphasized here because most of the recent immigrants
are over age 20. These people cannot afford the luxury of full-time

schooling; they must work. Therefore, classes must be held before or after work hours.

The English language classes offered by the U.S. Department of Health, Education and Welfare and the New York State Department of Education in New York are an example of this sort of program. The program can accommodate 500 students. Over 1,500 persons applied within a few days after classes were announced. Attendance is excellent. Absence from three classes without a good excuse means that the student is dropped and another eagerly takes his place. Classes are offered in the morning to accommodate the restaurant workers and in the evenings for the garment factory workers. It is heartening to see the eagerness with which these students come to classes, but it is more than disheartening to see them turned away because the classes are filled.

For those who are turned away from language classes, as well as those who live some distance from Chinatown, television classes are recommended. This method has been successfully tried in San Francisco and has been well received. The same video tapes can be repeated or rerun in other cities over educational channels. Television classes are not as effective as classroom instruction, however, because there is no teacher present for practice or interaction or correction of mistakes.

Bilingual Education

For those who have spent 10 to 12 years learning their native Chinese only to find that it is no longer useful because this is a land where it is not the medium of expression, bilingual education may be a transitional aid. The right to bilingual education was guaranteed by a Supreme Court ruling handed down in the Lau v. Nichols case in January 1974. In its ruling, the Supreme Court said, "Students who do not understand English are effectively foreclosed from any meaningful education."

The Congress has acted with the passage of the Bilingual Education Reform Act of 1974, but few plans have been formulated for its implementation.

NOTE

1. East/West, February 6, 1974.

3

The Chinese in the United States are clustered along the East and West Coasts and in the Hawaiian Islands. The only other significant concentrations are in the midwestern city of Chicago and, surprisingly, Houston, Texas, which lately seems to be attracting the Chinese.

AN URBAN POPULATION

This clustering phenomenon seems to be very intense with the Chinese. Not only are they an almost completely urban population (97 percent) but they tend to gravitate to a limited number of cities, primarily San Francisco, New York, Honolulu, and Los Angeles; and in these cities they tend to be found within the borders of a very distinct area called Chinatown.

Table 3.1 shows the 11 Standard Metropolitan Statistical Areas (SMSAs) that have the highest Chinese populations. In every one of these urban centers, the increase in population over a 20-year period was substantial and, in many instances, it doubled with each decade. The most impressive gain was in New York City, with an increase of 40,000, or 109 percent. San Jose, a town about 50 miles southeast of San Francisco, however, chalked up the most spectacular percentage increase. In 1950, it had a Chinese population of 192. This figure increased by more than 205 percent over the next decade and by 1,236 percent ten years later. In many ways, San Jose has become an extended suburb of San Francisco. Its electronics industries have attracted many professionally trained and technically skilled Chinese to the area.

TABLE 3.1

The Largest Centers of Chinese Population in the United States, 1950, 1960, and 1970

SMSA	1950	1960	1970	Percent Increase	
				1950–60	1960–70
San Francisco–Oakland	34,774	53,250	88,108	53	65
New York	20,550	36,503	76,208	78	109
Honolulu	15,409	36,875	48,288	139	31
Los Angeles–Long Beach	9,275	19,402	40,798	109	110
Chicago	3,737	5,866	12,653	157	116
Boston	2,897	5,564	12,025	92	116
Sacramento	3,852	6,457	10,444	67	62
Washington, D.C.–Maryland–Virginia	1,825	3,925	8,298	115	111
San Jose	192	585	7,817	205	1,236
Seattle	2,703	4,611	7,434	71	61
Philadelphia	n.a.	2,544	4,882	—	92

n.a. = not available

Note: The SMSA boundaries are not exactly the same from census to census. For example, the San Francisco–Oakland SMSA includes more counties in 1970 than in 1960.

Source: U.S. Department of Commerce, Bureau of the Census, direct query.

34

RANKING OF CHINESE-POPULATED CITIES

The ranking of the cities has also undergone important shifts. San Francisco always has held the lead as the oldest and largest center of Chinese population, but it attracted fewer persons during the decade from 1960 to 1970 than did New York. At the same time, former Chinese residents of San Francisco were moving out to Sacramento, San Jose, Stockton, or other nearby towns, maintaining ties with San Francisco but preferring a less congested place in which their children could grow up.

Over 92 percent of Hawaii's Chinese reside in Honolulu. In 1960 it was tied with New York City for second place. Ten years later, New York had pulled far ahead of Honolulu, with 76,208 Chinese residents to Honolulu's 48,288. Honolulu's growth had come about during the decade 1950-60. Since then, the increase has slowed down considerably. Immigrants are not going to Honolulu, and the young people are moving away from the island to the mainland (see Table 3.2).

Of the three ranking cities, New York is growing the most rapidly. During the census year 1970, it trailed San Francisco only slightly. By now, the absolute number of Chinese in the SMSA of New York may already exceed that of San Francisco. Attention to Chinese-American problems must, therefore, focus more upon this Eastern Seaboard city, rather than upon the traditional centers of Chinese population.

FACTORS INFLUENCING GROWTH

Before long, New York City may be the most concentrated center of Chinese population. A look at the intended city of residence (Table 1.4) will provide some answer to this dramatic shift. The num-

TABLE 3.2

Percentage of Chinese in Four Urban Centers to Total U.S. Chinese
Population, 1960 and 1970

SMSA	1960	1970
San Francisco	22	20
New York	16	18
Honolulu	16	11
Los Angeles	8	9

Source: U.S. Department of Commerce, Bureau of the Census, Subject Reports, PC(2)1C (1960), and PC(2)1G (1970).

TABLE 3.3

Age of the Chinese in the United States, 1970

Age	Total	Percent	Male	Percent	Female	Percent
All ages	431,583	100.0	226,733	100.0	204,850	100.0
Median age	26.8		27.8		25.8	
Under 5 years	35,813	8.3	18,315	8.1	17,498	8.5
5-9 years	39,159	9.0	19,898	8.8	19,261	9.4
10-14 years	39,955	9.1	20,517	9.0	19,438	9.5
15-19 years	43,607	10.1	22,867	10.1	20,740	10.1
20-24 years	45,884	10.6	22,996	10.2	22,888	11.2
25-29 years	32,228	7.5	15,860	7.0	16,368	8.0
30-34 years	33,758	7.8	17,715	7.8	16,043	7.8
35-39 years	30,659	7.1	16,696	7.4	13,963	6.8
40-44 years	28,617	6.6	14,386	6.3	14,231	6.9
45-49 years	25,423	5.9	14,480	6.4	10,943	5.3
50-54 years	19,087	4.4	10,526	4.6	8,561	4.2
55-59 years	17,118	4.0	9,512	4.2	7,606	3.7
60-64 years	13,419	3.1	7,721	3.4	5,698	2.8
65-69 years	11,107	2.6	6,190	2.7	4,917	2.4
70-74 years	7,698	1.8	4,576	2.0	3,122	1.5
75-79 years	4,422	1.0	2,561	1.1	1,861	0.9
80-84 years	2,106	0.5	1,130	0.5	976	0.5
85 years and over	1,523	0.4	787	0.3	736	0.4
Under 18 years	138,613	32.1	71,133	31.4	67,480	32.9
18 years and over	292,970	67.9	155,600	68.6	137,370	67.1
62 years and over	34,793	8.1	19,900	8.8	14,893	7.3
65 years and over	26,856	6.2	15,244	6.7	11,612	5.7

Source: U.S. Department of Commerce, Bureau of the Census, Subject Report PC(2)1G, Table 17.

36

ber of immigrants who go to Hawaii has become insignificant. At the
most, less than 400 have been immigrating to Hawaii each year over
the past ten years, and in some years it was less than 100. Yet, in
almost every year during the same period, the number immigrating
to New York has been roughly ten times the number going to Hawaii.

Hawaii is also losing its young Chinese men and women in the
25- to 35-year age group. There is an ever-growing number of young
Asians from Hawaii who now work or live on the mainland.

Los Angeles continues to attract immigrants, but the other
SMSAs with sizable Chinese populations seem to be increasing from
migration between the states, rather than immigration from China or
elsewhere abroad.

The difference in makeup of the Chinese population in the various
localities is very great. Many of the tables in this study were set up
—sometimes by city, sometimes by state, and sometimes by region
—to point out these differences so that specific problems would not be
camouflaged by national averages.

Table 3.3 gives an age breakdown of the Chinese population in
the United States. An important trend is discernible: with each
younger age group from 20 to 24 years on down, the numbers and percentages get smaller; with each younger five-year age group, we note
a decreasing population.

Later in our study, we will see that the number of children born
to Chinese parents over the ten-year period between 1959 and 1968
was only about 5,000 or 6,000 a year for the entire United States (see
Table 2.2). This fact is further substantiated by the number of children ever born to Chinese-American women ever married (see Table
6.7).

PRESENT IN ALL 50 STATES

The Chinese are heavily concentrated in a few cities, but they
are also widely dispersed. This statement is not a contradiction:
there are Chinese in all of the 50 United States. The 1970 census
enumerated about 165 Chinese in each of the Dakotas and 173 in the
state of Vermont. Even Alaska had 228.

In the late nineteenth century, the Chinese population of the
northwestern states of Washington, Idaho, and Wyoming was fairly
substantial. The early Chinese were engaged in mining gold in Idaho[1]
and coal in Wyoming, and in domestic service and produce farming
in Washington. Some vestiges of those early Chinese settlements
still remain, but others are fast disappearing. *

---

*In 1973 I visited Walla Walla and learned that the China building
had just been torn down and some of the old records and papers contained within had been carted away with the rubble.

TABLE 3.4

Chinese Population by State and Percent Change, 1960 and 1970

State	1960	1970	Percent Change	State	1960	1970	Percent Change
Total United States	237,292	435,062	83.3	Missouri	954	2,815	195.1
Alabama	288	626	117.4	Montana	240	289	20.4
Alaska	137	228	66.4	Nebraska	290	551	90.0
Arizona	2,936	3,878	32.1	Nevada	572	955	66.9
Arkansas	676	743	9.9	New Hampshire	152	420	176.3
California	95,600	170,131	78.1	New Jersey	3,813	9,233	142.1
Colorado	724	1,489	105.4	New Mexico	362	563	55.5
Connecticut	865	2,209	115.3	New York	37,573	81,378	116.6
Delaware	191	559	192.7	North Carolina	404	1,255	210.6
District of Columbia	2,632	2,582	-1.9	North Dakota	100	165	65.0
Florida	1,023	3,133	206.2	Ohio	2,507	5,305	131.5
Georgia	686	1,584	130.9	Oklahoma	398	999	151.0
Hawaii	38,197	52,039	36.2	Oregon	2,995	4,814	60.8
Idaho	311	498	60.1	Pennsylvania	3,741	7,053	88.5
Illinois	7,047	14,474	105.4	Rhode Island	574	1,093	90.4
Indiana	952	2,115	122.2	South Carolina	158	521	229.7
Iowa	423	993	134.8	South Dakota	89	163	83.1
Kansas	537	1,233	129.4	Tennessee	487	1,610	230.8
Kentucky	288	558	93.8	Texas	4,172	7,635	83.0
Louisiana	731	1,340	83.3	Utah	629	1,281	103.6
Maine	123	206	67.4	Vermont	68	173	154.4
Maryland	2,188	6,520	197.9	Virginia	1,135	2,805	147.1
Massachusetts	6,745	14,012	107.7	Washington	5,491	9,201	67.6
Michigan	3,234	6,407	98.1	West Virginia	138	373	170.3
Minnesota	720	2,422	236.4	Wisconsin	1,010	2,700	167.3
Mississippi	1,011	1,441	42.5	Wyoming	192	292	52.1

Source: U.S. Department of Commerce, Bureau of the Census, Subject Reports, PC(2)1C (1960), PC(2)1G (1970).

38

Table 3.4 breaks down the Chinese population by state for the census years 1960 and 1970, and shows the percentage change during the decade. The five leading states in Chinese population are California, New York, Hawaii, Illinois, and Massachusetts. Following at some distance are the states of Washington and Texas. This last state should be subjected to closer scrutiny as it has almost doubled its Chinese population in the last two decades.

Every state registered substantial gain, except for the District of Columbia with a -1.9 percent change. This figure is extremely misleading, however, since it reflects the movement of the Chinese out of the central city, or district proper, into the surrounding suburbs in Maryland and Virginia. The SMSA figures for the nation's capital shows that there were 8,298 persons of Chinese ancestry in 1970. The actual percentage increase from 1960 to 1970 for the Washington, D.C.-Virginia-Maryland SMSA is 111.

Is there any noticeable shift in the Chinese population from state to state or region to region? The large number of immigrants tends to overshadow the movement of those already residing in the United States, but some data from the census give an indication whether the Chinese are moving away from the West, whether they are still concentrating in the cities or trekking out to the suburbs like the rest of America, whether they are getting out of Chinatowns or expanding the boundaries of their own settlements to further accommodate the influx of immigrants, or whether they are filtering into states where they have never ventured before. As we look at the figures, we will try to discover what triggered the ingress or exodus.

HIGH MOBILITY

In 1970 only 43.2 percent of the Chinese were living in the same house as they had five years earlier, which means that 57 percent, or almost three out of five persons 16 years and over, moved between the years 1965 and 1970. They either had moved to a different house in the same county or to a different county or were abroad. In fact, about one out of five were immigrants. This rate varies by state and age. In Table 3.5 we see that only 4.5 percent of Hawaii's Chinese 16 years and over were abroad, whereas 24 percent of Illinois' Chinese were. This gives some idea of the disparity of characteristics of the Chinese from state to state. These figures also confirm what we already know: New York and Illinois have the highest percentages of immigrants.

In states like California and Hawaii, the Chinese who changed their residence from that of 1965 generally moved to a different house within the same county and they tended to stay in the West. But it is

TABLE 3.5

Physical Mobility of the Chinese in the United States, Age 16 Years and over, for Selected States, 1970

Residence in 1965	United States Number	United States Percent	California Number	California Percent	New York Number	New York Percent	Hawaii Number	Hawaii Percent	Illinois Number	Illinois Percent	Massachusetts Number	Massachusetts Percent
Same house	133,994	43.2	53,574	44.0	27,713	46.1	22,955	63.0	3,248	32.6	3,789	38.0
Different house in the United States	100,029	32.3	41,481	34.0	15,243	25.3	10,396	28.5	3,425	34.3	3,586	36.0
Same county[a]	57,649	57.6	26,861	64.8	7,057	46.3	8,907	85.7	2,226	65.0	1,860	51.9
Different county[a]	42,380	42.4	14,620	35.3	8,186	53.7	1,489	14.3	1,199	35.0	1,726	48.1
Northeast[b]	5,975	14.1	919	6.3	703	8.6	86	5.8	186	15.5	482	27.9
North Central[b]	4,556	10.8	1,069	7.3	504	6.2	211	14.2	220	18.4	237	13.7
South[b]	3,841	9.1	755	5.2	437	5.3	134	9.0	138	11.5	145	8.4
West[b]	28,008	66.1	11,877	81.2	6,542	79.9	1,058	71.1	655	54.6	862	49.9
Abroad	57,665	18.6	20,999	17.2	13,649	22.7	1,654	4.5	2,391	24.0	1,830	18.4
Moved in 1965, residence not reported	18,162	5.9	5,794	4.8	3,544	5.9	1,454	4.0	910	9.1	756	7.6
Total	309,850	100.0	121,848	100.0	60,149	100.0	36,459	100.0	9,974	100.0	9,961	100.0

[a]Percentages for these two categories add up to 100 percent of those who lived in a different house in the United States.
[b]Percentages for these four regions add up to 100 percent of those who moved to a different county.

Note: The U.S. Census Bureau cautions readers that its mobility figures for the western region may be inaccurate.

Source: U.S. Department of Commerce, Bureau of the Census, Subject Report, PC(2)1G (1970), Table 20.

significant that, whereas about one-fourth moved from the West to
New York, the reverse flow was much less. Again, it can be seen
that New York has greater magnetic force.

Where mobility has been tabulated by age group, the most mobile
group is 25 to 34 years. For all the states tabulated in Table 3.6, the
percentage of this age group who moved between 1965 and 1970 runs
from 60.8 percent for Hawaii to 84.5 percent for Illinois. This means
that from three to four out of five Chinese persons in this age group
changed their residence during this five-year interval, and, for a
large proportion of those who moved into these states, the jump was
a trans-Pacific one. In other words, they were not in this country
five years ago. The 20- to 24-year age group's mobility is only
slightly less spectacular. The significance of these figures is that
the adult Chinese population is essentially a recently uprooted one.

Of those who moved within the United States, about two-thirds
stayed in the same county, except for those living in New York.
There, the tendency leaned slightly toward moving out of Manhattan
into the suburban counties of the greater metropolis.

CONCENTRATION IN CHINATOWNS

To reduce the cultural shock and to ease the emotional pain of
their migration, the Chinese tend to seek out their own kind and to
congregate in certain sections of the urban centers that are popularly
called Chinatowns.

In the past, other factors, such as the Alien Land Acts, restric-
tive covenants, and white aversion to having an Oriental neighbor, also
contributed to the consolidation of these distinct ethnic enclaves.
Chinatowns were inevitably in the older sections of the core city. In
San Francisco, Chinatown is situated directly in the center of the business, financial, shipping, and civic districts (see Map 1). In cities
like Oakland and New York, they are located in the shadow of city
hall. New York's Chinatown is found in the lower tip of Manhattan
(see Map 2). It is apparent from these locations that the Chinese were
early residents of the major urban centers. They occupy what is now
prime real estate, but invariably the sections are rundown slums.

Do most Chinese live within Chinatowns? Are these places still
islands of Cathay in America? The answers to these questions vary
from city to city. Some Chinatowns are growing and expanding; some
are in various stages of decline or have disappeared—and for different
reasons.

Urban sprawl, urban renewal, eminent domain have all been
factors in the demise of many a Chinatown, but when there is a need,
a new one springs up. In Los Angeles, when the site of the old China-

TABLE 3.6

Chinese 16 Years and over Who Moved Between 1965 and 1970 as a Percent of Total Chinese Population, by Age Group, for Selected States

Age Group, 1970; Residence, 1965	United States	California	New York	Hawaii	Illinois	Massachusetts
16–19 years						
Different house	50.1	48.5	51.2	31.3	59.9	53.9
Abroad	17.8	17.9	21.8	5.8	14.4	20.1
20–24 years						
Different house	70.8	70.6	65.5	50.2	79.9	77.2
Abroad	29.6	39.3	31.4	9.0	36.0	27.8
25–34 years						
Different house	78.6	77.5	70.9	60.8	84.5	81.6
Abroad	27.3	21.2	31.9	7.8	35.3	26.1
35–44 years						
Different house	55.2	52.7	55.8	40.9	61.4	56.0
Abroad	14.8	14.6	23.2	3.7	14.1	8.6
45–64 years						
Different house	39.6	40.4	41.6	24.9	49.5	45.5
Abroad	11.1	11.8	15.3	2.5	14.6	13.1
65 years and over						
Different house	39.3	45.4	35.7	23.7	45.3	41.2
Abroad	9.0	10.2	11.8	1.3	15.6	8.4

Note: The U.S. Census Bureau cautions readers that its mobility figures for the West may be inaccurate.

Source: U.S. Department of Commerce, Bureau of the Census, Subject Report, PC(2)1G (1970), Table 20.

MAP 3.1

San Francisco Chinatown Proper, 1970

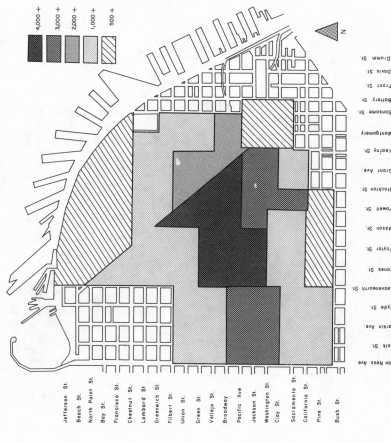

Note: Numbers refer to Chinese population within census tract.

Source: Compiled by Betty Lee Sung and Wai Leung.

43

MAP 3.2

Expanding Chinatown in New York, 1970

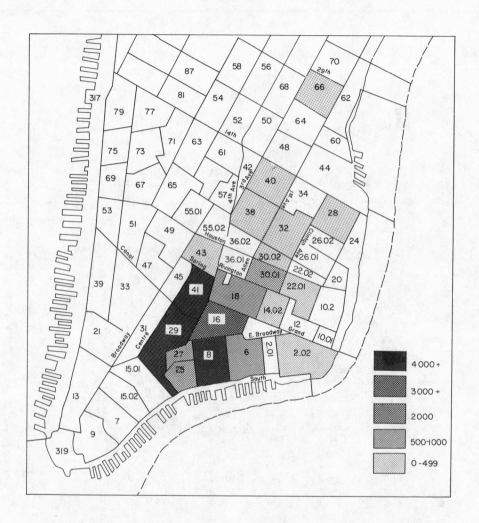

Note: Numbers refer to Chinese population within census tract. These tracts contain three-fourths of Manhattan's Chinese population, which is equal to the total Chinese population of Massachusetts and Illinois combined.

Source: Compiled by Betty Lee Sung and Wai Leung.

town was needed for a railroad station, the residents redistributed
themselves into three Chinatowns. Now the Los Angeles Chinatown has
reconsolidated into a major one along North Broadway.

In Pennsylvania:

> Philadelphia's Chinatown was seriously reduced in
> size when the city converted the main street of the
> ghetto into a thoroughfare leading into the Benjamin
> Franklin Bridge. . . . Pittsburgh's Chinatown was
> totally obliterated by the building of a modern ex-
> pressway.[2]

The old Chinatown in Chicago is centered at Cermak Road and
Wentworth Avenue on the South Side, but, with its population more
than doubled since 1960, it has no more room for expansion. Since
more Chinese are found on the North Side, an enterprising business
group has been quietly buying up a three-block stretch of property
along Argyle Street and is busily planning a fanciful new Chinatown.[3]

Boston's Chinatown has been mutilated by a superhighway—the
Massachusetts Turnpike. When that cement ribbon bisected Chinatown, half of the community life died and the people moved away. In
1940, 62 percent of Boston's Chinese resided in Chinatown. Each
decade since has seen a reduction: 57 percent in 1950 to 25 percent
in 1960 to 9 percent in 1970. Table 3.7 shows how widely scattered
the Chinese are in the metropolitan Boston area and the pattern of
their dispersion. Although only a small percentage of Chinese reside
within the Chinatown area, the locale still serves as a social and cultural center.

San Francisco's Chinatown

San Francisco's Chinatown burst its seams and spilled over into
North Beach, then spread out to the Inner Richmond district. In 1970
33,208 Chinese lived in this area, and the population density reached
from 120 to 180 persons per gross acre as compared to 24.6 persons
per gross acre citywide.[4] In a series of articles in March and April
of 1974, East/West stated that real estate prices were going through
the roof in the Richmond district and that 80 percent of the buyers
were Chinese. To give some idea of the rapid influx, East/West
said, "One block in the Richmond core area has seen 14 property purchases this year. Ten of them were made by Chinese."[5]

The houses in this area are primarily private dwellings and
among the attractions of the area are its excellent public transportation to the main Chinatown, better housing, and proximity to Golden

TABLE 3.7

Chinese Population in Chinatown, Other Parts of Boston, and
Surrounding Cities Within Approximate Vicinity of U.S. Route 495,
1940-70

	1940	1950	1960	1970
Chinatown	1,300	1,600	1,800	1,258
Other parts of Boston	300	400	3,600	5,500
Arlington	16	10	72	222
Belmont			31	164
Bedford				82
Beverly	14	16	40	62
Bellingham				18
Billerica				39
Braintree			23	37
Brookline	38	40	292	942
Burlington				86
Brockton	37	65	54	143
Cambridge	133	266	554	1,274
Chelsea	46	42	32	133
Concord				52
Canton				19
Dedham			5	22
Everett		5	16	25
Foxborough				4
Franklin				28
Framingham			33	186
Hingham				17
Holbrook				28
Holliston				28
Hudson				14
Lexington			48	189
Lowell		41	37	172
Lynn	63	62	116	207
Malden	13	19	62	132
Medford	13	15	28	150
Marborough		2	1	41
Melrose		12	38	98
Milton				18
Marshfield				20
Milford		1	5	31
Marblehead			55	14
Methuen			4	32

	1940	1950	1960	1970
Natick			29	69
Needham			48	86
Newton	17	36	133	414
Norwood			16	43
Nahant				14
Pembroke				17
Peabody	10	8	22	66
Quincy	27	29	61	191
Revere		6	15	26
Reading			18	36
Randolph			13	45
Rockland				22
Salem	28	50	37	82
Saugus			18	37
Swampscott				22
Scituate				18
Sharon				11
Stoughton				28
Stoneham			15	49
Sudbury				27
Somerville	21	30	51	351
Tewksbury				31
Waltham	10	39	67	150
Wellesley			37	98
Wakefield			3	25
Watertown			18	134
Wayland				63
Weston				54
Wilmington				11
Winchester			17	62
Woburn			4	46
Walpole				15
Westwood				27
Weymouth			11	68
Whitman				20
Winthrop			8	19
Total	2,086	2,788	7,337	13,994

Source: Action for Boston Community Development Inc., Planning and Evaluation Department, The Chinese in Boston, 1970.

Gate Park. Only 10,265 Chinese were counted in the Richmond district in 1970, but if the recent frenetic scramble for real estate in that area is any indication the numbers must have increased phenomenally. Still, Richmond is a bedroom community and has not cut its umbilical cord to the main Chinatown. Nor is there any way, at this moment, to ascertain whether new immigrants are snapping up the Chinatown premises vacated by movers to Richmond and other districts. If so, Chinatown proper's problems can only be aggravated by the rapid turnover of its tenants and the more acute needs of its recent arrivals.

New York's Chinatown

New York's Chinatown merits special attention because it will no doubt soon replace San Francisco as the most important center of the Chinese in the United States for reasons already set forth above.

When Calvin Lee wrote his book, Chinatown, U.S.A., in 1965, he predicted the decline of Chinatown and so did Rose Hum Lee, the eminent sociologist and former head of the Department of Sociology at Roosevelt College.[6] But these people were writing before the enactment of the Immigration Act of 1965, which changed the entire scenario for the Chinese in this country.

The New York Chinatown of 1975, compared with that of 1960, has increased in size threefold. Unlike the Chinatown in San Francisco or Chicago, where there was no adjacent room for expansion, New York's Chinese have been moving into other ethnic ghettos surrounding Chinatown. Little Italy and the Jewish stronghold off Delancey Street are slowly receding, while recent Chinese immigrants are replacing the former inhabitants of earlier immigration vintage. This turnover is but another repetition of the classic pattern wherein the newest immigrant groups take over the Lower East Side, while the former immigrant group moves up and out. With each passing year, however, the physical environment of the area deteriorates further and the social ills of the neighborhood progress.

The question is asked, "Why is it that a former model community like Chinatown is experiencing gang killings, muggings, school dropouts, and health problems unknown to the community a decade ago?" The answer is simple: Whenever a large immigrant group is uprooted and set down in the environment of a Lower East Side, the result will be what we see in Chinatown today and what we saw in the ghettos of the Irish, the Jews, the Italians, and the Puerto Ricans of yesteryear.

Chinatown proper in New York has traditionally been bound on the north by Canal Street, on the west by Mulberry Street, and on the east and south by the Bowery and Park Row. This area takes in census tracts 29 and 27. By 1960 the surrounding tracts 8, 16, 18, and 41 also had large Chinese populations. The City Planning Commission indicated that there were 10,604 Chinese residing in Chinatown in 1960.[7] In 1970 the census counted 21,796 Chinese for these same six census tracts, but the boundaries of residential Chinatown have extended to cover many more census tracts. Judging from the Chinese population by census tracts,[8] the boundaries of the enlarged New York Chinatown reach as far north as Houston Street, and there are already indications that Fourteenth Street will shortly be the new northern boundary. Expansion southeastward has also taken place to as far as the East River's edge.

Within this expanded area are found approximately three out of four of the Chinese living in Manhattan. In other words, instead of scattering as in Boston, New York's Chinese have tended toward greater concentration. In the eight-block census tract 29 alone, there are about 6,000 persons of Chinese extraction, which is more than the total number of Chinese found in the entire SMSA of Philadelphia. Two census tracts, 29 and 41, contain more Chinese than the states of Illinois and Massachusetts combined. And when one considers the Chinese community in New York, one has to think of 19 census tracts rather than the six of 1960. This is the extent to which New York's Chinatown has pushed its boundaries.

Obviously, then, some Chinatowns are fading away and their inhabitants scattering; some have undergone face-lifting, some have moved to different locations, and some are like a powerful magnet drawing the Chinese closer together, culturally and spatially. Each community must be viewed separately and dealt with separately within its own context. Here two questions might be raised: Why the differences in Chinatowns in different cities? If there is a decided propensity for the Chinese to stick together, why is this not consistently true?

Other questions that we will be seeking to answer as we analyze our data include: Does residence in or near a Chinatown affect the occupational prospect of the Chinese? How about residence in a particular state, city, or region? Wherever applicable, the tabulations have been broken down by region, state, or SMSA to see if place of residence or moving away from Chinatown has a significant effect upon occupation, income, and upward mobility of the American Chinese.

SUMMARY OF FINDINGS

1. The Chinese in the United States are highly concentrated on the East and West Coasts and on the islands of Hawaii, in large urban centers, and in Chinatowns.

2. A decided shift is taking place in the pattern of their demographic distribution. The older and better-known Chinese centers like Honolulu and San Francisco are proportionately losing people to newer settlements like New York, San Jose, and Houston. Three times as many immigrants are heading toward New York City than toward San Francisco. New York draws more immigrants than the nine other cities with sizable Chinese population combined. New York's influx is coming from immigration. These immigrants have made a trans-Pacific leap and, undoubtedly, will have tremendous problems of adjustment. The influx into San Jose and Houston is coming from intraregional movement caused by upward economic or social mobility.

3. Hawaii's Chinese population growth rate is much lower than that of the mainland states.

4. The age pyramid of the Chinese population is beginning to resemble more an age diamond—widest in the middle and tapering off at both ends. This means few teenagers, fewer children, and even fewer infants.

5. One out of five Chinese 16 years and over was not in this country in 1965, and three out of five moved within the five-year period of 1965 to 1970. The Chinese population has been a highly mobile one.

6. There are significant variations in employment patterns and economic characteristics of the Chinese based upon place of residence.

7. The Chinatowns throughout the United States are undergoing major transformations. The closed, staid, and "orderly" Chinatowns of the past have been dramatically affected by the recent large influx of immigrants.

RECOMMENDATIONS

The high concentration of Chinese within clearly defined geographical areas has its advantages and drawbacks. The advantages are that it is easy to deal with the group. A few strategically located agencies could reach a large proportion of the population. The existing communities already provide organizations, institutions, and channels to work through. Some sociologists contend that residential concentration is essential for political and economic leverage. Perhaps the group should use this leverage to insist upon some face-lifting for Chinatowns. Too many are slums with tourist-oriented veneers that mask physical decay. City planners and urban renewal officials should give top priority to more and better housing units for these areas.

The drawbacks to such heavy concentration may outweigh the advantages. In New York and San Francisco, more and more immigrants are pouring into Chinatown. They find secutiy and comfort in being among their own kind, but in the process they are creating over-crowding and an excessive dependence upon one another. The concen-tration also creates a favorable climate for exploitation of cheap labor.

It is also axiomatic that high concentration makes for high visi-bility of an identifiable minority group. Psychologically, this tends to generate fears that the majority's existence and way of life are be-ing threatened by the minority. It is recommended that the Chinese be gradually induced or aided to disperse, but account must be taken of their desperate need for some proximity to a Chinese center.

One means of accomplishing dispersion would be to offer attrac-tive occupations beyond the borders of Chinatowns and beyond the sea-board states. Employers should give serious consideration to this and take positive steps to seek out and recruit qualified Chinese per-sonnel.

NOTES

1. Sister M. Alfreda Elsensohn, Idaho Chinese Lore (Caldwell, Idaho: Caxton Printers, 1970).

2. Rose Hum Lee, The Chinese in the United States of America (Hong Kong: Hong Kong University Press, 1960), pp. 65-66.

3. East/West, April 3, 1974.

4. "San Francisco Chinese Community Citizen's Survey and Fact-Finding Committee Report" (1969), p. 54.

5. East/West, April 10, 1974, p. 8.

6. Rose Hum Lee, "Decline of Chinatowns in the U.S.," Amer-ican Journal of Sociology 54 (March 1949): 442.

7. D. Y. Yuan, "Chinatown and Beyond: The Chinese Popula-tion in Metropolitan New York," Phylon 27, no. 4 (1966): 321-32.

8. The author undertook a special study entitled "Minority Popu-lation by Census Tracts for Eleven SMSAs, 1970." These data were issued separately in three volumes by the Department of Asian Studies, City College of New York.

4

PERENNIAL STUDENTS

Case One: Jason Wu came to the United States in 1946. He was
among the second batch of bright young men selected by the Chinese
government immediately after the cessation of hostilities with Japan
to go abroad for specialized training in the United States. His field
was hydraulic engineering, and he looked forward to a promising future after the completion of his studies at the University of Illinois.

Jason already had a bachelor's degree from the Southwest Associated University in Chungking, China, before coming to the United
States. By 1948 he had earned his master's degree. The political
situation in China was very uncertain, and his parents had urged him
to prolong his stay in the United States. He decided to go for his doctorate.

A year later, the Nationalist government had fallen, and in 1950
the Korean War broke out. The United States immediately banned the
departure of all Chinese students with technical and scientific skills.
With his financial support from China cut off, Jason was caught in a
bind. What was he to do? He was not sure that he could ever get a
job as a hydraulic engineer in this country. Perhaps he should be more
practical and learn something that he could utilize to earn a living
somehow. He switched to accounting and, with the aid of Economic
Cooperation Administration (ECA) funds, managed to complete his
master's degree in that field.

The Korean War dragged on. Even with his accounting degree,
Jason could not find employment. His professor in engineering, real-
izing his plight, offered him a teaching assistantship along with the
chance to complete his doctorate. Jason grasped the opportunity.

By 1955 Jason had two master's degrees and a Ph.D., but still no job. He was not permitted to leave the United States, but neither was he permitted to work because he held a student visa. The only course open to him was to find a part-time teaching position and continue his student status by doing research.

Ten years after his graduation from college, he was still studying—not by choice, but by force of circumstances.

Case Two: It was the second time around for Kai-Ming Fong when he arrived in the United States in 1951. The first time was when he worked for a master's degree from Georgia Tech in 1945; he had gone back to Shanghai immediately afterward. Within a few years, he had become manager of Technical Services at the Shanghai airport. In 1949 Shanghai was liberated by Mao Tse-tung's troops, and Kai-Ming fled the city for Hong Kong. He considered himself highly fortunate to receive a coveted visa to the United States under the Refugee Relief Act.

During his first sojourn in the United States, he had not paid much attention to what was going on outside of campus. In spite of his education, his experience, and his know-how, Kai-Ming realized that he was a fish out of water. The task now was to survive in a foreign land. He accepted a lowly draftsman's position in an aerospace plant on Long Island and every night commuted to Brooklyn Polytech to pursue a Ph.D. degree in aeronautical engineering. His indomitable determination kept him going in spite of bone-weariness and mental fatigue. After work, it was classes; after classes, it was studying. There was no time for relaxation, no time for girls, no time for fun. By the time Kai-Ming received his doctorate, he had missed out a lot on life. He was 35 years old and still single.

Case Three: Dr. S. W. Lee had worked in the obstetrics and gynecology ward of the Canton General Hospital for many years before his arrival in the United States in the 1950s. His M.D. was earned from a Canadian university. But Dr. Lee could not practice medicine when he first came to this country for two reasons: He was not a citizen and his M.D. was not from an American university.

Employment for Dr. Lee was a matter of dire necessity. He had a wife and two young daughters with him. To tide them over, Mrs. Lee worked as a hostess in a restaurant. Dr. Lee finally found a position as medical researcher at Mt. Sinai Hospital. The pay was insignificant and the work was elementary, considering Dr. Lee's education and former experience.

Working at Mt. Sinai, however, entitled Dr. Lee to enroll for special courses in the medical school without tuition. So after his long trail of premed, medical school, internship, and residency totaling more than ten years, Dr. Lee was back in the classroom.

Case Four: Ronald Wong was born in Newark, New Jersey. He loved baseball, he loved rock music, he loved the outdoors, and he loved people. His family operated a restaurant, and after school he helped in the dining room, filling the soy sauce bottles and sugar bowls, drying the silverware, and taking in the dirty dishes.

Patrons would come in and sit at the bar to watch the baseball games on television and sip their drinks. Ronald soon became great pals with Maurice Cohen, the salesman who sold his father bottled liquor and wines. Ronald would listen to Maurice Cohen's stories of the places he went to and the commissions he earned, and Ronald decided that when he grew up he wanted to be a liquor salesman.

"What?" shouted his father and mother when he first mentioned the idea. "Absolutely not. We have labored all our lives so that we can afford to send you to college. You are our firstborn son. We want you to be educated, not like us who can barely read or write. You must go to the university to study. Be a doctor, be an engineer. But a liquor salesman! How can you possibly disappoint us so?" So Ronald went to the university and studied engineering for five years. Now he has a desk job and a nine-to-five schedule, drawing up blueprints that bore him stiff. All the while, he dreams of being out on the road, listening to the ball games while he's driving, and using his persuasive personality to sell the bar and liquor store owners five cases of bourbon when they only wanted four.

THE OVEREDUCATED

Cases one to four above explain in part why the Chinese are such a highly educated people. Add to that the high esteem in which scholars or men of learning are held in the Chinese culture and you can see why a full quarter of all Chinese males in the United States 16 years and over are college graduates or postgraduates (see Table 4.1). Even 16.5 percent of the females have attained this educational level. Following the column down under the 25- to 34-year age bracket—a time when most people have finished their formal education—an astounding 50.9 percent of the males and 35.2 percent of the females are in the college graduate or postgraduate levels. Note also that in this age bracket 85.3 percent of the males are high school graduates and the median years of school completed is more than 16. In other words, half the Chinese males 25 to 34 years old have 16 or more years of schooling.

A more detailed breakdown from the Public Use Sample Data reveals that 16 percent of Chinese males and 9 percent of the females have gone for postgraduate studies.

TABLE 4.1

School Years Completed by the Chinese in the United States, by Age Group and Sex, 1970

	Total 16 Years and over		16-19 Years		20-24 Years		25-34 Years		35-44 Years		45-64 Years		65 Years and over	
	Number	Percent	Number	Percent	Number	Percent	Number	Percent	Number	Percent	Number	Percent	Number	Percent
Male	163,893	100.0	18,757	100.0	22,996	100.0	33,575	100.0	31,082	100.0	42,239	100.0	15,244	100.0
Elementary														
Less than 5 years	15,744	9.6	166	0.9	339	1.5	844	2.5	2,013	6.5	6,587	15.6	5,795	38.0
5-7 years	13,494	8.2	236	1.3	302	1.3	1,032	3.1	2,474	8.0	6,290	14.9	3,160	20.7
8 years	7,962	4.9	492	2.6	192	1.0	581	1.7	1,500	4.8	3,556	8.4	1,641	10.8
High school														
1-3 years	24,703	15.1	10,000	53.3	1,664	7.2	2,472	7.4	3,593	11.6	5,568	13.2	1,400	9.2
4 years	32,910	20.1	5,137	27.4	4,750	20.7	6,241	18.6	6,579	21.2	8,685	20.6	1,518	10.0
College														
1-3 years	28,125	17.2	2,707	14.4	12,465	54.2	5,324	15.9	3,836	12.3	3,358	7.9	435	2.9
4 years or more	40,955	25.0	13	0.1	3,284	14.3	17,081	50.9	11,087	35.7	8,195	19.4	1,295	8.5
Median school years completed	12.6		11.5		14.0		16.1		12.9		11.5		6.7	
Percent high school graduates	62.2		41.9		89.1		85.3		69.2		47.9		21.3	
Female	145,012	110.0	17,099	100.0	22,888	100.0	32,411	100.0	28,194	100.0	32,808	100.0	11,612	100.0
Elementary														
Less than 5 years	22,202	15.3	194	1.1	520	2.3	1,682	5.2	4,238	15.0	8,907	27.1	6,665	57.4
5-7 years	12,292	8.5	236	1.4	716	3.1	1,788	5.5	3,258	11.6	4,677	14.3	1,617	13.9
8 years	6,294	4.3	452	2.6	340	1.5	982	3.0	1,349	4.8	2,336	7.1	835	7.2
High school														
1-3 years	19,623	13.5	8,773	51.1	1,762	7.7	2,655	8.2	2,638	9.4	3,099	9.4	696	6.0
4 years	35,101	24.2	4,648	27.1	5,405	23.6	7,920	24.4	8,325	29.5	7,907	24.1	896	7.7
College														
1-3 years	25,547	17.6	2,781	16.3	10,790	41.7	5,964	18.4	3,421	12.1	2,206	6.7	385	3.3
4 years or more	23,953	16.5	15	0.1	3,355	14.7	11,420	35.2	4,965	17.6	3,676	11.2	522	4.5
Median school years completed	12.3		11.6		13.8		13.6		12.3		9.5		4.4	
Percent high school graduates	58.3		43.5		85.4		78.1		59.3		42.0		15.5	

Source: U.S. Department of Commerce, Bureau of the Census, Subject Report, PC(2)1G (1970).

At this point, caution must again be advised against unqualified interpretation of the census data, for the numbers may be biased to a strong extent by the return of census questionnaires from the better educated. Nevertheless, in the absence of more reliable statistics, we must perforce use what we have with the understanding that the information is biased.

If the 25- to 34-year age group educational attainment is high, that of the future generations promises to be higher. In the age bracket immediately preceding, the 20- to 24-year-old group, illiteracy is minimal and the percentage of high school graduates is 85.4 for the females and 89.1 for the males. Those who are attending college or are graduates reach 68.5 percent for the males and 56.4 percent for the females.

THE UNDEREDUCATED

Age and sex are the crucial variables. At one extreme we have an extraordinarily well-educated group. At the other end of the age scale, especially among Chinese females, we have the opposite. In this same table, we see that 38 percent of the males and a whopping 57.4 percent of the females 65 years and over have five years of schooling or less. And in Table 4.2, we see that "less" means no schooling at all. In fact, 11 percent of the total Chinese population are illiterate. Thus, the educational profile, much like the employment pattern of the Chinese in the United States, runs to extremes with a large proportion of highly educated people and too many illiterates in either Chinese or English.

Comparing the educational level of the Chinese with that of the whites, blacks, and Japanese in Table 4.2, we find that the illiteracy rate for whites is 1.6 percent; for blacks, 3.3 percent; and for the Japanese, 1.8 percent; but for the Chinese, it is 11.1 percent—seven times greater than for whites and three times greater than for blacks.

Case Five: Gim Gok is one of the 14 percent in the 45- to 64-year age bracket who has had five years of schooling or less. She is 46 years old, been in this country four years, lives in a railroad apartment in New York's Chinatown, has four children, and works as a seamstress in a garment factory. Her husband is a chef in a New Jersey restaurant.

Every day her husband commutes to New Jersey and returns to Chinatown at two in the morning. The children—all four of them—sleep in one room, and the only place where they can do their homework is on the kitchen table. The kitchen also serves as living room and bathroom. The bathtub is right next to the kitchen sink.

Gim Gok would like to move to New Jersey to accommodate her husband and provide better living quarters for her children, but she is

TABLE 4.2

Years of School Completed by Persons 25 Years and over, by Race, 1970
(in percent)

	Chinese	White	Black	Japanese
Total number 25 years and over (100 percent)	227,165	109,900,000	10,375,000	353,707
No schooling	11.1	1.6	3.3	1.8
Elementary				
1-4 years	5.1	3.9	11.3	2.4
5-7 years	10.7	8.3	18.7	6.3
8 years	5.6	13.6	10.5	8.5
High school				
1-3 years	9.7	16.5	24.8	12.3
4 years	21.2	35.2	21.2	39.3
College				
1-3 years	11.0	10.7	5.9	13.6
4 years or more	25.6	11.6	4.4	15.9
Median school years	12.4	12.2	9.8	12.5
Percent high school graduates	57.8	52.3	31.4	68.8

Source: U.S. Department of Commerce, Bureau of the Census, Subject Reports, PC(1)C1, PC(2)1B, PC(2)1G (1970).

57

afraid. She does not speak English. When she ventures anywhere outside Chinatown, one of the children must accompany her. She knows that if she moved to New Jersey, she probably would not find another job. She takes English language classes one night a week, but learning a new language without the foundation of knowing how to read and write in one's mother tongue is doubly difficult.

EDUCATION AND WOMEN

When education must be paid for, a selective process comes into play and some groups are favored over others. Education was not publicly supported in China, nor is there tax-supported universal education in Hong Kong and Taiwan today. Neither is school compulsory. Under these circumstances, those financially better off give priority for schooling to their sons.

If the family can afford to send both sons and daughters, the latter may be educated if the family has shed the centuries-old concept that females are spoiled for wifehood or motherhood if they acquire some "book-learning." That females are not worthy of education is still a prevalent belief among the Chinese. This explains why approximately 15 percent of all Chinese females in the United States have less than five years of schooling and 10 percent have never entered a classroom. It is generally the foreign-born female who is the most deprived and, hence, the most handicapped. Her occupational sphere is, therefore, extremely circumscribed and limited to the most simple and menial jobs.

Illiteracy, then, is generally a problem with those over 45, especially the women. The younger generations are highly educated, regardless of sex.

EDUCATION AND NATIVITY

In this country, education is a birthright. In fact, in most states it is compulsory until age 16. The quality of education is another matter, but just using highest grade completed as a yardstick we find very few in the lower grade level among the native-born Chinese. In fact, the Chinese in this country have generally availed themselves as much as possible of the educational opportunities open to them, even in the days when a college education led only to a bartender's job or other menial work. The parents, in most cases, were the propelling force in goading their children on to higher educational achievement, even when they, themselves, were illiterate. The motivating factor is the high esteem accorded men of learning within the

TABLE 4.3

Years of School Completed by the Chinese in the United States, 25 Years and over, U.S. Total and Five Selected States, 1970

Years of School Completed	United States		California		New York		Hawaii		Illinois		Massachusetts	
	Number	Per-cent	Number	Per-cent	Number	Per-cent	Number	Per-cent	Number	Per-cent	Number	Per-cent
Total 25 years and over	227,165	100.0	88,307	100.1	44,993	100.0	28,310	99.9	7,337	100.0	7,084	99.9
No schooling	25,205	11.1	11,972	13.6	7,125	15.8	1,183	4.2	543	7.4	714	10.1
Elementary												
1–4 years	11,522	5.1	4,533	5.1	3,037	6.7	1,429	5.0	244	3.3	414	5.8
5–7 years	24,296	10.7	8,884	10.1	7,001	15.6	2,109	7.4	819	11.2	1,035	14.6
8 years	12,780	5.6	4,218	4.8	3,096	6.9	1,807	6.4	621	8.5	534	7.5
High school												
1–3 years	22,121	9.7	8,004	9.1	4,889	10.9	3,066	10.8	767	10.5	716	10.1
4 years	48,071	21.2	19,210	21.8	7,721	17.2	10,666	37.7	1,199	16.3	1,304	18.4
College												
1–3 years	24,929	11.0	12,759	14.4	3,121	6.9	2,948	10.4	663	9.0	465	6.6
4 years or more	58,241	25.6	18,727	21.2	9,003	20.0	5,102	18.0	2,481	33.8	1,902	26.8
Median school years	12.4		12.3		10.4		12.4		12.6		12.1	
Percent high school graduates		57.8		57.4		44.1		66.1		59.2		51.8

Note: Based on a 20 percent sampling.

Source: U.S. Department of Commerce, Bureau of the Census, Subject Report, PC(2)1G (1970), Table 18.

Chinese system of cultural values. In the social hierarchy in China, scholars stood at the top. That is why parents continually urge their children to study hard and reach higher levels in school. At the least, a high school education is a must, and more than a third of all native-born Chinese go on to college. A four-year college degree is the rule, while another 8 percent go on to graduate school (see Table 4.4).

The foreign-born educational profile is quite different: 12 percent are illiterate and another 10 percent finished only the eighth grade. These figures reflect the years of school completed for the Chinese 16 years of age or older. (If they had not gone higher than eighth grade after age 16, the likelihood of their going back to school is remote.) So, whereas more than one-third of the native-born are of college level, about one-third of the foreign-born are below the eighth grade level.

At the other extreme, better than 16 percent of the foreign-born are postgraduates. Add this percentage to the 21 percent enrolled in or graduated from college and you have a U-shaped educational curve instead of the normal bell shape.

EDUCATION AND EMPLOYMENT STATUS

The unemployment rate for the Chinese counted in the census is relatively low. Those who were omitted from the census are the ones likely to have unemployment difficulties, but their plight does not show up in our figures. What effect does education have on finding employment or holding a job? The logical assumption would be that the better educated have less difficulty, hence the unemployment rate would be lower. This fact is not substantiated for the Chinese.

In the last column in Table 4.4 we find a 10.5 percent unemployment rate for those with no education and the same percentage for those with postgraduate education. In other words, schooling may reach a point of diminishing returns. A very low 2.6 percent unemployment rate is registered for college graduates. After that, more education may create a problem of being overqualified; greater difficulty is experienced in finding a position commensurate with one's education. But overqualification seems not to be the prime reason why Chinese postgraduates cannot find employment. The more likely reason is that they are not permitted to work or that they must maintain their student status to remain in this country.

BETTER EDUCATION, BETTER JOB?

The Chinese professional, whether male or female, is extremely well educated, but so are Chinese male sales and clerical workers.

TABLE 4.4

Highest Grade Completed by the Chinese in the United States, 16 Years and over, by Sex, Nativity, and Employment Status, 1970
(in percent)

Highest Grade Completed	Sex		Nativity		Employment Status	
	Male	Female	U.S.-Born	Foreign-Born	Employed	Unemployed
None	6.0	10.4	1.8	12.0	6.4	10.5
Elementary						
Less than 5 years	3.0	3.9	2.4	4.1	2.6	0.0
5-7 years	7.9	9.2	4.3	11.1	7.9	11.8
8 years	4.8	4.5	3.8	5.2	4.0	9.2
High school						
1-3 years	15.9	14.3	18.2	13.2	12.8	11.8
4 years	20.8	25.4	31.6	17.5	24.0	30.3
College						
1-3 years	16.8	15.3	21.4	12.8	15.1	13.2
4 years	8.5	8.0	8.2	8.3	10.0	2.6
Postgraduate						
1 year	6.9	4.1	4.6	6.2	6.9	3.9
2 or more years	9.3	4.9	3.7	9.5	10.3	6.6
Total	100.0	100.0	100.0	100.0	100.0	100.0

Source: U.S. Department of Commerce, Bureau of the Census, Special Tabulation, Public Use Sample Data (1970).

For instance, 60 percent of the Chinese male bank tellers are college graduates, although this job actually requires only a high school degree, and 50 percent of Chinese males in file clerk jobs are college graduates. [1]

Chinese females, even those with a college education, are heavily concentrated in clerical jobs. Approximately half of those with one to three years of college, one-fourth of those who graduated, and one-eighth of those who are postgraduates remain at the clerical level. [2] This averages out to approximately one-third of all Chinese females who ever attended college (and we noted previously that almost one-fourth of the Chinese females 16 years and over have had some college education).

MORE SCHOOL, HIGHER PAY?

The general assumption is that a higher education commands a better job, which in turn means more pay. Does the correlation follow for the Chinese? After studying Table 4.5, we can say that, in some respects, the principle holds true. Those Chinese in the higher income brackets are better educated, but more education does not always result in better pay.

Of Chinese males 16 years or older, one out of five high school graduates earned more than $10,000 in 1969, whereas two out of five college graduates earned this same annual income. The proportion of those earning $10,000 or more increases to half of those with a postgraduate degree. But what about the three in five college graduates and the other half of the postgraduates who fall somewhat, or even substantially, below this income level? Is this the norm or is it below par? Let us compare these percentages with those for whites and blacks.

The data reveal that 59.6 percent of white male college graduates have a personal income of $10,000 or more, whereas the black and Chinese male trail far behind with 35.3 percent and 38.3 percent, respectively. On the postgraduate level, 67.1 percent of the white males go over the $10,000 mark, while the Chinese male falls behind the black male in earning capacity.

The disparity of income between male and female of any race is deplorable. Females with the same educational attainment never come near the earning power of their male counterparts, and the Chinese female postgraduate is at the bottom of the ladder. Her black sister seems to be doing better than either whites or Chinese.

On the whole, the Chinese have cracked open the doors of professional and technical occupations, but their income is in no way commensurate with their educational achievement.

TABLE 4.5

Personal Income of $10,000 or More in 1969, by Educational Level
and Sex for Whites, Blacks, and Chinese
(in percent)

	Male	Female
High school graduates		
White	32.5	2.4
Black	10.4	0.9
Chinese	20.9	2.6
College graduates		
White	59.6	10.2
Black	35.3	11.2
Chinese	38.3	9.3
Postgraduates		
White	67.1	27.7
Black	53.0	34.2
Chinese	50.9	13.3

Sources: For whites and blacks: U.S. Department of Commerce, Bureau of the Census, General Population Characteristics, vol. 2 (1970), Table 249; for Chinese: U.S. Department of Commerce, Bureau of the Census, Special Tabulation, Public Use Sample Data (1970).

SUMMARY OF FINDINGS

1. A large proportion of the Chinese population is highly educated: one-fourth of the males and one-sixth of the females are college graduates. The educational attainment for the younger age groups —those below 25 years of age—promises to be even higher.

2. At the other extreme, a large proportion of the Chinese population in the United States is illiterate: 11 percent, compared to 1.6 percent for whites and 3.3 percent for blacks.

3. The opposite-poles educational profile is generally found among the foreign-born Chinese. The majority of native born are neither illiterate nor do they go beyond college graduation to the degree that their foreign-born counterparts do.

4. The high educational attainment of such a large proportion of the Chinese is due partially to the cultural tradition of respect for scholarship but primarily to enforced classroom attendance mandated in large part by immigration regulations.

5. The highly educated Chinese male tends to gravitate toward a white-collar professional or technical job, but many are in positions beneath their qualifications.

6. More school does not mean better pay for the Chinese. In fact, they form the most poorly paid group at comparable educational levels.

7. Whether illiterate or postgraduate, the Chinese female is the most disadvantaged. One-third of the Chinese females who have ever attended college are in clerical work. The occupational sphere is extremely limited and the financial remuneration is far below that of Chinese males or that of her white and black sisters.

RECOMMENDATIONS

Since the Chinese population is one of extremes—many highly educated and a disproportionate number of illiterate and near-illiterate—recommendations cannot be applied to the group as a whole. For those with many years of schooling, it is suggested that more attention be given to learning the social amenities, such as playing golf with the boss on weekends or chatting about baseball at the water cooler. After all, holding a responsible job means more than mere technical or professional know-how.

The Chinese need to know more about the American government and the political process. They need citizenship or civic knowledge so that they can become acquainted with the forces that might affect their lives. They need a broadening of their horizon, rather than more specialization in their academic field.

Every Chinese in the United States should learn about his history and experiences of his people so that he can be comfortable with his identity. He need not feel that he is a foreigner in this country. If he has opted for American citizenship, this is his country as much as it is any other American's. He need not apologize for his parents' customs nor their humble origins. Their migration is, in itself, a heroic feat. This is an aspect of his education that must be reinforced.

Those at the lower end of the educational scale consist mainly of older men and, especially, women who have had no schooling whatsoever. It is extremely difficult, if not impossible, to set up the traditional structure imparting knowledge by books, classroom, and the blackboard for people who do not have any previous exposure to this type of education. Their learning has all been acquired through actual life situations.

For these people, training sessions should be offered to acquaint them with knowledge of the basic functions of daily life. The United States is a more highly technological society than the one most Chinese

have left in the Far East. Even such a routine thing as using the telephone may be a novel experience to the recent immigrant. Taking a
bus or knowing how to deposit or withdraw money from a bank are
other examples. Teaching them these techniques will reduce their
feelings of helplessness and their dependence upon an ethnic community and enhance their ability to function more effectively.

As far as this author is aware, no such training programs now
exist for immigrant groups whose adjustment to a new country is a
total and overwhelming reeducational process. Everything must be
learned at once, and this learning is not restricted to preparation for
a job per se.

The need for English language classes has already been documented and set forth in Chapter 2. More than any other aspect, the
Chinese must learn some rudiments of the English language.

Finally, we must reexamine our attitudes toward the female
gender. The census tabulation points out the unforgivable inequities
shouldered by the Chinese women. They are less favored with the opportunity for schooling, and too high a percentage are illiterate.
A large proportion of Chinese females with college degrees and Ph.D.s
are still working in occupations that insult their ability and intelligence.
At the same time, their income trails so far behind that of their
male Chinese counterparts that it is pitiful.

Most Chinese women are still reticent about challenging the
status quo. Without active involvement and support, the liberation
of the Chinese female can only reap the lean pickings of the wider
feminist movement.

NOTES

1. U.S. Department of Commerce, Bureau of the Census,
Special Tabulation, Public Use Sample Data (1970).
   2. Ibid.

RANGE OF OCCUPATIONS

Many Americans consider the choice of occupation as a basic
right. This belief is so fundamental that we give very little thought
to the fact that it is not universal and that sometimes, even in this
country, the choice is restricted by many factors and conditions.

Not until recent times have the Chinese had any choice of occupation. World War II triggered the change, but it was around the 1950s
that the Chinese started easing into other lines of work. By the 1960s,
the pace had turned into a spurt and the Chinese made rapid strides
forward. The object of this study is to find out how the Chinese have
regrouped occupationally. Our first task is to find out what size group
we are dealing with and what their employment pattern is at present.
Perhaps some light can be thrown on why they are in these positions.
In other words, what were the causative factors? From knowledge of
where we are, we will attempt to see if the pattern of Chinese employment can be expanded horizontally and vertically.

This is a large but necessary order because one's occupation
is the single most important basic aspect of one's life. Work takes
up the major portion of our waking hours and provides the wherewithal
for our daily existence. It determines where and how we live. It may
also circumscribe our social life. That is why a study of the occupational status of the Chinese is fundamental to the understanding of this
ethnic group.

LABOR FORCE

How large a group are we dealing with when we talk about the
occupational pattern of the Chinese? The number of civilians 16 years

and over who are employed or looking for work is
force. Excluded are persons such as housewives,
teer work, students, retirees, those who are unabl
those not actively seeking paid employment.

The Chinese labor force was approximately 19
against a total population of 437,000.* Using round r
190,000 labor force, 120,000 were males and 70,000
Approximately three-fourths of the males and one-half   ...es
16 years and over were in the labor force. The follow...g comparison
of labor force participation rate by whites and blacks is taken from the
1970 census:

	Percent Male	Percent Female
Chinese	73.2	49.5
White	80.6	43.4
Black	69.8	47.5

There is an appreciable difference in labor force participation
rates between the three ethnic groups. The percentage (80.6 percent)
of white males in the labor force is significantly higher than that for
the Chinese (73.2 percent) or blacks (69.8 percent). The Chinese occupy an intermediary position between the two groups. The reason
for the lower rates for Chinese males stems from the prolonged period
of their education, which keeps them out of the labor market but does
not mean that they are unemployed. This is obvious in Table 5.1,
which shows the percent of Chinese in the labor force by age group
and sex. Not until 25 to 34 years of age do the Chinese males start
coming into the labor force in numbers, and by the next age category,
35 to 44 years, they are into the labor market almost full force.

More Women Working

What is revealing about our findings is that a greater percentage
of Chinese women are in the labor force compared to the blacks or
whites. It has been popularly assumed that a large proportion of black
women are employed outside of the home, either because of low family
income or the absence of a male breadwinner, and that this situation
has had a deleterious effect on the black family. Our figures show a
larger percentage of Chinese women in the labor force, and the fact

*The size of the labor force has increased substantially since
that time because of the heavy influx of immigrants over recent years.

TABLE 5.1

Percent of Chinese 16 Years and over in the Labor Force, 1970

Age and Sex	United States	California	New York	Hawaii	Illinois	Massachusetts
Male	73.2	73.5	71.1	76.1	73.4	72.3
16–19 years	37.5	41.0	26.5	37.1	33.2	35.3
20–24 years	58.0	60.8	53.6	76.6	53.5	59.0
25–34 years	86.7	88.9	88.8	92.1	84.8	82.3
35–44 years	95.5	95.7	96.3	96.2	95.0	94.0
45–64 years	87.8	87.5	86.2	88.4	87.5	92.6
65 and over	24.8	23.6	21.9	26.6	32.9	26.0
Female	49.5	51.0	49.2	54.2	50.2	53.2
16–19 years	34.5	36.6	29.4	37.1	37.8	46.3
20–24 years	55.7	59.0	54.1	64.7	56.7	56.9
25–34 years	50.3	54.6	47.6	64.1	45.5	50.5
35–44 years	59.1	60.9	61.2	68.3	58.9	61.3
45–64 years	57.4	58.0	57.6	60.1	63.2	62.5
65 and over	12.0	11.1	14.8	6.8	14.9	20.2

Note: In labor force means the employed or those looking for work.

Source: U.S. Department of Commerce, Bureau of the Census, Subject Report PC(2)1G (1970), Table 19.

comes somewhat as a surprise. The impact of this development may be significant. The increasing participation of Chinese females in employment outside of the home is treated in greater length in Chapter 6.

Table 5.2 shows labor force and employment status of the Chinese, by sex, for the three states having the highest Chinese population and ten SMSAs. There does not seem to be any pattern in the labor force participation rates for Chinese males—the lowest being 68.3 percent, in Sacramento, California, and the highest, 78.5 percent, in San Jose, California.

There was a 10 percentage-point variation for these places, both of which are in the same state and fairly close to one another. Sacramento also registered the lowest labor force participation rate for Chinese females (44.3 percent) and had the greatest unemployment rate—11.1 percent. These figures are puzzling considering that Sacramento is the state capital and that government is a fairly stable and steady industry that employs a substantial proportion of clerical workers, teachers, and health workers. Because these are traditional female domains, these figures appear questionable.

MAJOR OCCUPATIONAL GROUPS

The variety and job titles identified by the Bureau of Census runs to 494, but they can be grouped under ten major occupational categories. As listed in Table 5.3, these range from professional and technical to private household workers. These major occupational groups simplify the handling of our statistics, but they mask many facts that must be examined in more detail. Nonetheless, it is important to view the whole before viewing the parts.

The striking fact that emerges from Table 5.3 is the heavy concentration in the professions and service work for the males. This is a twin-peak situation or a tendency toward extremes. Assuming that the ten occupational categories also reflect an ascending or descending scale of economic status associated with these occupational groups, we can say that the Chinese are both at the top and the bottom of the economic scale. For example, 28.9 percent of all Chinese males in the United States are in the professions, which is the top of the scale, while 23.6 percent are in service work, which is near the bottom. Again, we have a bifurcated group in economic status.

The proportions in each group vary from state to state, but the pattern holds true for these two categories, except in the state of Hawaii.* In some states, like Illinois, the extremes are even more

*In almost every table in this report, we can see that the figures for Hawaii differ noticeably from those for the mainland states. That

TABLE 5.2

Labor Force and Employment Status of the Chinese in the United States, by Sex, for Selected States and SMSAs, 1970

	Male				Female			
	Labor Force		Number	Percent	Labor Force		Number	Percent
	Number	Percent	Employed	Unemployed	Number	Percent	Employed	Unemployed
U.S. total	117,924	73.2	114,433	3.0	71,786	49.5	69,129	3.7
State								
California	46,008	72.5	44,164	4.0	29,983	51.0	28,575	4.7
New York	23,030	71.0	22,497	2.3	13,295	49.2	12,910	2.9
Hawaii	13,603	74.6	13,315	2.1	9,935	54.1	9,761	1.8
SMSA								
Boston	3,468	72.5	3,371	2.8	2,112	54.8	2,020	4.4
Chicago	3,475	74.5	3,389	2.5	1,967	50.9	1,916	2.6
Honolulu	12,627	74.5	12,364	2.1	9,331	54.6	9,174	1.7
Los Angeles–Long Beach	11,841	77.0	11,384	3.9	7,159	51.4	6,931	3.2
New York	21,584	71.1	21,075	2.4	12,685	49.8	12,325	2.8
Sacramento	2,553	68.3	2,499	2.1	1,588	44.3	1,412	11.1
San Francisco–Oakland	23,477	71.4	22,448	4.4	16,917	54.0	16,279	3.8
San Jose	2,309	78.5	2,227	3.6	1,192	45.8	1,119	6.1
Seattle–Everett	2,069	71.5	1,990	3.8	1,216	49.6	1,132	6.9
Washington, D.C.–Maryland–Virginia	2,084	73.3	2,055	1.4	1,355	49.5	1,303	3.8

Source: U.S. Department of Commerce, Bureau of the Census, Subject Report, PC (2)1G (1970), Tables 19, 28.

70

TABLE 5.3

Major Occupational Groups of the Chinese in the United States, by Selected States and Sex, 1970

Major Occupational Group and Sex	United States		California		New York		Hawaii		Illinois		Massachusetts	
	Number	Per-cent	Number	Per-cent	Number	Per-cent	Number	Per-cent	Number	Per-cent	Number	Per-cent
Males employed, 16 years and over	114,433	100.0	44,164	100.0	22,497	100.0	13,315	100.0	3,914	100.0	3,858	100.0
Professional and technical	33,119	28.9	11,400	25.8	4,866	21.6	2,883	21.7	1,438	36.7	1,121	29.1
Managers and administrators	13,061	11.4	4,989	11.3	2,278	10.1	1,878	14.1	338	8.6	391	10.1
Sales workers	5,021	4.4	2,385	5.4	946	4.2	866	6.5	134	3.4	54	1.9
Clerical workers	10,762	9.4	5,388	12.2	1,813	8.1	1,499	11.3	274	7.0	248	6.4
Craftsmen	8,367	7.3	3,463	7.8	963	4.3	2,595	19.5	137	3.5	125	3.2
Operatives	11,998	10.5	4,943	11.2	3,367	13.0	1,229	9.2	355	9.1	313	8.1
Laborers	3,787	3.3	1,784	4.0	360	1.6	697	5.2	89	2.3	82	2.1
Farm workers	830	0.7	481	1.1	14	0.1	146	1.1	14	0.4	6	0.2
Service workers	27,010	23.6	9,100	20.6	7,784	34.6	1,516	11.4	1,125	28.7	1,518	39.4
Private household workers	478	0.4	231	0.5	106	0.5	6	0.1	10	0.3	0	0.0
Females employed, 16 years and over	69,129	100.0	28,575	100.0	12,910	100.0	9,761	100.0	2,228	100.0	2,255	100.0
Professional and technical	13,402	19.4	4,332	15.2	2,004	15.5	1,860	19.1	610	27.4	409	18.1
Managers and administrators	2,636	3.8	987	3.5	479	3.7	534	5.5	36	1.6	16	0.7
Sales workers	3,531	5.1	1,558	5.5	430	3.3	890	9.1	55	2.5	86	3.8
Clerical workers	21,989	31.8	10,453	36.6	3,246	25.1	3,619	37.1	626	28.1	639	28.3
Craftsmen	846	1.2	351	1.2	182	1.4	190	2.0	39	1.8	0	0.0
Operatives	15,556	22.5	6,567	23.0	5,426	42.0	778	8.0	460	20.7	843	37.4
Laborers	592	0.9	199	0.7	92	0.7	100	1.0	26	1.2	10	0.4
Farm workers	361	0.5	250	0.9	6	0.1	54	0.6	0	0.0	7	0.3
Service workers	8,842	12.8	3,259	11.4	769	6.0	1,650	16.9	348	15.6	213	9.5
Private household workers	1,374	2.0	619	2.2	276	2.1	86	0.9	28	1.3	32	1.4

Source: U.S. Department of Commerce, Bureau of the Census, Subject Report, PC(2)1G (1970), Table 22.

pronounced: 36.7 percent are in the professions and 28.7 percent in service work. States like New York and Massachusetts have a much greater percentage of males in service work, but the percentage in the professions is substantial as well.

A twin-peak situation also holds for the Chinese female, but the peaks are closer together toward the middle of the economic scale. The largest numbers are found in clerical work and the second largest come under the heading "operatives." These two occupational groups combined include from approximately one-half to two-thirds of all females employed.

Variation by City

The opposite-poles employment picture prevails even in breakdown by cities (see Table 5.4), but it is accentuated in some cases by an even greater concentration in either the professions or service work for the males. For example, 47.9 percent of the Chinese males in Washington, D.C., are in the professions, whereas 41.5 percent of those in Boston are in service work. The lowest percentage in the professions is found in New York City (18.6 percent), and 36 percent of the males are in service work.

There is no departure in the twin-peak female pattern of employment either, except for the same concentration of either clerical workers or operatives, depending upon the city: 43.6 percent are in clerical position in Sacramento, whereas 43.7 percent are operatives in New York City. The few exceptions are found in Washington, D.C., San Jose, California, and Honolulu, where female professionals exceed the numbers in the operatives category.

Four SMSAs shown in Table 5.4 are within the state of California. They are Los Angeles, Sacramento, San Francisco-Oakland, and San Jose. The latter three are fairly close to one another, but the variation in the percentages of the various occupation groups is pronounced. For instance, only 10.9 percent of the females in San Francisco are in professional jobs, whereas in San Jose, 50 miles south, the percentage is 32.4; and 12 percent of the females in that city are farm laborers, whereas in some places women in farming are few or almost nil.

---

is because Hawaii's Chinese were unfettered by American racism until the islands became a territory of the United States in 1898. Even then, the social climate was more favorable than that found on the mainland. As a consequence, the Chinese were able to move up and out into other occupations more quickly.

TABLE 5.4

Major Occupational Groups of the Chinese in the United States, by Percent Distribution for Selected SMSAs and Sex, 1970

Major Occupational Group	Boston	Chicago	Hono-lulu	Los Angeles-Long Beach	New York	Sacra-mento	San Francisco-Oakland	San Jose	Seattle-Everett	Washington, D.C.-Virginia-Maryland
Males employed, 16 years and over	100.0	100.0	100.0	100.0	100.0	100.0	100.0	100.0	100.0	100.0
Professional and technical	27.5	31.7	22.2	32.0	18.6	25.5	19.8	50.5	25.1	47.9
Managers	10.2	9.4	14.1	10.9	10.3	14.5	10.3	9.1	13.7	10.1
Sales workers	1.2	3.7	6.5	5.7	4.5	3.6	5.9	4.9	3.9	1.2
Clerical workers	6.8	7.8	11.4	10.5	8.3	13.5	14.8	7.3	9.2	6.1
Craftsmen	2.4	4.0	20.0	6.1	4.3	5.4	9.7	6.0	7.6	3.6
Operatives	7.9	9.4	8.9	12.3	15.7	9.8	12.3	5.5	4.9	3.8
Laborers, except farmers	2.3	2.2	5.2	3.5	1.7	6.2	3.5	2.3	2.2	2.8
Farmers, managers and laborers	0.2	0.4	0.6	0.2	0.1	2.6	0.3	7.0	0.2	0.2
Service workers	41.5	31.1	11.2	18.6	36.0	19.0	22.7	7.1	33.2	23.4
Private household workers	0	0.3	0	0.3	0.5	0	0.7	0.3	0	0.9
Females employed, 16 years and over										
Professional and technical	15.6	22.7	18.9	20.3	14.0	13.3	10.9	32.4	18.6	34.4
Managers	0.6	1.7	5.4	3.5	3.6	3.9	3.2	2.7	2.5	4.3
Sales workers	3.8	2.4	9.4	5.3	3.4	3.5	5.8	5.4	5.9	4.4
Clerical workers	28.5	30.4	37.5	33.9	25.4	43.6	38.2	29.9	24.2	29.9
Craftsmen	0	2.0	1.9	0.7	1.4	0.8	1.6	0.8	0.4	0.8
Operatives	39.6	23.4	8.2	25.6	43.7	14.1	26.3	7.7	29.6	5.7
Laborers, except farmers	0.5	1.4	1.0	0.4	0.7	1.4	0.5	1.3	1.5	0.4
Farmers, managers, and laborers	0.3	0	0.5	0.1	0	1.3	0.3	12.0	0.8	0
Service workers	9.9	14.8	16.5	8.3	5.6	13.8	11.1	6.4	14.9	14.2
Private household workers	1.2	1.2	0.7	2.1	2.1	4.2	2.2	1.4	1.6	5.9

Source: U.S. Department of Commerce, Bureau of the Census, Subject Report, PC(2)1G (1970).

Aside from the professions and service work, the Chinese males appear to have a healthy percentage of 10 to 15 percent under the managerial category. But closer scrutiny will reveal that these managers, more often than not, are owner-operators of small businesses such as restaurants, gift shops, or grocery stores.

Some comment is in order on the other major occupational categories and the conspicuous absence of Chinese from certain types of jobs—sales work, for example. A national percentage of 4.4 percent of the males and 5.1 percent of the females are in sales work. Again, more often than not, these sales workers are employed in the Chinatown curio shops, which cater to the tourists, or they are salespeople who cater to their own people, such as insurance salesmen whose clients are of their own ethnic group. Sales work calls for extensive dealing with the public, and there has been reluctance on the part of both the employers and the Chinese to vanquish fears about how clients will react to a salesperson of Chinese ancestry.

Craftsmen

The crafts is one field to which the Chinese would be ideally suited. Crafts are skilled and other manual occupations. Approximately 30 million blue-collar workers are employed in this occupational category in the United States. Craftsmen transform the ideas of scientists and the plans of engineers into goods and services. They operate transportation and communication systems. They build homes and factories and machines. They are the mechanics and the repairmen, the carpenters and the bricklayers. In the crafts, one works with materials and with the hands more than with ideas or with the public.

However, crafts are heavily unionized, and entry into these occupations is extremely difficult. (This subject will be dealt with more fully in Chapter 8.) As a result, Chinese representation in the crafts is insignificant. For example, it was but 4.3 percent in New York State in 1970. In actual numbers, it was less than a thousand Chinese males for the entire Empire State.

Laborers, Farmers, and Household Workers

At one time, laborers, farmers, and household workers were the predominant occupations of the Chinese in the United States. Today, the Chinese have almost disappeared from these major occupational groups. This rapid decrease is seen in Table 5.5, which shows the occupational grouping of the Chinese for the four decennial censuses.

TABLE 5.5

Major Occupational Groups of the Chinese in the United States,
1940–70
(in percent)

Major Occupational Group	1940	1950	1960	1970
Total employed	36,454	48,409	98,784	181,190
Professional and technical	2.8	7.1	17.9	26.5
Managers	20.6	19.8	12.7	8.9
Sales workers	11.4	15.9	6.6	4.3
Clerical workers	11.4	15.9	13.8	16.8
Craftsmen	1.2	2.9	5.2	5.4
Operators	22.6	17.1	15.0	14.8
Laborers, except farmers	0.7	1.7	1.3	2.3
Farmers	3.8	2.6	1.0	0.6
Service workers	30.4	28.8	18.8	19.6
Private household workers	6.2	2.6	1.0	0.8
Not reported	0.3	1.5	6.5	—

Note: Between 1960 and 1970, some job titles were shifted from one occupational group to another, especially in the service work category.

Source: U.S. Department of Commerce, Bureau of the Census, Decennial Censuses (1940, 1950, 1960, 1970).

Private household workers went from 6.2 percent, in 1940, to 0.8 percent, in 1970. Farmers went from 3.8 percent, in 1940, to 0.6 percent, in 1970. Laborers increased from a tiny 0.7 percent, in 1940, to 2.3 percent in 1970, and we may see a slight increase in this category in 1980 as a result of the recent influx of immigrants, but the increase will never be significant to any degree.

The most spectacular finding from this table is the phenomenal increase in the professional and technical percentages from a mere 2.8 percent, in 1940, to 7.1 percent, in 1950, to 17.9 percent, in 1960, and a whopping 26.5 percent in 1970. At the same time, the work force increased five times within this 30-year time span. The decrease in the managerial and sales positions can be explained again by the fact that the small owner-operated stores are dwindling rapidly.

How do these percentages measure against those for whites, blacks, and Japanese? Table 5.6 gives a comparison. The Chinese

TABLE 5.6

Percent Distribution of Employed Persons in Major Occupational
Groups, by Race, 1970

Major Occupational Group	Chinese	White	Black	Japanese
Professional and technical	26.5	14.8	8.3	19.0
Managers	8.9	11.4	2.2	8.2
Sales workers	4.3	6.7	2.2	6.4
Clerical workers	16.8	18.0	13.8	20.2
Craftsmen	5.4	13.5	9.1	11.8
Operators	14.8	17.0	23.6	11.7
Laborers, except farmers	2.3	4.1	9.3	5.9
Farmers	0.6	4.0	3.1	3.8
Service workers	19.6	9.4	20.0	11.0
Private household workers	0.8	1.3	8.3	1.8

Source: U.S. Department of Commerce, Bureau of the Census,
Subject Report (1970).

are far ahead of all three other ethnic groups by percentage in the
professions; they trail far behind all three groups in the crafts; and
they are on an even keel with the blacks in service work.

Detailed Occupations

To get down to specifics, exactly what professions or occupations are the Chinese engaged in? Table 5.7 gives a selected list of
those occupations in which the Chinese are to be found to a greater
degree.

In studying the figures and percentages in this table, we see
some decided areas of concentration. There are 8,862 engineers
and another 3,631 engineering and science technicians for an approximate total of 12,500. Educators, both at college and precollege levels, run close to another 10,000. Professional health personnel add
up to about 8,000. These three groups already total about 40,500
out of 48,000 professionals.

There are reasons why the Chinese are predisposed toward
these three professions. Some of the reasons were mentioned at the
beginning of this chapter. To recapitulate briefly, one reason is the
importance attached to science and technology in Chinese educational

TABLE 5.7

Selected Occupations of the Chinese in the United States, 1970

Selected Occupations	Male	Female	Total	Percent
Total 16 Years and Over	113,929	67,261	181,190	100.0
Professional, Technical, and Kindred Workers	34,436	13,565	48,001	26.5
Accountants	2,073	823	2,896	1.6
Architects	596	44	640	0.4
Computer specialists	1,288	414	1,702	0.9
Engineers	8,780	82	8,862	4.9
Aeronautical and astronautical	510	0	510	0.3
Chemical	531	0	531	0.3
Civil	2,222	40	2,262	1.2
Electrical and electronic	2,588	22	2,610	1.4
Industrial	148	0	148	0.1
Mechanical	892	20	912	0.5
Lawyers and judges	327	45	372	0.2
Librarians, archivists, and curators	234	561	795	0.4
Mathematical specialists	122	154	276	0.2
Life and physical scientists	2,244	582	2,826	1.6
Biological	382	126	508	0.3
Chemists	1,353	417	1,770	1.0
Physicists and astronomers	278	19	297	0.2
Personnel and labor relations workers	340	83	423	0.2
Physicians, dentists, and related practitioners	3,344	586	3,930	2.2
Dentists	423	0	423	0.2
Pharmacists	591	156	747	0.4
Physicians, medical and osteopathic	2,200	408	2,608	1.4
Registered nurses, dieticians, and therapists	156	1,413	1,569	0.9
Health technologists and technicians	373	1,073	1,446	0.8
Religious workers	196	27	223	0.1
Social scientists	285	94	379	0.2
Social and recreational workers	372	461	833	0.5
Teachers, college and university	4,059	1,005	5,064	2.8
Biology	99	57	156	0.1
Chemistry	244	74	318	0.2
Physics	389	0	389	0.2
Engineering	545	0	545	0.3
Mathematics	318	88	406	0.2
Health specialties	181	121	302	0.2
Psychology	54	24	78	0.0
Economics	103	21	124	0.1
History	116	40	156	0.1
English	96	79	175	0.1
Foreign language	150	104	254	0.1

(continued)

TABLE 5.7 (continued)

Selected Occupations	Male	Female	Total	Percent
Teachers, except college and university	1,209	3,332	4,541	2.5
Elementary school	198	1,866	2,064	1.1
Prekindergarten and kindergarten	0	379	379	0.2
Secondary school	807	675	1,482	0.8
Engineering and science technicians	3,189	442	3,631	2.0
Chemical	244	64	308	0.2
Draftsmen	1,457	170	1,627	0.9
Electrical and electronic engineering	839	0	839	0.5
Writers, artists, and entertainers	2,020	651	2,671	1.5
Designers	467	257	724	0.4
Editors and reporters	190	125	315	0.2
Painters and sculptors	407	68	475	0.3
Photographers	282	20	302	0.2
Public relations men and publicity writers	108	66	174	0.1
Writers, artists, and entertainers, n.e.c.	293	75	368	0.2
Research workers not specified	1,961	766	2,727	1.5
Managers and Administrators Except Farm	13,189	2,868	16,057	8.9
Bank officers and financial managers	375	239	614	0.3
Buyers, wholesale and retail trade	303	200	503	0.3
Managers and superintendents, building	200	119	319	0.2
Officials and administrators, public administration, n.e.c.	397	66	463	0.3
Federal public administration and postal service	336	45	381	0.2
Restaurant, cafeteria, and bar managers	3,207	546	3,753	2.1
Sales managers and department heads, retail trade	352	0	352	0.2
Managers and administrators, n.e.c., salaried	3,328	596	3,924	2.2
Construction	181	0	181	0.1
Durable goods, manufacturing	228	0	228	0.1
Nondurable goods including not specified manufacturing	391	79	470	0.3
Transportation	267	66	333	0.2
Wholesale trade	333	0	333	0.2
Retail trade	1,051	293	1,344	0.7
General merchandise stores	116	52	168	0.1
Food stores	571	132	703	0.4
Finance, insurance, and real estate	200	0	200	0.1
Business and repair services	180	36	216	0.1
Personnel services	320	20	340	0.2
Managers and administrators, n.e.c., self-employed	4,020	847	4,867	2.7
Wholesale trade	277	28	305	0.2
Retail trade	2,161	434	2,595	1.4
Food stores	1,805	317	2,122	1.2
Personnel services	1,203	324	1,527	0.8

Selected Occupations	Male	Female	Total	Percent
Sales Workers	4,690	3,180	7,870	4.3
Insurance agents, brokers, and underwriters	504	98	602	0.3
Real estate agents and brokers	236	34	270	0.1
Stock and bond salesmen	306	20	326	0.2
Salesmen and sales clerk, n.e.c.	3,107	2,812	5,919	3.3
Sales representatives, wholesale trade	569	72	641	0.4
Sales clerks, retail trade	2,066	2,458	4,524	2.5
General merchandise stores	275	1,102	1,377	0.8
Food stores	1,047	450	1,497	0.8
Apparel and assessories stores	128	176	304	0.2
Clerical and Kindred Workers	9,768	20,736	30,504	16.8
Bank tellers	117	600	717	0.4
Bookkeepers	731	2,166	2,897	1.6
Cashiers	1,354	2,485	3,839	2.1
Counter clerks, except food	267	253	520	0.3
Estimators and investigators, n.e.c.	182	257	439	0.2
Expediters and production controllers	240	83	323	0.2
File clerks	521	552	1,073	0.6
Library attendants and assistants	252	510	762	0.4
Mail carriers, post office	517	32	549	0.3
Office machine operators	649	1,605	2,254	1.2
Postal clerks	706	302	1,008	0.6
Receptionists	22	410	432	0.2
Secretaries	153	2,924	3,077	1.7
Shipping and receiving clerks	482	66	548	0.3
Statistical clerks	207	450	657	0.4
Stenographers	21	247	268	0.1
Stock clerks and storekeepers	613	294	907	0.5
Telephone operators	69	327	396	0.2
Ticket, station, and express agents	130	164	294	0.2
Typists	206	2,958	3,164	1.7
Craftsmen and Kindred Workers	8,789	1,060	9,849	5.4
Bakers	278	85	363	0.2
Construction craftsmen	1,748	19	1,767	1.0
Carpenters	569	19	588	0.3
Electricians	580	0	580	0.3
Plumbers and pipe fitters	255	0	255	0.1
Mechanics and repairmen	2,463	143	2,606	1.4
Aircraft	370	46	416	0.2
Automobile mechanics	718	21	739	0.4
Radio and television	508	17	525	0.3
Metal craftsmen except mechanics	566	26	592	0.3
Machinists	215	8	223	0.1

(continued)

TABLE 5.7 (continued)

Selected Occupations	Male	Female	Total	Percent
Printing craftsmen	464	116	580	0.3
Tailors	333	106	439	0.2
Telephone installers and repairmen	231	0	231	0.1
Operatives Except Transport	9,914	15,025	24,939	13.8
Assemblers	269	332	601	0.3
Checkers, examiners, and inspectors—manufacturing	284	138	422	0.2
Clothing ironers and pressers	1,408	686	2,094	1.2
Cutting operatives, n.e.c.	123	120	243	0.1
Dressmakers and seamstresses, except factory	17	222	239	0.1
Garage workers and gas station attendants	734	0	734	0.4
Laundry and dry cleaning operatives, n.e.c.	1,921	860	2,781	1.5
Meat cutters and butchers, except manufacturing	1,572	81	1,653	0.9
Metalworking operatives, except precision machines	280	104	384	0.2
Packers and wrappers, except meat and produce	256	583	839	0.5
Sewers and stitchers	185	9,801	9,986	5.5
Transport Equipment Operatives	1,824	32	1,856	1.0
Deliverymen and routemen	484	13	497	0.3
Truck drivers	389	19	408	0.2
Laborers, except farm	3,597	650	4,247	2.3
Freight and material handlers	152	66	218	0.1
Stock handlers	1,417	305	1,722	1.0
Farmers and Farm Managers	421	78	499	0.3
Farm Laborers and Farm Foremen	260	217	477	0.3
Service Workers, Except Private Household	26,724	8,742	35,466	19.6
Cleaning service workers	1,545	445	1,990	1.1
Food service workers	22,302	5,567	27,869	15.4
Bartenders	764	43	807	0.4
Busboys	1,390	94	1,484	0.8
Cooks, except private household	11,433	1,350	12,783	7.1
Dishwashers	1,127	442	1,569	0.9
Food counter and fountain workers	119	220	339	0.2
Waiters	6,211	2,532	8,743	4.8
Food service workers, n.e.c., except private household	1,258	886	2,144	1.2
Health service workers	340	764	1,104	0.6
Personal service workers	625	990	1,615	0.9
Hairdressers and cosmetologists	27	431	458	0.3
Protective service workers	377	62	439	0.2
Private Household Workers	317	1,108	1,425	0.8

n.e.c. = not elsewhere classified

Source: U.S. Department of Commerce, Bureau of the Census, Subject Report, PC(2)7A (1970).

institutions in an effort to catch up with the West. Another reason is that engineering and science are courses of study more likely to be chosen by students who have problems expressing themselves in English or who are shy about dealing with people. The more impersonal disciplines of engineering and science or mathematics meet their needs in that respect. A third reason is that Chinese parents understand what an engineer or teacher or doctor is. They do not quite know what a psychologist or anthropologist is. Therefore, the parents tend to push their sons into these traditional disciplines. A fourth reason pertains to the educators or teachers. In social status, the scholar or man of learning enjoys top prestige, hence the penchant toward teaching as a career.

Entry into these professions is also somewhat easier for the Chinese in the United States. Professional competence is an important criterion in these fields, and the Chinese can handle this requirement better than the more illusive ones, such as the ability to socialize or play office politics.

If the Chinese are culturally inclined toward these professions and have succeeded very well in them, there is little reason why anyone should question their inclination, except that when there is such a heavy concentration in a limited number of professions the group is extremely vulnerable to economic or social change.

Service Work

As the term implies, workers in this occupational group provide a service, such as food preparation, cleaning and maintenance, health care, personal care, or protection. Ten million Americans are in these occupations, and about 35,000 Chinese fall under this heading. Service work traditionally has been the most important occupational group for the Chinese in this country because it includes those jobs that fall within the heading of restaurants and laundries.

In some cities, like Boston, New York, and Seattle, service work is still the leading occupational group for the Chinese. And it is the male, much more so than the female, who is in service work. For the Chinese in particular, service work today is almost synonymous with such restaurant jobs as cook, waiter, bartender, dishwasher, and the like (see Table 5.7).

From 1950 to 1960, service work among the Chinese declined significantly from 28.8 percent to 18.8 percent of the total Chinese employed. The 1970 census registers a slight increase to 19.6 percent. This author's projection is that this category will increase in importance in 1980 because of the huge influx of immigrants who will be going into these occupations.

It is further suggested that the percentage and numbers in restaurant work is even greater than the 19.6 percent figure. A later table (Table A.3), showing employment breakdown by industry, reveals that approximately 30,000 out of a working labor force of 180,000, or one out of every six Chinese persons employed, are connected with eating or drinking places.

Actually, the 3,753 who classified themselves as managers of restaurants, cafeterias, and bars, may also be classified as restaurant workers because, by and large, the managers are self-employed owners who invariably double as cooks, headwaiters, or bartenders. Persons such as cashiers and bookkeepers, generally listed under the clerical category, also come under the province of restaurant work.

Thus we see that this one line of work employs 23,000 persons and far exceeds any other type of employment for the Chinese

The Disappearing Laundryman

Not too many years ago, more Chinese were in laundries than in any other line of work.[1] Today, the laundry business has been edged out by home washers and dryers, permanent press fabrics, and the disdain by the Chinese themselves for laundry work. Listed under clothing, ironers and pressers, and laundry and dry cleaning operatives are 4,800 for the entire United States (see Table 5.7). Others may be in laundries as truck drivers or "managers." Chinese laundries still in business are run primarily by older immigrants. In the 1950s and early 1960s, laundries were popular with newly arrived immigrants because laundry work did not require much capital or skill. Today, one cannot give one away.

Retail food stores—even supermarkets—are also losing ground with the Chinese. Less than 1 percent of the Chinese remain in this line of work. At one time, it ranked just behind laundries and restaurants as the most important occupation. Of the three, only restaurant work remains in the forefront, and it is outstripping all other types of work by the number of people engaged in it.

Garment Industry

The newly arrived female immigrant today goes to work in the garment factory. About 10,000 are employed as operatives, meaning predominantly sewing machine operators. The Chinese now have supplanted the Jewish and Italian operators in the garment industry.

In New York City, 43.7 percent of all employed Chinese females are operatives. There are about 230 garment factories scattered around the fringe of New York's Chinatown. Some have only 10 or 12 sewing machines; others operate on a larger scale. A good number of these factories are owned by Chinese contractors who bid for job lots on Seventh Avenue, and the competition is very keen. The operators work on a piecework basis. The New York garment workers are unionized, and there are union regulations governing hours and wages; but the competition is so great that both the boss and workers wink at the clock and the payscale and operate as competitively as possible.

In Boston, the percentage of Chinese females employed as operatives is 39.6 percent; in Chicago, 23.4 percent; in San Francisco-Oakland, 26.3 percent; and in Seattle, 29.6 percent. These high percentages give us some idea of the importance of the garment industry in the employment picture of Chinese females.

When interviewed about why they went into the garment factories, workers gave the following reasons:

1. Ease of getting a job;
2. Do not have to ride the bus or subway to get to work;
3. Flexible schedule;
4. Do not speak English;
5. Can learn job proficiently in about a week; and
6. Social and informal atmosphere in factory.

Clerical Work

U.S.-born Chinese females or the better educated ones are found in such clerical jobs as bookkeeper, cashier, secretary, office machine operator, typist, and file clerk. The concentration of Chinese females in the clerical category is even more pronounced than that in the operatives category. Nearly 22,000 out of a labor force of 70,000, or 31.8 percent, are in this occupational group alone. In California and Hawaii, the percentage is even greater, running from 36 to 37 percent. Considering the educational attainment of the Chinese female, she is grossly underemployed.

Construction

Seven out of ten craft jobs held by the Chinese are in California or Hawaii. Yet, even in these areas, the Chinese are underrepresented in the building trade crafts: carpentry, masonry, electrical work, and plumbing. Altogether, only 1 percent of the Chinese labor force is found in the construction crafts jobs, and the small percentage does not mean that they do not seek this type of work.

AGE AND EMPLOYMENT

Ordinarily, advancing years bring commensurate advancement in occupation. With the Chinese, it is those in the 25- to 34-year age bracket who are occupying the upper strata jobs, whereas those in the upper age brackets are concentrated toward the lower end of the occupational scale.

For Chinese males 45 years and over, service work leads all the other categories. (We already have discussed the nature of these jobs.) These are the older immigrants who came here before World War II and perhaps recent immigrants who have difficulty with the language. The likelihood of these men shifting their occupational field is remote.

That there are 17 percent 45 years and over who call themselves managers looks favorable, but this is somewhat deceptive. Time has enabled these men to accumulate some capital, and no doubt many have invested it into a small business of their own—a restaurant or gift shop perhaps. A good third of the managers are of this type. The professions are still strong with those in the 45- to 64-year age bracket.

The number of women working is greater in the 45- to 64-year age bracket than for any other group. By 45 years of age, a woman's children are grown or in their teens, and she is not tied down to domestic or maternal duties. Of the 18,000 Chinese women working, one-third are in operative jobs. These jobs are flexible, fairly easy to come by, and do not need much skill. No knowledge of the English language is necessary, and the jobs are located on the fringes of Chinatown. The coworkers are people like themselves, and garment factories fulfill a social function as well as one of employment.

Now let us swing to the other end of the scale and consider the teenage group of 16- to 19-year-olds. Their situation is different from the regular workers because those in this age group are still enrolled in school. Whatever jobs they hold are part-time, after-school, or weekend jobs. Teenagers take jobs for spending money or to help pay for their educational expenses. They take what they can get for short periods of time. It would be ideal if these young people could utilize this period in their lives to experiment and sample the real world of work.

There are roughly 35,000 Chinese young people in this age group. They make up 8 percent of the total Chinese population. One-third of them hold some type of job. This is a smaller percentage than that of white teenagers of the same age bracket, but a higher percentage than that of the blacks.

The most outstanding fact that comes to light when the occupational pattern is broken down by age group is the high percentage in

TABLE 5.8

Major Occupational Groups of Chinese in the United States, by Sex and Age Groups, 1970

Occupational Group	Total		16-19 Years		20-24 Years		25-34 Years		35-44 Years		45-64 Years		65 and over	
	Number	Per-cent	Number	Per-cent	Number	Per-cent	Number	Per-cent	Number	Per-cent	Number	Per-cent	Number	Per-cent
Male	114,433	100.0	6,434	100.0	11,526	100.0	28,058	100.0	28,962	100.0	35,869	100.0	3,584	100.0
Professional and technical	33,119	28.9	364	5.7	2,610	22.6	13,679	48.8	9,505	32.8	6,531	18.2	430	12.0
Managers, administrators	13,061	11.4	42	0.7	428	3.7	2,110	7.5	3,687	12.7	6,161	17.2	633	17.7
Sales workers	5,021	4.4	473	7.4	554	4.8	965	3.4	1,072	3.7	1,636	4.6	321	9.0
Clerical workers	10,762	9.4	1,346	20.9	2,189	19.0	2,213	7.9	2,054	7.1	2,692	7.5	268	7.5
Craftsmen	8,367	7.3	228	3.5	842	7.3	1,872	6.7	2,276	7.9	2,984	8.3	165	4.6
Operatives	11,998	10.5	989	15.4	1,319	11.4	1,926	6.9	2,709	9.4	4,625	12.9	430	12.0
Laborers	3,787	3.3	948	14.7	603	5.2	515	1.8	633	2.2	964	2.7	124	3.5
Farmers and farm managers	478	0.4	10	0.2	25	0.2	57	0.2	115	0.4	224	0.6	47	1.3
Farm laborers	352	0.3	76	1.2	29	0.3	38	0.1	62	0.2	123	0.3	24	0.7
Service workers	27,010	23.6	1,941	30.2	2,922	25.4	4,652	16.6	6,776	23.4	9,659	26.9	1,060	29.6
Private household	478	0.4	17	0.3	5	0.0	31	0.1	73	0.3	270	0.8	82	2.3
Female	69,129	100.0	5,578	100.0	12,205	100.0	15,714	100.0	16,124	100.0	18,218	100.0	1,290	100.0
Professional and technical	13,402	19.4	192	3.4	2,243	18.4	5,855	37.3	2,270	17.1	2,225	12.2	137	10.6
Managers, administrators	2,636	3.8	46	0.8	169	1.4	412	2.6	785	4.9	1,165	6.4	59	4.6
Sales workers	3,531	5.1	877	15.7	680	5.6	408	2.6	620	3.8	879	4.8	67	5.2
Clerical workers	21,989	31.8	2,912	52.2	6,126	50.2	4,837	30.8	4,280	26.5	3,719	20.4	115	8.9
Craftsmen	846	1.2	20	0.4	78	0.6	142	0.9	214	1.3	330	1.8	62	4.8
Operatives	15,556	22.5	371	6.7	1,018	8.3	2,374	15.1	5,105	31.7	6,209	34.1	479	37.1
Laborers	592	0.9	72	1.3	75	0.6	79	0.5	98	0.6	243	1.3	25	1.9
Farmers and farm managers	114	0.2	0	0.0	19	0.2	6	0.0	26	0.2	59	0.3	4	0.3
Farm laborers	247	0.4	37	0.7	20	0.2	33	0.2	36	0.2	106	0.6	15	1.2
Service workers	8,842	12.8	974	17.5	1,630	13.4	1,370	8.7	1,910	11.8	2,708	14.9	250	19.4
Private household	1,374	2.0	77	1.4	147	1.2	198	1.3	300	1.9	575	3.2	77	6.0

Source: U.S. Department of Commerce, Bureau of the Census, Subject Report, PC(2)1G (1970), Table 22.

the professions among the 25- to 44-year age group for both males and females. These age groups consist of men and women who have completed their formal education and have made a choice of careers. Almost half of the males in the 25- to 34-year age group are in professional and technical work, and another 7 percent are in the managerial classification. About two out of every five Chinese women are similarly situated in these two top occupational categories. If these figures are any indication of the potential of the Chinese, the future looks optimistic. Meanwhile, for the present, some real problems exist.

SUMMARY OF FINDINGS

1. Stereotypes have boxed the Chinese in the public mind. The view is that they are suitable for only certain types of work. The truth is that during their 130 odd years of history in this country, they have run the gamut of the major occupational groups, concentrating in large numbers in one area or another, depending upon the social or political attitude toward them at the time.

2. In 1970, the Chinese-American labor force numbered approximately 190,000. Three-fourths of the males and one-half of the females 16 years and over are in the labor market. The male labor force participation rate is considerably lower than the national average. The female rate is somewhat higher.

3. The occupational pattern for Chinese males by major group breakdown tends toward extremes—a concentration in the professional category and another concentration in the service work group. For females, the twin-peak concentrations are the clerical and operatives categories.

4. The middle-class occupations of sales workers and craftsmen are conspicuously few among the Chinese. Clerical work is prevalent with U.S.-born females and the better-educated foreign-born females.

5. Categories from which the Chinese are almost totally absent are farmer, unskilled laborer, and private household worker. Yet, at one time, these were the predominant occupations of the Chinese.

6. The most spectacular increase has been in the professional and technical field, rising from 2.8 percent, in 1940, to 26.5 percent, in 1970. For the males, the percentage is even greater—28.9 percent—and for males in the 25- to 34-year age group the percentage is 48.8. Of the professional careers, engineers and educators lead the field, followed by personnel in health work.

7. The restaurant business is the single most important source of employment for the Chinese; 30,000 are engaged in this field alone.

8. Ten thousand Chinese females, usually foreign-born immigrants, are employed as operatives, predominantly in the garment industry.

9. Laundries and food stores are fading out as traditional Chinese enterprises.

10. An age breakdown of occupations held by the Chinese reveals that the older generations generally hold lower echelon jobs, but there is a record-breaking penetration of the professional and technical levels by the younger generations.

RECOMMENDATIONS

A Chinese labor force of 190,000 for the entire United States presents no employment threat to anyone. Moreover, the Chinese are concentrated in only a few occupations, many of them noncompetitive. The most notable example is the restaurant business, which hires almost one out of every six Chinese employed. Other areas of concentration are teaching, engineering, clerical work, and the garment industry.

Dispersal is recommended to effect a more balanced distribution throughout the occupational spectrum. A breakthrough is called for to gain entry into other fields. However, many presently entrenched in these occupations are going to put up strong resistance to admitting Chinese to their ranks. The Chinese cannot fight this battle alone. Recent legislation and directives, such as Equal Employment Opportunity, Contract Compliance, and Affirmative Action, have given the Chinese good leverage. Such actions show that government can legislate change.

Teachers are already in oversupply and future demand is steadily decreasing. Chinese educators would do well to consider preparing for other professions. An alternative to clerical work for Chinese females would be in the field of health, a rapidly growing industry. To thin the ranks of Chinese females in garment work and help them diversify into other lines of work, it is recommended that studies be undertaken immediately to examine the difficulties these females operate under and to either introduce these women to other industries or bring the industries to the vicinity of Chinatown.

The better solution would be to help these women go a short distance beyond the Chinatown borders, but this is easier said than done. Most of these women are so afraid of venturing out that they would prefer to accept lower wages and horrible working conditions than to expand their working as well as living horizons. This fear is not confined to the Chinese female; it is the same for the male. Restaurants in the suburbs that need cooks, or bartenders, or waiters must send a car to Chinatown daily to pick up their help. Otherwise they could not find employees. Since this is, at present, an accepted practice for the males, it could be employed in a modified form for the females. Any plant or enterprise wishing to use Chinese female workers could arrange for scheduled transportation from Chinatown with a station wagon picking them up in the morning and taking them back in the evening. Over a period of time, after the workers had gotten used to the idea of going beyond Chinatown, some of their fears would be dispelled and they could be weaned to public transportation. It is also recommended that employees be hired in small groups, for in numbers they would find courage—one bolstering the other.

Another solution would be to try to bring light industry to the vicinity of Chinatown. It is not recommended that another agency be set up to undertake this job. There are many already in existence. The knot in this situation is the lack of awareness among the public that the Chinese do indeed have employment problems. There are public and private facilities to help the Chinatown communities diversify into other lines of work. Every state has similar agencies, but in the New York State Department of Commerce alone there are:

1. New York Job Development Authority—makes long-term second mortgage loans for construction of new or expanded production facilities.

2. Job Incentive Program—approves state tax credits for firms constructing new plants or expanding facilities and providing job opportunities in low-income areas and operating approved training programs.

3. Industrial Location Service—specialist in helping firms, large and small, to find the right location for their plants, in strict confidence and at no cost.

4. New York Business Development Corporation—a quasi-public corporation that may lend financial assistance to industry in New York State when requirements are beyond the limitation of conventional an lending institutions.

5. Small Business Administration—loans money to business for equity or long-range financing.

6. International Commerce—promotional efforts to develop foreign trade sales opportunities.

Private organizations such as the Executive Volunteer Corps, where retired executives offer the benefit of their experience and expertise, and commercial banks are other organizations that can help the Chinese community expand its employment horizons and increase its economic potential.

NOTE

1. Betty Lee Sung, <u>The Story of the Chinese in America</u> (New York: Colliers, 1971), chap. 11.

Even in the year 1976, women are not thought of seriously in terms of occupation or career. They work 12 to 16 hours a day, perpetuating the human race, clothing and feeding their families, keeping the wheels of daily life running smoothly, and providing their males with support to enable them to carry on their careers. "Women's work" runs the gamut and is never done. That is why it is not even looked upon as an occupation, nor given its proper due. For centuries, women were considered shadows, chattels, or adjuncts to their menfolk. It is only within the last few decades that women everywhere have begun to assert themselves.

The drawback to this assertiveness is that, although women are now competing in the labor market outside the home and, in every instance, have proven themselves competent to any task performed by men, they still are saddled with the work of their former status. They have gained in one respect without being relieved of their duties in the other, thus giving them a double role and double burden.

WOMANPOWER PLANNING

In manpower planning for the masculine sector, one considers such factors as education, occupation, industry, income, economic conditions, labor force size, and so on. All of these factors apply equally to the feminine sector, but there are other dimensions as well. The female is endowed by nature to bear children and nurture them. She cannot forsake this role, nor does she want to. Most women today will still assign first priority to being wife and mother. She is the central figure in any family. When we talk about womanpower, we must look also at marital status, family characteristics, birth and fertility rates, and the husband's attitude or position. Women's employment decisions are predicated primarily upon the family's welfare.

Women have only begun to figure in the U.S. labor force since World War II. In 1940, only 27.4 percent of the total U.S. female population was employed outside the home. By 1950, this percentage had increased to 31; by 1960, to 37; and by 1970, to 43.[1] Among Chinese females 14 years and over, those in the labor force in 1960 were 44 percent, and in 1970, when the age bracket was upped to 16 years and over, the percentage was 50.

FEMALE LABOR FORCE

The proportion of Chinese females gainfully employed is higher than the national average, and this does not take into account unpaid family workers in the family-type restaurants, groceries, and laundries who do not classify themselves as "employed." Suffice it to say that the Chinese female has always been an important member of the "rice-winning" team in the family.

The presence of Chinese women on the American scene is a recent phenomenon. Around the turn of the century, there were about 15 males to every Chinese female. The ratio improved by 1940 to 3:1.[2] Today the sex ratio is 111 males to every 100 females—a substantial improvement, but still out of proportion (see Table 6.1).

In the 1970 census we have, for the first time, meaningful employment figures for Chinese females (see Table 6.2). Close to one-half of those 16 years and over are in the labor force (either working or looking for work). The unemployment rate is very low—only 3.7 percent. Obtaining employment does not seem to be a difficulty with Chinese females; the problem is more what type of job and at what pay. Recent immigrants, fresh off the plane, can walk into one of the small garment factories scattered throughout Chinatown or its peripheral area and start working the next day. Piecework at low rates is always available.

A comparison of labor force status with whites, blacks, and Japanese shows that a larger percentage of Oriental women (50 percent) work outside the home than do black (48 percent) or white women (41 percent). Black and white women also have higher unemployment rates—7.7 and 4.8 percent, respectively—compared to 3.7 for Chinese and 3.0 percent for Japanese women.

One naturally assumes that fewer married women l· ·   ...
their husbands work. That is not so. In 1940, 15 percer
U.S. women living with their husbands held outside jobs.
the rate was 41 percent.[3]

TABLE 6.1

Chinese Population in the United States, by Sex and Sex Ratio, Total and by States, 1970

State	Male	Female	Sex Ratio, Males: 100 Females	State	Male	Female	Sex Ratio, Males: 100 Females
Alabama	347	279	124.4	Missouri	1,559	1,256	124.1
Alaska	144	84	171.4	Montana	168	121	138.8
Arizona	2,025	1,853	109.3	Nebraska	355	216	155.1
Arkansas	374	369	101.4	Nevada	535	420	127.4
California	87,835	82,296	106.7	New Hampshire	215	205	104.9
Colorado	807	682	118.3	New Jersey	4,902	4,331	113.2
Connecticut	1,173	1,036	113.2	New Mexico	346	217	159.4
Delaware	296	263	112.5	New York	43,919	37,459	117.2
District of Columbia	1,405	1,177	119.4	North Carolina	711	544	130.7
Florida	1,660	1,473	112.7	North Dakota	88	77	114.3
Georgia	892	692	128.9	Ohio	2,815	2,490	113.1
Hawaii	26,097	25,942	100.6	Oklahoma	548	451	121.5
Idaho	279	219	127.4	Oregon	2,584	2,230	115.9
Indiana	1,174	941	124.8	Pennsylvania	3,789	3,264	116.1
Illinois	7,767	6,707	115.8	Rhode Island	582	511	113.9
Iowa	560	433	129.3	South Carolina	287	234	122.6
Kansas	703	530	132.6	South Dakota	86	77	111.7
Kentucky	307	251	122.3	Tennessee	879	731	120.2
Louisiana	752	588	127.9	Texas	4,072	3,563	114.3
Maine	113	93	121.5	Utah	745	536	139.0
Maryland	3,363	3,157	106.5	Vermont	92	81	113.6
Massachusetts	7,529	6,483	116.1	Virginia	1,474	1,331	110.7
Michigan	3,474	2,933	118.4	Washington	4,801	4,400	109.1
Minnesota	1,355	1,067	127.0	West Virginia	192	181	106.1
Mississippi	766	675	113.5	Wisconsin	1,484	1,216	122.0
				Wyoming	160	132	121.2
U.S. Total	228,565	206,497	110.8				

Source: U.S. Department of Commerce, Bureau of the Census, General Population Characteristics (1970).

TABLE 6.2

Employment Status of the Chinese 16 Years and over in the United
States and Five Selected States, by Sex, 1970

	Percent Male			Percent Female		
	In Labor Force*	Em- ployed	Unem- ployed	In Labor Force*	Em- ployed	Unem- ployed
United States	73.2	97.0	3.0	49.5	96.3	3.7
California	73.5	96.0	4.0	51.0	95.3	4.7
New York	71.1	97.7	2.3	49.2	97.1	2.9
Hawaii	76.1	97.9	2.1	54.2	98.2	1.8
Illinois	73.4	97.3	2.7	50.2	97.5	2.5
Massachusetts	72.3	97.4	2.6	53.2	96.0	4.0

*Employed or looking for work. Not in labor force refers to
students, retired persons, housewives, or inmates of institutions.

Note: Based on a 20 percent sampling.

Source: U.S. Department of Commerce, Bureau of the Census,
Subject Report, PC(2)1G (1970), Table 19.

Almost half the Chinese women living with their husbands work
(see Table 6.3), and the percentage increases as their stay in the
United States lengthens. In a state like Hawaii, where the Chinese
population is more acculturated, significantly more women work when
they are married, live with their husbands, and have children under
six years of age. What is happening in Hawaii could be indicative of
what will eventually happen to Chinese females in New York.

WORKING MOTHERS

One-third of Chinese mothers who live with their husbands and
have children under six hold jobs outside the home. Young children,
therefore, have not kept these mothers from employment. The percentage of black mothers in the same category is much higher (43.7);
of white mothers it is much lower (25.0). Keep in mind that the figures are for women who live with their husbands, and so, presumably,
have some other means of support.

When the youngest child marches off to school, the mothers march off to work. The overall figures for mothers in the United States shows a fantastic leap in the labor force at this juncture in their lives. The percentage goes from 30 percent of those with children under 6 to 49 percent of those with children from 6 to 17 years old. This last percentage exceeds even those women married and living with husbands who have no children.[4] One could interpret these figures to mean that mothers may have to work to ensure adequate family support.

The foregoing raises questions about marriage and children and the increasing tendency of women to enter the labor force. Is there—should there be—some recognition of sex differences in occupation, industry, hours worked, income, and so on? How can women deal with their desire for marriage and a family and a career as well? Men have always had all three, but with a helpmeet to take care of the domestic side. A career woman has to juggle all three—all the while building up a huge guilt complex that she is neglecting her husband and children.

The wisdom of "me-tooism" or chasing after male-established standards and goals is questionable. Women are not men and to try to go after everything that men do is silly at times. For example, the first woman who passed the New York City examination for a maintenance job had to lift and carry a 120-pound sack for a certain distance. This is not equality. There are biological differences that must be recognized, and the maternal role is to be taken into account.

Women must strive for marriage, family, and career on a more equitable basis. Since her childbearing role cannot be shared, she can be compensated by part-time work, by day-care centers, by more flexible hours, and, more important, by changed male attitudes toward domestic responsibilities. The unfortunate part of it is that women have either shouldered the extra burden or compromised their roles as wives and mothers.

LATE MARRIAGES

Marrying at a later age is one way in which the Chinese females are trying to meet these challenges. In Table 6.4 we see that 68.6 percent are still single in the age bracket of 20 to 24 years. By comparison, only 36 percent of the American females have not yet tied the knot. An astonishingly large proportion of Chinese women maintain their single status until they reach 30 to 34 years of age. Then the percentage of those married shoots up to the 90s. Eventually as many as 96 percent do get married, which means that Chinese do not eschew marriage—they just postpone it.

TABLE 6.3

Employment Status of Chinese Females with Husbands Present and Children Under Six for the United States and Five Selected States, 1970

	United States	California	New York	Hawaii	Illinois	Massachusetts
Total females 16 years and over	145,012	58,782	27,014	18,349	4,556	4,427
Number in labor force	71,786	29,983	13,295	9,935	2,285	2,350
Percent in labor force	49.5	51.0	49.2	54.1	50.2	53.1
Number employed	69,129	28,575	12,910	9,761	2,228	2,255
Percent employed	96.2	95.3	97.1	98.1	97.5	96.0
Wives employed, husbands present	40,051	15,967	7,854	5,815	1,269	1,345
Percent all wives, husbands present	46.9	47.6	47.5	53.6	45.6	52.2
With children under six	9,110	3,654	1,490	1,349	297	324
Percent husband/wife families with children under six	32.6	35.2	27.8	46.8	29.1	32.4

Source: U.S. Department of Commerce, Bureau of the Census, Subject Report, PC(2)1G (1970), Tables 18, 19, 23.

SIZE OF FAMILIES

In the olden days in China, large families were a source of pride and a symbol of status. The Chinese met their social, economic, and religious needs through the family. In an agricultural economy, many hands were needed to till the land. Social security was provided through the communal and collective efforts of a broad-based family. The larger the family, the more members it had with which to cope with the contingencies of life. Smaller families were the exception, and the barren woman was much pitied. A woman was naught in China until she had given her husband a son; once a son was produced, her position in the family was fixed. She could never be cast out.

One would expect some vestige of this cultural heritage and desire for large families to carry over into the Chinese-American family. Yet, in looking at the number of children under 18 in Chinese families (see Table 6.5), one finds that more than a third of the 95,000 families had no children; one or two offspring was the norm; and a sharp drop registered after the third child.

Table 6.6 shows the fertility rate of Chinese women of childbearing age. These figures confirm that the average Chinese woman gives birth to between two and three children. It is puzzling, in view of the fact that Westernization is usually accompanied by a lower fer-

TABLE 6.4

Chinese Women in the United States 15 Years and over, Single or
Ever Married, 1970

Age Group	Single		Ever Married	
	Number	Percent	Number	Percent
15–19 years	20,107	96.6	714	3.6
20–24 years	15,949	68.6	7,289	31.4
25–29 years	3,435	20.8	13,053	79.2
30–34 years	1,392	8.6	14,877	91.4
35–39 years	921	6.6	13,086	93.4
40–44 years	534	3.7	14,096	96.3
45–49 years	469	4.3	10,411	95.7
50–54 years	361	4.2	8,275	95.8
55–64 years	574	4.3	12,808	95.7
65 years and over	608	5.2	10,995	94.8

Source: U.S. Department of Commerce, Bureau of the Census, Subject Report, PC(2)3A (1970).

TABLE 6.5

Chinese Families with Own Children Under 18, by Number of Children, for the United States and Five Selected States, 1970

Own Children Under 18	United States		California		New York		Hawaii		Illinois		Massachusetts	
	Number	Per cent	Number	Per cent	Number	Per cent	Number	Per cent	Number	Per cent	Number	Per cent
All families	94,931	99.9	37,437	100.0	18,546	100.0	12,304	99.9	2,920	99.9	2,920	99.9
None	35,069	36.9	13,941	37.2	7,034	37.9	4,961	40.3	979	33.5	943	32.3
1	18,899	19.9	7,191	19.2	3,698	19.9	2,263	18.4	602	20.6	699	23.9
2	19,454	20.5	7,736	20.7	3,844	20.7	2,169	17.6	699	23.9	542	18.6
3	12,377	13.0	5,020	13.4	2,405	13.0	1,503	12.2	375	12.8	375	12.8
4	5,825	6.1	2,225	5.9	1,095	5.9	854	6.9	183	6.3	213	7.3
5	2,422	2.6	965	2.6	399	2.2	387	3.1	45	1.5	132	4.5
6 or more	855	0.9	359	1.0	71	0.4	167	1.4	37	1.3	16	0.5

Source: U.S. Department of Commerce, Bureau of the Census, Subject Report, PC(2)1G (1970), Table 23.

TABLE 6.6

Fertility of Chinese Women in the Childbearing Ages, 1970

Children Ever Born to Women Ever Married	United States	California	New York	Hawaii	Illinois	Massachusetts
15–24 years old	8,099	2,897	1,612	895	294	280
Children per 1,000 women ever married	786	762	922	806	731	946
25–34 years old	27,692	9,953	5,146	2,499	1,102	963
Children per 1,000 women ever married	1,778	1,815	1,833	2,351	1,652	1,746
35–44 years old	26,711	11,499	5,106	3,165	856	671
Children per 1,000 women ever married	3,005	2,966	2,955	3,206	3,114	3,250

Source: U.S. Department of Commerce, Bureau of the Census, Subject Report, PC(2)1G (1970), Table 18.

tility rate, that the fertility rate of Chinese women in Hawaii is higher than that of the mainland states, especially in the more productive 25- to 34-year age bracket. Hawaii has a more balanced Chinese population and is farther ahead in assimilation.

POSTPONING CHILDREN

A comparison (see Table 6.7) with white, black, and Japanese women shows that Chinese women are having far fewer children than their sisters of other races. The Chinese are not only postponing marriage but also they are postponing children. At ages 20 to 24, 45.9 percent of married Chinese women have no children at all. At ages 25 to 29, almost one-third are still childless, whereas the same percentage of white females already have two children. By the time a woman reaches 30 years of age, her childbearing span has already been halved, and the prospect that she will give birth to more than two or three children is quite remote. It seems that the Chinese and Japanese families are the most limited of all.

Do foreign-born Chinese women tend to have more children than those U.S.-born? According to Table 6.8, it does not appear so. The percentages for U.S.-born and foreign-born are almost parallel. Nativity is not the decisive factor; time and the circumstances are greater determinants.

The younger generation Chinese female is limiting her family severely. Only the older women have larger families. For example, of those in the 45- to 49-year age bracket, about 16 percent have five or six children; 14 percent of those 65 years or over have seven or more children. The difference is a span of only about 15 to 35 years. Within this short period of historical time, we are witnessing a social change of far-reaching consequence. One of the pillars of Chinese culture has been toppled.

WHY FEWER CHILDREN?

Why Chinese females are marrying later and limiting their families may be indicated in the prolonged years of schooling. They wait for graduation before getting married or having children. Table 6.9 shows fertility of Chinese women by level of education and reveals an inverse correlation between education and the number of children born. In other words, the less schooling, the more children. No college graduate or postgraduate has seven or eight children. One-fourth of the females at this educational level have no children at all, and three out of four have no more than two children. The decision

TABLE 6.7

Percent of Women Ever Married by Children Ever Born of the Chinese in the United States, 1970

Age Group and Race	Children Ever Born					5 and 6	7 or More
	0	1	2	3	4	5 and 6	7 or More
15-19 years							
Chinese	55.3	35.9	7.1	1.7	0	0	0
Japanese	52.1	39.1	7.1	0	0.5	1.1	0
White	53.6	37.0	7.2	1.2	0.3	0.2	0
Black	32.6	42.5	17.8	4.9	1.3	0.6	0
20-24 years							
Chinese	45.9	33.9	14.4	4.2	1.5	0	0.8
Japanese	46.1	38.3	12.2	2.4	0.4	0.3	0.3
White	37.0	34.0	20.0	5.0	1.0	0.25	0.5
Black	20.6	32.8	24.4	12.7	5.6	3.1	0.6
25-29 years							
Chinese	32.3	29.5	23.9	10.5	3.4	1.1	0.2
Japanese	29.1	32.4	25.9	8.6	2.7	0.8	0.2
White	16.0	21.0	32.0	18.0	7.0	3.0	0.4
Black	12.6	20.2	22.8	17.5	11.9	11.4	3.4
30-34 years							
Chinese	11.3	18.4	31.7	21.9	10.6	5.0	0.7
Japanese	15.8	18.7	35.5	19.4	7.0	3.0	0.3
White	8.0	11.0	27.0	25.0	15.0	9.0	2.0
Black	9.5	16.6	17.9	16.5	13.5	18.0	10.8
35-39 years							
Chinese	8.0	10.7	25.0	25.7	16.1	12.5	1.7
Japanese	15.8	14.9	27.5	22.3	11.2	6.4	1.6
White	6.0	9.0	23.0	24.0	17.0	13.0	4.0
Black	9.8	12.4	15.1	14.4	12.7	18.2	17.1
40-44 years							
Chinese	7.6	8.3	20.9	23.8	20.0	15.3	3.8
Japanese	16.6	14.2	26.4	22.6	12.2	6.8	1.0
White	8.1	11.0	24.0	22.0	15.0	12.0	5.0
Black	13.1	14.1	14.6	13.0	10.7	15.6	18.6
45-49 years							
Chinese	10.5	11.3	20.6	19.5	18.2	16.2	3.5
Japanese	13.2	12.5	26.8	23.7	13.6	8.6	1.3
White	9.8	13.0	26.0	21.0	12.0	10.0	4.0
Black	18.0	16.1	14.9	12.1	9.3	13.0	16.3
50-54 years							
Chinese	9.2	14.8	21.3	18.2	17.1	13.7	5.4
Japanese	11.0	14.0	25.0	22.7	15.0	9.6	2.3
White	12.9	16.0	27.0	19.0	10.0	8.0	4.0
Black	23.1	18.2	14.7	10.7	8.0	11.0	14.1
55-64 years							
Chinese	9.7	16.2	22.5	17.2	14.3	14.0	5.8
Japanese	12.3	12.9	21.0	18.3	13.6	14.4	7.2
White	17.9	19.0	25.0	15.0	8.0	7.0	4.0
Black	27.1	19.2	14.0	10.0	7.2	9.3	13.0
65 years and over							
Chinese	8.0	14.0	18.6	16.8	11.3	16.9	14.0
Japanese	9.2	9.9	14.3	13.8	13.3	21.1	18.1
White	17.6	17.0	21.0	15.0	9.0	10.0	8.0
Black	25.6	17.4	13.5	9.9	7.8	10.1	15.3

Source: U.S. Department of Commerce, Bureau of the Census, Subject Report, PC(2)3A (1970).

TABLE 6.8

Children Ever Born to Chinese Women Ever Married, 15 Years
and over, by Nativity, 1970

| Children Ever Born | Women Ever Married | | | |
| | U.S.-Born | | Foreign-Born | |
	Number	Percent	Number	Percent
0	7,600	18.6	11,800	16.4
1	5,700	14.0	12,600	17.5
2	9,800	24.0	16,500	23.0
3	7,300	17.9	11,400	15.9
4	4,800	11.8	9,400	13.1
5	2,100	5.1	5,200	7.2
6	1,500	3.7	2,600	3.6
7	1,200	2.9	1,400	1.9
8 or more	800	2.0	900	1.3

Note: Based on a 1 percent sampling.

Source: U.S. Department of Commerce, Bureau of the Census,
Special Tabulation, Public Use Sample Data (1970).

may lie with the Chinese males who think along the same lines. If
the male decides that he cannot get married or have children until he
graduates, his marital partner may have little choice but to go along
with his decision. As we saw in Chapter 4, he, too, is prolonging his
education well beyond the normal range. In the cycle of events, the
ultimate culprit may be the immigration restrictions placed upon work
for students. How can a student think about establishing a family if
he has no way to support it? Again, the Chinese population in the
United States may be structured by legal, rather than cultural, controls.

The total Chinese female labor force in 1970 was about 72,000.
Of this number, about 30,000 are in California, 13,000 in New York,
and 10,000 in Hawaii. In other words, they are highly concentrated.
Again, the reader is cautioned that these figures are now different.
The heavy immigration of recent years must be taken into account,
especially since New York is getting the major share of the new immigrants.

Occupations of the Chinese females are extremely limited. Over
30,000 of the 72,000 are in the seven occupations shown, in order of
importance, in Table 6.10. (They may be represented in other fields
but not in large numbers.) By broad occupational group, the breakdown may be regrouped, as shown in Table 6.11.

TABLE 6.9

Fertility of Chinese Women Ever Married, 15 Years and over, by Level of Education and Percent, 1970

Number of Children Ever Born	No Schooling			Elementary (1-8)			High School (9-12)			College-Postgraduate			Horizontal Total 100 Percent
	Number	Percent Vertical	Percent Horizontal	Number	Percent Vertical	Percent Horizontal	Number	Percent Vertical	Percent Horizontal	Number	Percent Vertical	Percent Horizontal	
0	1,200	7.9	6.2	2,500	10.0	12.9	7,800	19.2	40.2	7,900	24.8	40.7	19,400
1	1,600	10.6	8.7	3,300	13.2	18.0	6,500	16.0	35.5	6,900	21.6	37.7	18,300
2	3,500	23.2	13.3	4,700	18.8	17.9	10,300	25.4	39.2	7,800	24.5	29.7	26,300
3	3,200	21.2	17.1	3,900	15.6	20.9	6,600	16.3	35.3	5,000	15.7	26.7	18,700
4	1,900	12.6	13.4	4,700	18.8	33.1	5,200	12.8	36.6	2,400	7.5	16.9	14,200
5	1,200	7.9	16.4	3,200	12.8	43.8	1,800	4.4	24.7	1,100	3.4	15.1	7,300
6	1,000	6.6	24.4	1,000	4.0	24.4	1,300	3.2	31.7	800	2.5	19.5	4,100
7	900	6.0	34.6	1,100	4.4	42.3	600	1.5	23.1	0	0.0	0.0	2,600
8 or more	600	4.0	35.3	600	2.4	35.3	500	1.2	29.4	0	0.0	0.0	1,700
Vertical total 100 percent	15,00			25,000			40,600			31,900			112,600

Note: Based on a 1 percent sampling.

Source: U.S. Department of Commerce, Bureau of the Census, Special Tabulation, Public Use Sample Data (1970).

TABLE 6.10

Seven Ranking Occupations of Chinese Women

Specific Occupation	Number
Seamstress	10,023
Food service worker	5,567
Teacher to 12th grade	3,332
Typist	2,954
Secretary	2,924
Sales clerk	2,812
Cashier	2,485
Total	30,097

Source: U.S. Department of Commerce, Bureau of the Census, Subject Report, PC(2)7A (1970).

The pattern seems to be that foreign-born or poorly educated women go into the garment factories and food service work, whereas the U.S.-born and educated go into clerical and sales work. In the professions and technical occupational group, Chinese females gravitate toward teaching and health service work. The narrow range of jobs for Chinese females is very apparent.

TABLE 6.11

Number of Workers in Four Major Occupational Groups of Chinese Women, 1970

Occupational Group	Number
Clerical	20,736
Operative	15,025
Service worker	8,742
Sales worker	3,180
Total	47,683

Source: U.S. Department of Commerce, Bureau of the Census, Subject Report, PC(2)7A (1970).

INCOME

This topic already has been dealt with and will be dealt with throughout this study, but it cannot be overemphasized that females earn about half as much as males. Table 6.13 shows that almost three out of four females have a personal income of less than $5,000 per year and that their median income was $2,686, compared to $5,223 for Chinese males, which is already low. A closer scrutiny of work and pay follows in Chapter 9.

SUMMARY OF FINDINGS

1. Women of all races are entering the labor force at an increasing rate. A larger proportion of Chinese females are employed than either black or white females.

2. The unemployment rate for Chinese females, at 3.7 percent, is comparatively low. The type of work they perform—piecework at low rates—is always available.

3. Chinese females are postponing marriage until their late 20s or early 30s. Matrimony does not take a woman out of the labor market. Half of the Chinese wives living with their husbands are employed. One-third of Chinese mothers with children under six are employed.

4. Even though large families are a deeply rooted cultural tradition of the Chinese, the size of families among the Chinese in the United States has shrunk to an average of four persons.

5. Births have fallen off to a crude birthrate of less than 1.5 (replacement rate is 2.1). Chinese females are having their first child at a much older age, and they are having fewer children than any other racial group identified by the census. The low birthrate prevails among both foreign-born and U.S.-born Chinese females.

6. Chinese female employees are highly concentrated in a limited number of occupations. The better educated are in the professional and clerical fields—predominantly the latter. The recent immigrants and less educated are in garment factories and food service.

7. About three out of four Chinese females earned less than $5,000 in 1969.

RECOMMENDATIONS

Employers must recognize that female employees are split between job and home duties. It now behooves labor planners and negotiators to consider the special situation of female workers by setting

TABLE 6.12

Size of Chinese Families in the United States, Total and Five Selected States, 1970

	United States Number	United States Per cent	California Number	California Per cent	New York Number	New York Per cent	Hawaii Number	Hawaii Per cent	Illinois Number	Illinois Per cent	Massachusetts Number	Massachusetts Per cent
Number of families	94,931	100.0	37,437	100.0	18,546	100.0	12,304	100.0	2,920	100.0	2,920	100.0
Size of families												
2 persons	23,389	24.6	9,074	24.2	4,667	25.2	2,739	22.3	682	23.4	658	22.5
3 persons	17,873	18.8	6,888	18.4	3,480	18.8	2,367	19.2	501	17.1	521	17.8
4 persons	19,802	20.9	7,758	20.7	3,776	20.4	2,545	20.7	669	22.9	608	20.8
5 persons	15,445	16.3	6,394	17.1	3,034	16.3	2,047	16.6	444	15.2	420	14.4
6 persons	9,802	10.3	3,871	10.3	1,962	10.6	1,341	11.0	333	11.4	424	14.5
7 persons	6,083	6.4	2,371	6.3	1,348	7.3	803	6.5	213	7.3	242	8.3
8 persons	1,485	1.6	692	1.8	188	1.0	249	2.0	31	1.1	25	0.9
9 persons	591	0.6	209	0.6	62	0.3	139	1.1	19	0.7	19	0.6
10 persons or more	461	0.5	180	0.5	29	0.2	74	0.6	28	1.0	3	0.1
Total persons in families	380,393		150,938		73,651		50,689		11,977		12,050	
Average per family	4.01		4.03		3.97		4.12		4.10		4.13	

Note: Based on a 20 percent sampling.

Source: U.S. Department of Commerce, Bureau of the Census, Subject Report, PC(2)1G (1970), Table 23.

TABLE 6.13

A Comparison of Personal and Family Income of the Chinese in the United States, 1969

Income	Personal Income				Family Income	
	Male 16 and over		Female 16 and over			
	Number	Percent	Number	Percent	Number	Percent
Total persons or families	146,969	100.0	95,332	100.0	94,931	100.0
$1-999 or less	17,799	12.1	23,744	24.9	2,378	2.5
$1,000-1,999	17,286	11.8	16,209	17.0	2,449	2.6
$2,000-2,999	12,707	8.7	11,237	11.8	3,021	3.2
$3,000-3,999	12,332	8.4	10,304	10.8	4,037	4.3
$4,000-4,999	11,216	7.6	8,654	9.1	4,737	5.0
$5,000-5,999	9,619	6.5	7,057	7.4	5,393	5.7
$6,000-6,999	8,821	6.0	5,216	5.5	5,543	5.8
$7,000-7,999	8,215	5.6	3,748	4.0	5,638	5.9
$8,000-8,999	7,491	5.1	2,933	3.1	5,413	5.7
$9,000-9,999	6,247	4.3	1,687	1.8	5,494	5.8
$10,000-14,999	21,419	14.6	3,478	3.6	23,869	25.1
$15,000 or more	13,817	9.4	1,065	1.1	26,979	28.4
Median income (in dollars)	5,223		2,686		10,610	
Mean income (in dollars)	6,877		3,512		12,210	
Less than $5,000	71,340	48.5	70,148	73.6	16,622	17.5
$5,000-10,000	40,393	27.5	20,641	21.7	27,481	28.9
$10,000-15,000	21,419	14.6	3,478	3.6	23,869	25.1
$15,000 or more	13,817	9.4	1,065	1.1	26,979	28.4

Source: U.S. Department of Commerce, Bureau of the Census, Special Report, PC(2)1G, Tables 19 and 24.

up more part-time jobs on a regular basis. Vacation time, fringe benefits, seniority, union dues, and leave accruals should be prorated for these jobs so that women who work less than full time need not work in the disadvantaged position now common to part-time work.

Day care should be considered an essential societal institution, a service no less important than schools, libraries, or even police protection.

Finally, husbands and fathers must be willing to accept and share the duties of home and childrearing on a more equitable basis.

The fact that, in the United States, over 10,000 Chinese women in a labor force of 72,000 are in one occupation alone—garment workers—is disquieting. The apparel industry is facing stiff competition from imports—ironically, from the Far East where they are made by even cheaper Asian labor. The garment worker is in a highly vulnerable position. Effort must be made to diversify the extremely limited field of occupations of the less-educated, non-English-speaking, recent female immigrants. They can and should be taught other skills and introduced to other lines of work.

As we saw in Chapter 4, about one-third of the Chinese females 16 years and over have been to college or are college graduates. These women achieve white-collar status, but little else. Out of a work force of 72,000, 20,736 are in the clerical positions of bookkeepers, secretaries, typists, file clerks, and so on. They are qualified for better jobs, but are victims of sexism as well as racism. A high priority objective should be to make available to them higher as well as wider employment opportunities.

NOTES

1. U.S. Department of Commerce, Bureau of the Census, Statistical Abstract (1971), Table 331.

2. Betty Lee Sung, The Story of the Chinese in America (New York: Collier Books, 1971), pp. 117, 320.

3. U.S. Department of Commerce, Bureau of the Census, op. cit.

4. Ibid., Table 332.

7

CHINESE IN
GOVERNMENT WORK

For centuries, the Chinese regarded government service as the apex of the occupational scale. The high social status attached to government service was transferred from the old country to the new. This explains the high percentage—19, or almost one out of every five Chinese employed in the United States—who work for either the federal, state, or local governments. And it is all the more remarkable when one considers that the Chinese population consists predominantly of foreign-born aliens who are excluded from government service by the citizenship requirement.

Table 7.1 gives the number of Chinese employed in government service by selected states. In Hawaii, with 96 percent of her Chinese population citizens, 30 percent are in government service. In California 14,000 Chinese, or 18 percent, work for the government. The percentages are rather insignificant in New York and Massachusetts, where the foreign-born proportion is higher and the history of the Chinese is more recent.

AGE VARIABLE

The mature (age 30 and over) second- or third-generation U.S.-born Chinese is more likely to have aimed for a career in government. Some 20 or 30 years ago, he stook little chance of getting a position other than menial work in private industry outside his community. Since civil service is based primarily on a merit system, his chances in government were better. Looking at Table 7.2, it is very apparent that Chinese-Americans in the upper age groups are more into government service.

TABLE 7.1

Chinese Employed as Government Workers as Percent of Civilian
Labor Force for Five Selected States, 1970

| | Chinese in Civilian Labor Force | |
	Number	Percent
Male	19,700	18
Female	13,900	19
California	14,000	18
New York	3,100	9
Hawaii	6,500	30
Illinois	1,300	19
Massachusetts	300	6
U.S. total	34,500	19

Note: Based on a 1 percent sampling.

Source: U.S. Department of Commerce, Bureau of the Census,
Special Tabulation, Public Use Sample Data (1970).

TABLE 7.2

Number and Percent of Chinese Government Workers,
by Age Group, 1970

	Number	Percent
16-19 years	1,744	5
20-24 years	5,299	15
25-34 years	10,271	30
35-44 years	8,337	24
45-64 years	8,671	25
65 years and over	383	1
Total 16 years and over	34,705	100

Source: U.S. Department of Commerce, Bureau of the Census,
Subject Report, PC(2)1G (1970), Table 21.

LEVEL OF GOVERNMENT

Government is one of the fastest growing industries in the
United States. In 1940 federal government jobs stood at about 1 million; by 1950 it was 2 million; and in 1970 it was close to 3 million.
The number of state and local government jobs available are four
times the number of federal jobs.[1]

Table 7.3 shows that state governments hire more Chinese than
does either the federal or local, although the federal government does
not trail too far behind. In the federal government, roughly one-third
of the Chinese males employed are professionals and technicians,
one-third are in clerical work, and one-fifth are in the crafts. The
federal government is the one place where Chinese have managed to
penetrate the craft occupations. Chinese females in federal government service are overwhelmingly concentrated in clerical jobs.

In state governments, the Chinese have fared better: 80 percent
of the males and 60 percent of the females are in the professional-
technical category; 30 percent of the distaff workers are concentrated
in clerical work.

In local government, the Chinese female has outdone herself.
Two-thirds are in the professions, whereas only one-half of the males
are in this category. How does this translate? It is simply that this
large percentage of Chinese females in the professions represent
schoolteachers and librarians.[2] Education is a function of local government.

FEDERAL GOVERNMENT JOBS AND PAY

A series of recent publications put out by the Civil Service Commission, Minority Group Employment in the Federal Government, gives
a breakdown of workers employed by broad ethnic groups. This data
should be highly accurate because it is taken from payroll information. The Chinese figures, however, are submerged under the more
general heading "Oriental," so we must look at them in this context.
Asian groups share the same general occupational experiences, but
each group has problems unique to itself. In the absence of a more
detailed breakdown, the Oriental subcategory must suffice.

Table 7.4 shows the gradual change in grade rank for four years
since 1967. No data were available for 1968. The viewer can per-
ceive a gradual decrease in the lower grade levels and just as gradual
an increase in the general service (GS) 14-15 levels. Very few are
in the GS 16-18 levels. By and large, Oriental workers in the federal
government are clustered around the entry levels of GS 5, 9, and 11.
A comparison with other ethnic groups is found in Table 7.5. As a
group, Orientals seem to have come off fairly well.

TABLE 7.3

Chinese Government Workers in Federal, State, and Local Governments, by Number and Percent at Each Level, 1970

	Federal		State		Local	
	Number	Percent of Government Workers	Number	Percent of Government Workers	Number	Percent of Government Workers
Male	8,400	43	8,200	42	4,000	20
Female	3,300	24	5,200	37	5,400	39
California	5,200	37	3,500	25	5,300	38
New York	800	26	800	26	1,500	48
Hawaii	2,900	45	2,600	40	1,000	15
Illinois	200	15	900	69	200	15
Massachusetts	*	*	200	67	100	33
U.S. total	11,700	34	13,400	39	9,400	27

*None reported in census.

Note: Based on a 1 percent sampling.

Source: U.S. Department of Commerce, Bureau of the Census, Special Tabulation, Public Use Sample Data (1970).

TABLE 7.4

Oriental Employees in the Federal Government General Service Pay System (All Agencies), by Numbers and Percent, 1967-71

GS Rank	1967 Number	1967 Percent	1969 Number	1969 Percent	1970 Number	1970 Percent	1971 Number	1971 Percent
1			11	0.0	9	0.0	12	0.0
2	2,078	22.4	138	1.3	110	1.0	98	1.0
3			688	6.6	647	6.1	698	6.2
4			1,156	11.1	1,151	10.8	1,157	10.2
5			1,206	11.6	1,230	11.6	1,315	11.6
6	2,790	30.1	539	5.2	606	5.7	638	5.6
7			931	9.0	916	8.6	918	8.1
8			251	2.4	248	2.3	313	2.8
9			1,474	14.2	1,495	14.1	1,658	14.6
10	2,630	28.4	193	1.9	210	2.0	195	1.7
11			1,464	14.1	1,440	13.6	1,519	13.4
12			1,101	10.6	1,169	11.0	1,241	11.0
13			683	6.6	720	6.8	783	6.9
14			348	3.3	439	4.1	503	4.4
15	1,771	19.1	178	1.7	196	1.8	267	2.3
16			9	0.0	13	0.0	13	0.0
17			2	0.0	1	0.0	3	0.0
18			2	0.0	1	0.0	—	0.0
Total GS	9,269	100.0	10,374	100.0	10,601	100.0	11,331	100.0

Source: U.S. Civil Service Commission, Study of Minority Group Employment in the Federal Government (SM70–67B; SM70–69B; SM70–70B; SM70–71B).

111

TABLE 7.5

Ethnic Composition of U.S. Federal Government Employees in the General Service Pay System, by Percentage Comparison, 1967-71

GS Rank	Blacks		Spanish Surname		American Indians		Orientals		All Others	
	Number	Percent	Number	Percent	Number	Percent	Number	Percent	Number	Percent
1967 total	133,626	100.0	21,450	100.0	9,606	100.0	9,269	100.0	1,096,100	100.0
1-4	75,846	56.8	9,687	45.2	5,500	57.3	2,078	22.4	276,857	25.3
5-8	40,494	30.3	6,688	31.2	2,476	25.8	2,790	30.1	296,572	27.1
9-11	12,631	9.5	3,631	16.9	1,147	11.9	2,630	28.4	276,521	25.2
12-13	3,893	2.9	1,102	5.1	381	4.0	1,401	15.1	181,737	16.6
14-15	696	0.5	333	1.6	97	1.0	363	3.9	59,008	5.4
16-18	66	0.0	9	0.0	5	0.0	7	0.0	5,405	0.4
1969 total	137,918	100.0	23,681	100.0	9,752	100.0	10,374	100.0	1,107,381	100.0
1-4	67,252	48.8	9,180	38.8	5,051	51.8	1,993	19.2	228,566	20.6
5-8	47,837	34.7	7,855	33.2	2,616	26.8	2,927	28.2	306,172	27.6
9-11	16,318	11.8	4,548	19.2	1,465	15.0	3,131	30.2	295,678	26.7
12-13	5,370	3.9	1,618	6.8	473	4.9	1,784	17.2	204,016	18.4
14-15	1,078	0.7	466	2.0	140	1.4	526	5.1	67,727	6.1
16-18	63	0.0	14	0.0	7	0.0	13	0.1	5,222	0.5
1970 total	142,466	100.0	24,764	100.0	11,071	100.0	10,601	100.0	1,095,089	100.0
1-4	65,716	46.1	9,074	36.7	5,838	52.7	1,917	18.1	212,446	19.4
5-8	52,257	36.7	8,513	34.4	2,962	26.8	3,000	28.3	307,200	28.1
9-11	16,849	11.8	4,767	19.2	1,532	13.8	3,145	28.7	290,247	26.5
12-13	6,174	4.3	1,875	7.6	573	5.2	1,889	17.8	209,123	19.1
14-15	1,378	1.0	517	2.1	161	1.5	635	6.0	70,617	6.4
16-18	92	0.0	18	0.0	5	0.0	15	0.1	5,456	0.5
1971 total	148,957	100.0	26,757	100.0	12,377	100.0	11,331	100.0	1,116,054	100.0
1-4	63,833	42.9	9,487	35.5	6,478	52.3	1,965	17.3	210,607	18.9
5-8	58,024	39.0	9,325	34.9	3,380	27.3	3,184	28.1	317,997	28.5
9-11	18,262	12.3	5,175	19.3	1,688	13.6	3,372	29.8	290,838	26.1
12-13	7,028	4.7	2,150	8.0	646	5.2	2,024	17.9	217,337	19.5
14-15	1,697	1.1	597	2.2	176	1.4	770	6.8	73,681	6.6
16-18	113	0.0	23	0.0	9	0.0	16	0.1	5,594	0.5

Source: U.S. Civil Service Commission, Minority Group Employment in the Federal Government (SM70-67B, SM70-69B, SM70-70B, SM70-71B).

112

AGENCIES EMPLOYING CHINESE

Of the 20,889 Orientals employed in the federal government in 1971, 11,700 are Chinese.[3] Since no data are available on the Chinese alone, we will use the Oriental figures as a guideline. Table 7.6 was set up to show the agencies in which Orientals are found. The largest number are found in the Department of Defense, which includes the Army, Navy, Air Force, Supply, and the Office of the Secretary. One-half the Orientals employed in the federal government work in the Department of Defense. The data on type of work these people engage in were unavailable at the time of this writing, but an agency such as the Corps of Engineers is a likely place to utilize the services of engineers and technicians. The auditing divisions and the medical services in the armed forces are also areas in which Orientals are likely to be found.*

Oriental employees in the Veterans Administration have increased the most. The functions of this agency are primarily medical, educational, and insurance-oriented. Again, these are traditional fields for the Oriental professional.

POSTAL SYSTEM

Of approximately 730,000 post office jobs in the nation, between 3,000 and 4,000 are held by Orientals. Orientals include the Chinese, Japanese, Koreans, and other nationalities like Vietnamese. It is this author's guess that most of the postal employees under the heading "Orientals" are Japanese rather than Chinese. Even when lumped together, there were but 3,947 Orientals in the Postal System in 1969. The figure rose to 4,232 in 1970, but declined the year following to 3,952.

In 1967, 89 percent of the Oriental postal workers were in the lower PFS 1-4 ranks. By 1971, most had moved out of these ranks, but only into the next two higher ranks—PFS 5 to 9. They were conspicuously absent from the higher ranks extending upward to PFS 21 (see Table 7.7). The obvious conclusion that can be drawn from these figures is that the vast employment network of the U.S. Postal System is a highly segregated bloodline of the federal government.

---

*By way of comparison, the Department of Defense has always taken up a disproportionate share of the federal civilian payroll. Out of 2.9 million, 41 percent work for this department.

TABLE 7.6

Orientals Employed in Agencies of the U.S. Federal Government, General Service Pay System, 1967-71

Agency	1967	1969	1970	1971
State Department	208	203	184	178
Treasury	501	504	596	687
Defense total	11,791	12,126	11,386	10,268
Office of Secretary of Defense	278	390	131	132
Army	3,436	3,602	3,430	3,403
Navy	6,027	5,842	5,677	4,847
Air Force	1,987	2,043	1,905	1,651
Supply	—	249	243	235
Justice	88	132	154	171
Post Office	3,766	3,962	4,250	3,964
Interior	463	462	414	411
Agriculture	395	437	442	464
Commerce	214	272	306	287
Labor	42	49	49	65
Health, Education and Welfare	684	677	792	879
Housing/Urban Development	82	104	105	135
Transportation	365	398	405	660
Atomic Energy	12	21	30	35
Federal Reserve System	2	3	4	4
Management and Budget	1	3	2	5
Canal Zone	7	6	6	8
Civil Aeronautics	1	2	2	2
Civil Service Commission	33	29	38	45
Equal Employment Commission	1	2	7	10
Federal Communication Commission	5	5	5	8
Federal Deposit Insurance Corporation	7	8	14	13
Federal Home Loan	7	8	7	7
Federal Power Commission	13	12	13	16
Federal Trade Commission	6	6	7	5
General Accounting	11	16	20	20
General Service Administration	404	389	380	378
Government Printing	7	10	12	13
U.S. Information Agency	136	155	145	147
Interstate Commerce Commission	2	6	5	7
National Aeronautics and Space Administration	179	202	193	184
National Labor Relations Board	16	15	18	23
National Science Foundation	1	7	7	5
Office of Economic Opportunity	15	15	23	23
Panama Canal Company	4	10	11	11
Railroad Retirement Board	6	4	6	5
Securities and Exchange Commission	3	5	4	5
Selective Service Commission	21	26	34	34
Small Business Administration	28	16	23	82
Smithsonian Institution	12	10	9	12
U.S. Soldiers Home	1	2	3	0
Tennessee Valley Authority	16	23	30	28
Veterans Administration	837	1,089	1,262	1,581
Federal Courts	0	1	2	4
Total all agencies	20,393	21,432	21,405	20,889

Source: U.S. Civil Service Commission, Minority Group Employment in the Federal Government (SM70-67B; SM70-69B; SM70-70B; SM70-71B).

114

TABLE 7.7

Ethnic Comparison of U.S. Postal System Employees, by Percent, 1967-71

Postal Field Schedule Rank	Black Number	Black Percent	Spanish Surname Number	Spanish Surname Percent	American Indian Number	American Indian Percent	Oriental Number	Oriental Percent	All Other Number	All Other Percent
1967 total	132,011	100.0	14,776	100.0	1,057	100.0	3,758	100.0	546,744	100.0
1-4	123,632	93.7	13,626	92.2	917	86.8	3,337	88.8	459,648	84.1
5-8	7,805	5.9	1,034	7.0	124	11.7	374	10.0	68,409	12.5
9-11	467	0.3	87	0.6	13	1.2	39	1.0	14,379	2.6
12-15	97	—	27	0.2	3	0.3	7	0.2	3,916	0.7
16-18	7	—	2	—	0	—	1	—	359	—
19-20	3	—	0	—	0	—	0	—	33	—
1969 total	136,322	100.0	17,494	100.0	1,182	100.0	3,947	100.0	541,359	100.0
1-4	124,173	91.1	15,847	90.1	992	83.9	3,312	84.0	451,330	83.4
5-8	11,343	8.3	1,485	8.5	165	14.0	575	14.6	70,743	13.1
9-11	623	0.5	127	0.7	22	1.9	44	1.1	14,543	2.7
12-15	170	0.1	33	0.2	3	0.2	15	0.4	4,288	0.8
16-18	11	—	2	—	0	—	1	—	418	—
19-20	2	—	0	—	0	—	0	—	37	—
1970 total	138,753	100.0	19,045	100.0	1,271	100.0	4,232	100.0	550,678	100.0
1-4	124,549	89.8	17,124	89.9	1,056	83.1	3,485	82.3	457,754	83.1
5-8	13,176	9.5	1,730	9.1	185	14.6	662	15.6	72,844	13.2
9-11	771	0.5	150	0.8	27	2.1	66	1.6	15,014	2.7
12-15	241	0.2	37	0.2	3	0.2	18	0.4	4,514	0.8
16-18	14	—	4	—	0	—	1	—	515	0.1
19-20	2	—	0	—	0	—	0	—	37	—
1971 total	130,350	100.0	18,175	100.0	1,224	100.0	3,952	100.0	542,108	100.0
1-4	30,444	23.3	3,108	17.1	197	16.1	473	12.0	57,711	10.6
5-8	98,004	75.2	14,532	80.0	878	71.7	3,341	84.5	417,140	76.9
9-11	1,190	0.9	266	1.5	51	4.2	91	2.3	23,280	4.3
12-15	410	0.3	60	0.3	8	0.6	25	0.6	5,841	1.1
16-18	46	—	8	—	3	0.2	3	—	775	0.1
19-20	2	—	1	—	1	—	1	—	81	—
21	6	—	0	—	0	—	0	—	36	—
4th class	99	—	103	0.6	36	2.9	4	—	6,476	1.2
Rural carriers	149	0.1	97	0.5	50	4.1	14	0.3	30,768	5.7

Note: Dashes indicate the percentage to be less than 0.1 percent.

Source: U.S. Civil Service Commission, Minority Group Employment in the Federal Government (SM70-67B; SM70-70B; SM70-71B).

115

TABLE 7.8

San Francisco Government Employees of Oriental Extraction, by
Major Occupational Group and Sex, as of December 31, 1971

Major Occupational Group	Total		Male		Female	
	Number	Percent	Number	Percent	Number	Percent
Officials and managers	14	2.0	12	2.6	2	0.9
Professional	326	47.0	207	45.1	119	50.9
Technical	87	12.6	82	17.9	5	2.1
Official and clerical	140	20.2	37	8.1	103	44.0
Craftspersons	35	5.1	35	7.6	0	0.0
Operatives	36	5.2	36	7.8	0	0.0
Laborers	0	0.0	0	0.0	0	0.0
Uniformed protective service	9	1.3	9	2.0	0	0.0
Service workers	42	6.1	37	8.1	5	2.1
Agricultural and horticultural workers	4	0.6	4	0.9	0	0.0
Total	693	100.0	459	100.0	234	100.0

Source: Commission on Human Rights, San Francisco, Racial
and Ethnic Employment Pattern Survey, City and County of San Francisco Employees (December 31, 1971).

SAN FRANCISCO COUNTY AND CITY GOVERNMENT

The charm of this gateway city to the Pacific Ocean has always
been its Chinatown with its large Chinese-American population. Out
of a city population of approximately 700,000, over 8 percent are
Chinese and 2 percent Japanese. To administer the affairs of government, San Francisco employs a work force of more than 20,000. Of
this number on the regular payroll in December 1971, only 693 were
Orientals.

At the state and local government levels, Orientals are primarily
in professional and technical jobs; clerical jobs follow slightly behind.
Their numbers in administrative and managerial positions are insignificant, as is their presence in all the other major occupational categories (see Table 7.8 for a detailed breakdown).

Pay for Oriental males from the San Francisco government in 1971 clustered around the $880- to $1,250-per-month brackets. Females were more evenly distributed in the pay scale, although 50 percent held professional positions (see Table 7.9).

NEW YORK CITY GOVERNMENT

Let us span the continent and go to the second largest center of Chinese population on the East Coast—New York City. The population of the five boroughs of the metropolitan area is 7.8 million, and, according to the 1970 census, there are 70,182 Chinese. This is not even 1 percent of the population. Nevertheless, the Chinese are a highly concentrated, visible group that forms a viable community because of this consolidation.

The New York City government employed a work force of 273,881 in 1971. Of this number 817 were Chinese. Two-thirds of this number were in education or health services. The rest were lightly scat-

TABLE 7.9

Income of Orientals in San Francisco County and City Government Service, 1971

Monthly Income (in dollars)	Male		Female	
	Number	Percent	Number	Percent
301–400	1	0.2	4	1.1
401–500	70	11.7	47	12.6
501–600	43	7.2	48	12.8
601–700	34	5.7	48	12.8
701–800	33	5.5	61	16.3
801–1,000	140	23.4	75	20.1
1,001–1,250	150	25.1	63	16.8
1,251–1,500	80	13.4	21	5.6
1,501 and up	47	7.9	7	1.9
Total*	598	100.0	374	100.0

*Includes temporary employees.

Source: Commission on Human Rights, San Francisco, Racial and Ethnic Employment Pattern Survey, City and County of San Francisco Employees (December 31, 1971).

TABLE 7.10

Number of Chinese in New York City Government Agencies, 1971

Agency	Total City Employees	Chinese Employees		
		Total	Male	Female
Administration, Office of	114	0	0	0
Art Commission	2	0	0	0
Borough President Offices	201	2	2	0
Budget, Bureau of the	279	2	0	2
City Clerk	54	0	0	0
City Planning, Department of	368	4	3	1
City Sheriff	109	0	0	0
Collective Bargaining, Office of	25	0	0	0
Comptroller, Office of the	1,176	5	3	2
Consumer Affairs, Department of	335	0	0	0
Correction, Department of	3,681	4	3	1
County Clerk--Queens	51	0	0	0
District Attorney Office	662	2	1	1
Economic Development Administration	508	2	2	0
Education, Board of	88,641	231	62	169
Environmental Protection Administration	19,411	21	19	2
Estimate, Board of Bureau of Franchises	19	1	1	0
Estimate, Board of Bureau of the Secretary	24	0	0	0
Finance Administration	2,043	5	2	3
Fire, Department of	14,873	0	0	0
Health and Hospitals Corporation	40,646	286	137	149
Health Services Administration	6,374	43	26	17
Housing and Development Administration	4,863	23	19	4
Housing Authority	11,312	15	9	6
Human Resources Administration	25,503	93	65	28
Human Rights, Commission on	54	0	0	0
Investigation, Department of	83	0	0	0
Jamaica Planning and Development, Office of	13	0	0	0
Law, Department of	698	3	0	3
Lower Manhattan Development, Office of	12	0	0	0
Mayor, Office of the	201	0	0	0
Midtown Planning and Development, Office of	22	2	2	0
Model Cities Administration	442	3	2	1
Municipal Services Administration	3,917	16	13	3
Parks Recreation and Cultural Affairs Administration	4,895	3	3	0
Personnel, Department of	406	0	0	0
Police, Department of	35,310	15	8	7
Public Administrators	45	0	0	0
Public Events, Department of	18	0	0	0
Standards and Appeals, Board of	34	0	0	0
Staten Island Development, Office of	6	0	0	0
Surrogate's Court--Richmond County	18	0	0	0
Tax Commission	22	0	0	0
Teachers Retirement Board	110	1	0	1
Transportation Administration	255	14	10	4
Triborough Bridge and Tunnel Authority	5,429	1	1	0
Veterans Affairs, Division of	26	0	0	0
Water Supply, Board of	591	20	20	0
Total	273,881	817	413	404

Source: New York City, Commission on Human Rights, The Employment of Minorities, Women and the Handicapped in City Government: Report of a 1971 Survey.

tered throughout the 50–odd agencies of the municipal government
(see Table 7.10). Even in the Board of Education and the Health and
Hospitals Corporation, where the Chinese were strongest in numbers,
they were few in comparison to the total personnel in those two agencies.

Three important services of the municipal government are sanitation and fire and police protection. Sanitation, listed under the Environmental Protection Administration, employed 19,411 persons in
1971, of which 21 were Chinese. The Police Department payroll was
35,310, of which 15 were Chinese. The Fire Department employed
14,873, and there was not a single Chinese to be found in the entire
lot.

The absence of Asians in these three municipal agencies is a
common pattern in all metropolitan areas in the United States. In an
intensive affirmative action investigation by the California Fair Employment Practices Commission, it was found that Asians were woe-
fully underrepresented in or completely absent from the Police and
Fire Departments of Los Angeles, Oakland, Santa Clara, and Bakers-
field.[4]

Of those Chinese who do work for the city government, three
out of four are professionals and another 8 percent are paraprofes-
sionals. Knowing that the Chinese are found predominantly in the
Board of Education or the Health and Hospitals Administration, we
can surmise that they are either teachers or medical care personnel
(see Table 7.11).

Table 7.12 shows the salary level of Chinese employed in the
New York City government. Since three–fourths of the jobs held by
Chinese are in the professional ranks, it is not surprising to find
that three–fourths of them earned salaries in the $10,500–17,999
range. These salaries are below those for comparable positions in
private industry or professional service. It is this author's personal
belief that a disproportionate number of Chinese doctors work in the
city hospitals, mainly because they have not met the residence or citizenship requirements to practice.

DECLINE IN GOVERNMENT SERVICE

There is a slight indication that government service may be losing its appeal for Chinese Americans. At one time, it was the best
channel for them to move out of their few traditional lines of work in
the service category and into the professional, technical, and clerical
ranks. Today, private industry is more amenable to hiring Chinese,
and the challenge and opportunities offered by private industry must
be weighed against the cultural status and security of civil service.

TABLE 7.11

New York City Government Employees of Chinese Extraction, by Sex
and Occupational Classification, 1971

Occupational Classification	Total		Male		Female	
	Number	Percent	Number	Percent	Number	Percent
Officials and administrators	20	2.4	11	2.7	9	2.2
Professionals	614	75.1	328	79.4	286	70.8
Technical workers	11	1.3	9	2.2	2	0.5
Inspectors and investigators	9	1.1	1	0.2	8	2.0
Protective service workers	7	0.9	7	1.7	0	0.0
Paraprofessionals	68	8.4	12	2.9	56	13.9
Clerical workers	29	3.6	7	1.7	22	5.5
Craftsmen	4	0.5	4	1.0	0	0.0
Operatives	3	0.4	3	0.7	0	0.0
Service workers	48	5.9	27	6.5	21	5.2
Laborers	4	0.5	4	1.0	0	0.0
Total	817	100.1	413	100.0	404	100.1

Source: New York City, Commission on Human Rights, The
Employment of Minorities, Women and the Handicapped in City Government: Report of a 1971 Survey.

Not all jobs in government are obtained through competitive
civil service examinations. There are noncompetitive positions—
usually at the higher levels—that are filled on the basis of a person's
experience, skills, and background. Then there are the appointed
positions made on the basis of political considerations, as well as
qualifications, and, finally, there are the elected officials.

The Chinese have managed very well to gain entry into the competitive positions, carrying out the routine functions of government
responsibly and efficiently. But the ranks of jobs filled by election,
appointment, or personal considerations are very thin for the Chinese
indeed.

To sum up, the Chinese found in government service a wedge to
break out of their ghetto occupations. They are primarily in the pro-

TABLE 7.12

Salary Level of New York City Government Employees of Chinese
Extraction, by Sex, 1971

Salary Level (in dollars)	Total		Male		Female	
	Number	Percent	Number	Percent	Number	Percent
Under 5,200	21	2.5	6	1.5	15	3.7
5,200-7,299	112	13.7	41	9.9	71	17.6
7,300-10,499	55	6.8	25	6.1	30	7.4
10,500-12,999	366	44.8	138	33.4	228	56.4
13,000-17,999	228	27.9	185	44.8	43	10.6
18,000-24,999	12	1.4	11	2.7	1	0.3
25,000 and up	3	0.3	2	0.5	1	0.3
Unknown	20	2.4	5	1.2	15	3.7
Total	817	99.8	413	100.1	404	100.0

Source: New York City, Commission on Human Rights, The
Employment of Minorities, Women and the Handicapped in City Government: Report of a 1971 Survey.

fessional and technical jobs, performing the highly skilled tasks in the
daily operations of governmental functions, but, when it comes to pro-
motions into the supervisory or managerial ranks, they are skipped
over on the pretext that they are deficient in English or socially not
presentable.

SUMMARY OF FINDINGS

1. Almost one out of five Chinese persons employed work in
government service. They are found primarily in Hawaii and California. This percentage is unusually high considering that, until very
recent times, government employment required U.S. citizenship and
the Chinese population in the United States is heavily foreign-born and
alien. The reason lies in the status attached to government service
and the lower racial bars of the civil service system.

2. In state and local governments, the Chinese are predominantly
professionals and technicians. Translated into specific occupations,
they are teachers, engineers, and medical personnel.

3. In grade level and earnings, the Chinese may be classified as in the middle or upper-middle echelons. The Chinese have had a better showing than other ethnic minorities in government service, but very few have managed to penetrate the upper grades.

4. Large areas of government employment, such as the Postal System, the Sanitation, Fire, and Police Departments, have very few, if any, Orientals on their payrolls.

RECOMMENDATIONS

Government service has expanded occupational opportunities for the Chinese people and it has given them upward mobility into the middle ranks. Having proven themselves, the Chinese are ready to move forward. The problem today is not getting in but going up. Promotion criteria must be reviewed to remove some of the myths and stereotypes about the Chinese. There is too much presumption that whites will not take orders from a Chinese, that a Chinese might not be able to handle himself in the social milieu, that the Chinese speak only pidgin English or have a heavy accent.

The issue of whether government employees must be citizens of the United States was resolved at the state and local level by guidelines issued by the Civil Rights Commission late in 1969. The guidelines state that the citizenship requirement discriminates against persons because of national origin and, therefore, is in violation of Title VII of the Civil Rights Act. The U.S. Civil Service Commission has taken exception to this interpretation and has not removed the citizenship ban. This question was discussed in detail in Chapter 2. It is recommended that the federal government as an employer should itself comply with its own guidelines handed down for the state and local governments, except in positions involving national security and defense.

The bulk of the Chinese employed in government are in jobs filled by competitive examinations. The higher level jobs are filled either on a noncompetitive basis, by appointment, or by election. These are the managerial, administrative, or policy-making jobs. This area was not covered because there are so few Chinese in the upper echelons. The appointive and elective jobs require involvement in the political processes, and the Chinese have been reluctant to participate. It behooves the Chinese to realize that the United States is a democracy where the people are expected to be informed and involved, and to take an active part in the political processes of government. If they expect to have a voice in the determination of affairs that affect their lives and their interests, they must take a more active political role.

NOTES

1. U.S. Department of Labor, <u>Occupational Outlook Handbook</u> (Washington, D.C.: Government Printing Office, 1972), p. 841.

2. U.S. Census Bureau, Special Tabulation, Public Use Sample Data (1970).

3. Ibid.

4. Vicki Seid, "Police, Fire Departments Lack Asians, Says FEPC," <u>East/West</u>, August 21, 1974, p. 3.

CHAPTER

8

UNIONS

The strongest bastion against entry into the skilled crafts—particularly the building and construction industry—is the unions. Peculiar to this line of work is the fact that hiring is done, not by contractors, but through the unions, and union cards are hard to come by.

The craft unions, as opposed to industrial unions, are strong exclusionists, and it is their intention to keep their numbers low, their wages high, and their influence in the trades absolute. If one were to look at the structure of the unions and their hiring practices, one would realize how entrenched their position is, for they can determine the size and composition of the work force, the hiring and the firing, the qualifications for entry into the crafts, when and under what circumstances their numbers can work, and, to a large extent, the benefits and wages.

Table 8.1 shows the qualifications needed to become an apprentice in selected unions in New York City. It must be remembered, however, that the prime governing factors are nepotism and the determination by the unions as to how many new men they will admit.

MANAGEMENT SURRENDERED RIGHT TO HIRE

A booklet published by the New York City Commission on Human Rights called "Bias in the Building Industry" flatly stated that:

> The contractors continue to shirk their responsibility
> to include minority group workers in their work force.
> . . . Their LEGAL responsibility is set forth in a re-
> cent National Labor Relations Board ruling . . . which
> re-affirmed four basic legal doctrines:

124

TABLE 8.1

Apprenticeship in New York Area: Qualification, Training Period, and Wages, 1974

	Physical Examination	Age	Qualifications Education (grade)	Years Residence	Test	Citizenship	Years Apprenticeship	Starting Wage (in dollars)	Journeymen's Wage (in dollars)
Auto mechanic	Yes	18-26	—	—	Yes	—	4	3.35/hr.	5.15/hr.
Baker	Yes	18 and over	—	—	Yes	—	3	75./wk.	178./wk.
Bricklayer	Yes	17-21	9th	3	Yes	—	4	4.60/hr.	9.20/hr.
Carpet and linoleum layer	Yes	17-27	9th	—	Yes	Yes	4	4.60/hr.	8.40/hr.
Building construction carpenter	Yes	17-27	9th	—	Yes	Yes	4	5.65/hr.	9.15/hr.
Shop and mill carpenter	Yes	17-27	9th	—	Yes	Yes	4	5.31/hr.	9.17/hr.
Cement mason	Yes	18-21	8th	1	—	Yes	3	4.93/hr.	9.85/hr.
Electrician	Yes	19-22	High school	2	Yes	Yes	4	3.05/hr.	8.75/hr.
Iron worker, ornamental	Yes	18-30	10th	3	Yes	Yes	3	5.86/hr.	8.40/hr.
Iron worker, rigger and machine	Yes	18-28	10th	—	Yes	—	3	4.50/hr.	7.30/hr.
Iron worker, structural	Yes	18-28	10th	—	Yes	Yes	3	5.25/hr.	8.50/hr.
Metal lather	Yes	18-25	10th	1	Yes	Yes	3	3.85/hr.	8.75/hr.
Millwright	Yes	17-27	9th	—	Yes	Yes	4	4.60/hr.	8.40/hr.
Painter, decorator, paper hanger	Yes	18-25	10th	—	Yes	—	3	4.41/hr.	7.35/hr.
Plasterer	Yes	18-21	9th	1	—	—	3	162./wk.	299./wk.
Plumber (Local 1)	Yes	17-21	High school	3	Yes	—	5	5.49/hr.	8.25/hr.
Plumber (Local 2)	Yes	18-24	High school	3	Yes	Yes	5	2.85/hr.	7.02/hr.
Painter, caulker, and cleaner	Yes	18 and over	7th	—	—	—	3	2.50/hr.	5.60/hr.
Sheet metal worker	Yes	18-25	High school	—	Yes	—	4	5.58/hr.	11.52/hr.
Sheet metal worker (signs)	Yes	18-22	High school	—	Yes	Yes	5	2.90/hr.	5.80/hr.
Steamfitter	Yes	18-24	High school	1	Yes	Yes	5	3.42/hr.	8.65/hr.
Stone rigger	Yes	18-28	10th	1	Yes	Yes	3	4.75/hr.	8.75/hr.
Structured steel and bridge painter	Yes	18-26	High school	—	Yes	—	2	4.53/hr.	9.47/hr.

Source: New York State Employment Service, Apprenticeship Information Center.

1. Hiring is a management responsibility that cannot be delegated to unions.
2. Union membership cannot be imposed as a condition of initial employment because this creates a closed shop in violation of federal labor law.
3. Labor contract clauses on hiring cannot be so rigged as to create or perpetuate an illegal closed shop. . . .
4. The satisfactory completion of union tests or other requirements cannot be made a condition of employment.

More than ten years after this ruling, the labor needs of the contractors are still met by asking the union to send out X number of men. The booklet goes on to say that "it is beyond credulity that a union official or business agent will seek out any non-union men. . . . If there is a shortage of men the contractors will pay overtime rates to union men or accept referrals from out-of-town locals."

When confronted by the complete surrender of their right to hire, the contractors protested that, if any nonunion men were on the job, the union men would walk off. In this way the contractors take further refuge within the unions. It is not the concept of the labor movement that is questioned, but its exclusionist policy against non-whites that is deplored. Table 8.2 reveals how few Chinese there were in ten construction unions in San Francisco in 1970. Similar figures compiled by the Equal Employment Opportunity Commission (EEOC) for the New York region in 1972 show that out of a total membership of 175,934 for 317 locals, there were only 229 Asian-Americans (see Table 8.3). A closer look at the nonwhite union membership will reveal that a good portion of the work force is in the laborer category.

GOVERNMENT INTERVENTION

Since the contractors are reluctant to cooperate in opening the doors of employment in the crafts to minorities, the various levels of government have passed laws and issued executive orders and decrees to try to open up a wedge. The Civil Rights Act of 1964 has been on the law books for a decade, and Title VII of the act declares racial discrimination in private employment unlawful. Until 1972, however, the Equal Employment Opportunity Commission (EEOC), set up under the act to implement the law, found its effectiveness seriously hampered by its inability to enforce any violation of the law.

TABLE 8.2

Racial Composition of Ten Construction Unions in San Francisco, 1970

Union	Total	White	Black	Spanish Surname	Oriental	Indian
Carpet Linoleum and Tile Layers Union Local 1238	430	323	12	86	4	5
Electrical Workers Union Local 6	1,204	1,061	35	75	31	2
Elevator Constructors Union Local 8	600	547	16	28	3	6
Glaziers Union Local 718	305	341	1	4	1	3
Iron Workers Union Local 377	1,162	934	1	96	9	12
Lathers Union Local 65	184	24	5	40	15	0
Operating Engineers Union Local 3	32,000	31,175	72	454	270	29
Plumbers Union Local 28	2,748	2,583	19	121	20	5
Sheet Metal Workers Union Local 104	960	895	8	42	12	3
Tile Setters Union Local 19	299	284	2	10	0	3

Source: East/West, December 23, 1970 (taken from HUD tabulation).

TABLE 8.3

Union Membership in the Building Trades, by Minority Group in New York Region, 1972

Unions in Building Trade	Total (100 percent)	Black		Spanish Surname		Asian-American		American Indian	
		Number	Percent	Number	Percent	Number	Percent	Number	Percent
All building trades (317 locals)	175,934	21,839	12.4	8,925	5.1	229	0.1	1,186	0.7
Mechanical trades	59,016	3,399	5.8	3,674	6.2	18	–	815	1.4
Electrical workers	30,639	2,264	7.4	2,787	9.1	3	–	53	0.2
Iron workers	11,387	902	7.9	751	6.6	11	0.1	719	6.3
Plumbers and pipefitters	11,339	87	0.8	49	0.4	3	–	14	0.1
Sheet metal workers	2,534	26	1.0	13	0.5	0	0.0	7	0.3
Other mechanical trades	3,117	120	3.8	74	2.4	1	–	22	0.7
Trowel and miscellaneous trades	65,554	4,691	7.2	2,062	3.1	107	0.2	113	0.2
Asbestos workers	499	5	1.0	2	0.4	0	0.0	2	0.4
Bricklayers	6,151	314	5.1	50	0.8	1	–	9	0.1
Carpenters	40,658	3,002	7.4	1,509	3.7	104	0.3	46	0.1
Operating engineers	13,135	748	5.7	304	2.3	2	–	55	0.4
Plaster and cement workers	4,211	582	13.8	190	4.5	0	0.0	1	–
Other trowel and miscellaneous trades	900	40	4.4	7	0.8	0	0.0	0	0.0
Laborers, painters, and roofers	51,364	13,749	26.8	3,189	6.2	104	0.2	258	0.5
Laborers	43,305	12,944	29.9	2,565	5.9	97	0.2	234	0.5
Painters and allied trades	6,497	604	9.3	611	9.4	7	0.1	6	0.1
Roofers	1,562	201	12.9	13	0.8	0	0.0	18	1.2

Note: Dashes indicate the percentage to be less than 0.1 percent.

Source: Equal Employment Opportunity Commission, News Release, July 14, 1974.

At the federal level, Presidential Executive Order 11246 set up the Office of Federal Contract Compliance and imposed on the contractor in all federal contracts and federally assisted construction contracts the obligation to take affirmative action to ensure that applicants are employed and employees treated equitably without regard to their race, creed, or national origin. Affirmative action mandates positive effort on the part of the employer or contractor to recruit nonwhites and to see that they are given equal opportunity for advancement. To enforce compliance, the government can cancel the contract or prohibit the contractor from bidding on any future contract. The executive order was eventually further strengthened by requiring the employer to show that he had met definite goals in hiring minority workers in his work force before he was permitted to bid on government-assisted contracts.

It was further recognized that the pattern of discrimination and exclusion began at the apprenticeship level. In 1967, the U.S. Department of Labor announced that various trade union locals would be denied federal certification unless they reconsidered their refusal to admit nonwhites to their apprenticeship programs.

Without these government measures, it is doubtful that the unions or contractors would have opened up their ranks to nonwhites at all, and, even with these measures, there is serious doubt that they have made much of an impact. Benjamin W. Wolkinson, in an exhaustive study, concludes that remediation has been insignificant.[1] Of the 75 cases of complaints brought before the Equal Employment Opportunity Commission mentioned in his study, agreements were executed in only 18. Of these, the compliance in many instances was perfunctory and did not get at the root of systematic exclusion of minorities from the unions.

HOMETOWN PLANS

In some instances, the industry and local unions themselves offered to upgrade their commitment to bringing minority workers into the trades when they realized that the social climate would no longer accept their exlusionist position. At the same time, governmental pressures were making it a bit uncomfortable for them. When a tight money market reduces private construction to a minimum, public construction may be the only type of work available. In this way a number of hometown plans came into being.

Funded by federal, state, and city monies, these plans set up trainee programs to teach minority members the trades. Unfortunately, the graduates of the training programs still found themselves jobless unless they were affiliated with a union. By 1973, the hometown plans were considered a failure.

FEW CHINESE IN CONSTRUCTION CRAFTS

Where do the Chinese fit into this picture? Hardly at all, and that is precisely the point we want to make. If we turn back to Table 5.7, we see that in 1970 the percentage of Chinese engaged in the crafts was 5.4 percent. However, only 1,767, or 1 percent of the Chinese labor force, were in the construction crafts. Of this number Hawaii alone claimed a large proportion—one out of every five persons in the labor force in that state was in the crafts. That leaves but a scattered few for the entire U.S. mainland.

The scant numbers are quite evident by the figures given in Tables 8.2 and 8.3. Out of a total of 365 Orientals* in the ten construction unions in San Francisco, 270 of these are in one union alone. Only 20 are in the plumbers union in a city where Orientals make up about 10 percent of the population.

For the New York region we have later figures for 1972, encompassing union membership in the building trades for 317 locals. For a much larger area and under a broader definition, "Asian-American," there is a total of 229 persons, or one-tenth of 1 percent, who are in the construction crafts. There are three plumbers of Asian descent in New York.

These figures say something, and they say it loud and clear: Asian-Americans are definitely not in the construction crafts. Is it because they choose not to go into this line of work or have they been effectively excluded? This question was answered for me by David Wong, director of the Recruitment and Training Program in Westchester, New York, which serves as watchdog for the Office of Federal Contract Compliance.

In a personal interview, he said,

> I had an opening to refer a plasterer. I put one ad
> in the Chinese newspaper and made a spot announce-
> ment over the local FM station that broadcasts once
> a week on Saturdays. Thirty Chinese applicants came
> to me for that job.
>
>   My territory is Westchester, but whenever I have
> a little time, I come down to Chinatown to volunteer

---

*Note that in some of our tables the term "Oriental" is employed and in others "Asian-Americans" is used. These terms are not synonymous, nor do they give us any breakdown for the Chinese. In the absence of other data, the figures are given as indicators. The term Oriental generally means the Far Eastern peoples such as the Chinese, Japanese, and Koreans. Asian-Americans take in the Filipinos and Indians, as well as the Vietnamese, Indonesians, Malayans, and so on.

my services. I've been with the Recruitment and
Training Program for about five years and I have
personally placed 44 Asian-Americans in the various
trades. When the DeMatteis Construction Firm was
awarded the Confucius Plaza* contract two years ago,
I mentioned to the Board of Urban Affairs and Mr. De-
Matteis that they should give some consideration to
putting Asian-Americans into a project that is going
up in our own community. I sent about 20 people up
to the State Employment Office to register for trainee
positions, but not one of those people were called.
After the protest demonstration, suddenly everyone
looked bewildered and said, "Look, we did not know
any Asian-Americans were interested."

Now we come to the question about qualifications
and knowledge of the English language. I have found
out since last year that the 15 Chinese who took the
sheet metal test and steamfitters' test scored the
highest of all the minorities. They came in first in
math, first in spatial relations, and even first in English. So far, none has gone to work yet.

If somebody tells me that they don't know where
to find qualified Asian-Americans for construction
work, I can supply them with 135 names to select
from now. We have skilled carpenters, bricklayers,
electricians, and tilemen from the old country with
many years of experience. They just need some
training in the building codes and methods used in
this country.

CHINESE NOT A MINORITY

Minorities have a hard enough time battling the fortress of the
trade unions, but in this fight, where all the ethnic minorities are in
the same boat, the Chinese or Asians are left out in the cold. The
anomaly is that the minorities could not penetrate the construction
industry without government pressure in the form of Affirmative Action or Contract Compliance; yet, when machinery was set up to aid
minorities, the Asians were not recognized as minorities.

According to James McNamara of the Office of Federal Contract
Compliance, in testimony before the Civil Rights Hearings for Asian-
Americans,

---

*New housing and commercial complex in New York's Chinatown.

Orientals simply have not been recognized by the
government agencies, by the unions, or by the contractors as a group that are considered minorities and a
group that is considered disadvantaged. . . . The
New York State Commission on Human Rights . . .
does not consider Orientals to be entitled to that
kind of special treatment known as a dispensation
from the State laws against discrimination. . . . On
the federal level, we have had some recent experiences
with the U.S. Attorney's Office in the Southern District. . . . The problem is, again, they do not recognize Orientals in the definition of minorities, at least
in the two cases that our office had some involvement
in.

As a consequence of this ruling, Asians are outside of Affirmative Action and Contract Compliance—the entire equal employment opportunity umbrella. They have to compete disadvantageously not only
with whites but also with other nonwhite minorities who are given government backing through these special programs.

MINORITY WITHIN A MINORITY

Even in instances where the Asian has been recognized as a
minority coming under the umbrella of Affirmative Action and Contract Compliance, he faces competition with other minority groups
scrambling for the limited number of slots. Again, the construction
of Confucius Plaza is an excellent example.

Before awarding any public-monies contracts in New York,
contractors must demonstrate that they are in compliance with minority hiring goals. When the Chinese community leaders asked for re-
assurances on this score at the signing of the contract, they were told
by the attorneys, "Don't worry, the government will make sure of
that." When the work got under way, the Chinese discovered that only
four people out of a work force of 71 were Chinese; one was the architect, two were laborers, and the fourth, an office worker. When queried about a $42 million construction project going up in Chinatown with
no provision by the contractor to utilize Chinese craftsmen, the contractor replied, "We are in compliance. Our percentage of minority
employees exceeds the recommended goals."

A spokesman for the Equal Employment Opportunity Commission
maintained that the law and executive orders did not specify proportionate representation among the minorities. "We cannot break minorities
up into categories, so many blacks, so many Puerto Ricans, so many

Asian-Americans, etc. When a contractor shows us that his work force is 40 percent black and Puerto Rican, he has shown us he is in compliance."

True, the letter of the law was fulfilled, but there was absolutely no sensitivity to the feelings or position of the Chinese craftsmen, who realize that if they are excluded from their line of work right on their own front steps by the contractors, the unions, and other minorities they stand little chance when they have to compete elsewhere.

SUMMARY OF FINDINGS

1. Occupations like the building and construction crafts are controlled by the unions. The control is almost absolute because the unions determine the size and composition of the work force, the hiring and the firing, the qualifications for entry into the crafts, when and under what circumstances their members can work, and to a large extent the benefits and the wages. This has been very effective in keeping minority groups out of the industry.

2. Title VII of the Civil Rights Act has not proven effective in righting these wrongs because the Equal Employment Opportunity Commission could only conciliate complaints and did not have enforcement powers until 1972. Federal Contract Compliance was also impotent until it was strengthened by the stipulation of preaward compliance by unions and contractors.

3. Hometown plans, whereby the industry and unions offered to police themselves, have not been successful and are being terminated in favor of mandatory goals.

4. If the blacks and numerically larger nonwhite minorities have had a tough time breaking into the industry, the Chinese are having a worse time of it. They are conspicuously absent from the craft occupations.

5. Rationalizations that the Chinese do not want to go into the crafts or that they are unqualified are simply not true. They are willing, able, and eager to enter the construction crafts.

6. In instances where minorities are being helped to scale the barriers put up by the unions and construction industry by such government programs as Affirmative Action, Equal Employment Opportunity, and Contract Compliance, the Chinese are outside the purview of these aids because they are not considered a minority. There is no clear-cut interpretation and determination. Even where they are recognized as a minority, the Chinese are edged out by the more vocal, activist, and numerically stronger minorities.

RECOMMENDATIONS

From this observer's viewpoint, it seems that there are two er-
roneous approaches in the efforts of government, contractors, and
everyone involved to increase minority representation in the building
and construction industry:

1. Using old methods to fit new conditions—trying to push minorities into union-established channels for training, apprenticeship,
union membership, and job referrals—has not yielded encouraging results. It is simply futile and unrealistic to think that the "haves" in
terms of union membership are going to willingly and voluntarily relinquish their privileges and prerogatives to the "have nots."
2. There has been too much concentration on the trainee aspect
without providing for employment opportunities at the end of the training period. The trainee period is a long one. It is also parallel to
the apprenticeship programs. If the trainees are subordinated to the
apprentices in job preference, trainees will be discouraged from entering or completing their training. If the trainees see no hope at the
end of their period of training, the training programs serve no useful
purpose.

The bottleneck is at the union hiring halls, where the membership holds the keys to job referrals. If the hiring halls continue to
resist integration or dole out a few token slots to minorities, this is
where the government must direct its efforts to increase the flow.
Since management or the contractors have long relinquished their right
of hiring to the unions, they may just as well relinquish it to a third
party who will try earnestly to open up the industry to workers without
regard to skin color.

Bypass the Union

My recommendation is to bypass not only the union's exclusionist apprenticeship program but also its hiring halls in job referrals
and placement. Since contractors must pledge to aim toward a goal
of minority representation in their work force prior to contract award,
they could just as well allocate these job slots to an organization like
the Recruitment and Training Program (RTP) now under contract to
the Office of Federal Contract Compliance. This program is privately
run and has had an outstanding record of providing supportive services
to enable minorities to seek and hold jobs in the construction industry.
RTP could be entrusted also with the actual placement in jobs of minority workers who have finished training and those already qualified by

virtue of holding diplomas from vocational schools, by being licensed, or by having long years of experience in the trade. The essential criteria are to prove that the worker is qualified.

The RTP as it is presently set up merely warms up the minority applicants in anticipation of getting into the game. It seeks out and prepares applicants to take the examinations given by the unions; it helps the applicant obtain necessary papers and documents such as birth certificates, high school diplomas, and citizenship papers; and it helps minority members register at the state employment office. But the criteria and procedures are still union-established and union-controlled. As a result, a large number of the beneficiaries of RTP efforts are still sitting in the dugout, waiting to be called.

After recruiting and ascertaining that the applicants are qualified, the RTP should be empowered to place the minority workers into slots set aside for them. Its task would be no different from that of the union hiring halls, except that they would be motivated toward getting minority representation into an industry that has traditionally been lily-white.

For the Chinese, who are neither here nor there—not part of the majority, but not adjudged a minority by some political jurisdictions—there must be some recognition that all minorities are not alike, although all minorities are disadvantaged by racial discrimination. There is special need in the Chinese communities at present because of the unprecedented increase in the Chinese-American population within the last few years.

Many Chinese immigrants were skilled craftsmen before they came to the United States. They are looking for jobs in their line of work and are hard-working and reliable. They also are qualified, willing, and able. They should not be denied the chance to break into the trade.

Suggestions were solicited from a number of people in Chinatown working in the manpower area on how to facilitate the entry of Chinese-Americans into the crafts. The opinion seems to be that the Chinese are unfamiliar with how to go about getting into the industry and that they need a little more "handholding" at this point.

The Chinese are conditioned somewhat by their cultural background to be reticent and noncompetitive. In China, humility is considered a virtue. In this country, such character traits are viewed as weaknesses and are decided drawbacks if today's contemporaries are to be in the vanguard for penetrating the union strongholds. Consequently, it is recommended that branch Recruitment and Training Programs be established in the Chinatowns of New York and San Francisco to serve the Asian populations of the East and West Coasts. Proposals for such Chinatown-based programs have been submitted to the Department of Labor for three consecutive years and have been turned down each time. As mentioned previously, handholding is vitally necessary for the initial thrust. Once the Chinese gain entry into the crafts they will be able to hold their own by their performance. Their record will be their own best advertisement.

Maintain Standards

Minority workers must never permit themselves to lower the standards of job performance. To do so would be self-defeating. No one should be able to point a finger at the minority craftsmen and call them inferior. No one wants his apartment house or office building to go up with shoddy workmanship. No one wants to pay extra for inefficiency in the construction of public works through heavier taxes. Nor should any employer be compelled to accept unproductive workers. Minority workers must be judged by their performance. They should be given no dispensation for poor skills or bad work habits. It is not recommended that minority workers be hired merely because they are black or of Spanish origin or Asian or Chinese.

The fact remains that there are qualified minority workers who cannot enter the crafts because of racial discrimination. This is clearly evident from the case cited where Chinese applicants scored highest in mathematics, highest in spatial relations, and even highest in English, but were never called. This evidence is reinforced when a metropolis like New York City, with a population of close to 10 million, counted only 229 Asian craftsmen in its union locals in 1972.

NOTE

1. Benjamin W. Wolkinson, Blacks, Unions and the EEOC (Lexington, Mass.: D. C. Heath, 1973), p. 99.

9

Dollars and cents figures as a measurement of income are not always reliable and may not even be comparable. According to the Census Bureau, the rate of nonresponse to the question on income ran about 10.6 percent in 1960 and was considerably higher for 1970.[1] The concept of income for many Chinese is entirely different from the one generally accepted in this country. For those who work for their own countrymen, and a substantial proportion do, remuneration on a job calls for room and board, payment of all social security and income taxes, plus a pay envelope. What is in the pay envelope is considered income. The dollars may be fewer, but the total package may favor the employee.

On the other hand, those who work for non-Chinese firms generally regard as their income the gross amount before deductions, not to mention what they will have left after spending for food and rent. With these qualifications in mind, we can take a look at the income figures from the census.

Table 9.1 shows family income of the Chinese in the United States and five selected states. There seems to be wide disparity in family income from state to state. California, with its larger Chinese population, approximates the national pattern of income distribution— about 5 percent for each $1,000 aggregate, except at the lower and higher extremities. The Chinese in New York are noticeably poorer, and those in Hawaii, significantly better off.

There is a close relationship between income and length of stay in this country. Those who have been in this country for some time are doing well, while the recent arrivals are having a hard time. The Chinese in New York are faring the worst. Their median income is close to $6,000 below that of Chinese in Hawaii. That is a very big gap. The Chinese in Massachusetts are only a little better off. In

TABLE 9.1

Family Income of the Chinese in the United States, Total and Five Selected States, 1969

Family Income (in dollars)	United States Number	United States Percent	California Number	California Percent	New York Number	New York Percent	Hawaii Number	Hawaii Percent	Illinois Number	Illinois Percent	Massachusetts Number	Massachusetts Percent
All families	94,931	100.0	37,437	100.0	18,546	100.0	12,304	100.0	2,920	100.0	2,920	100.0
Less than 1,000	2,378	2.5	857	2.3	535	2.9	175	1.4	88	3.0	86	2.9
1,000-1,999	2,449	2.6	1,011	2.7	626	3.4	188	1.5	77	2.6	67	2.3
2,000-2,999	3,021	3.2	1,294	3.5	695	3.7	230	1.9	52	1.8	91	3.1
3,000-3,999	4,037	4.3	1,543	4.1	999	5.4	239	1.9	155	5.3	192	6.6
4,000-4,999	4,737	5.0	1,523	4.1	1,514	8.2	330	2.7	141	4.8	235	8.0
5,000-5,999	5,393	5.7	1,912	5.1	1,539	8.3	421	3.4	172	5.9	177	6.1
6,000-6,999	5,543	5.8	2,142	5.7	1,506	8.1	428	3.5	123	4.2	176	6.0
7,000-7,999	5,638	5.9	2,012	5.4	1,437	7.7	496	4.0	155	5.3	276	9.5
8,000-8,999	5,413	5.7	1,994	5.3	1,335	7.2	548	4.5	180	6.2	181	6.2
9,000-9,999	5,494	5.8	2,221	5.9	1,145	6.2	510	4.1	174	6.0	195	6.7
10,000-11,999	11,028	11.6	4,830	12.9	1,892	10.2	1,263	10.3	371	12.7	325	11.1
12,000-14,999	12,841	13.5	5,572	14.9	1,848	10.0	1,823	14.8	513	17.6	315	10.8
15,000-24,999	20,361	21.4	8,215	21.9	2,722	14.7	3,916	31.8	567	19.4	493	16.9
25,000 or more	6,598	7.0	2,311	6.2	753	4.1	1,737	14.1	152	5.2	111	3.8
Median income (in dollars)	10,610		10,915		8,316		14,179		10,771		8,884	
Mean income (in dollars)	12,210		12,188		10,028		15,936		11,754		10,475	

Note: Based on a 20 percent sampling.

Source: U.S. Department of Commerce, Bureau of the Census, Subject Report, PC(2)1G (1970), Table 24.

TABLE 9.2

Comparison Between Average Income of the Chinese and the National
and State Averages, 1969
(in dollars)

	Family Income	
	Median	Mean
United States	9,590	10,999
Chinese in the United States	10,610	12,210
California	10,732	12,227
Chinese in California	10,915	12,188
New York	10,617	12,491
Chinese in New York	8,316	10,028
Hawaii	11,554	13,077
Chinese in Hawaii	14,179	15,936
Illinois	10,959	12,338
Chinese in Illinois	10,771	11,754
Massachusetts	10,835	12,283
Chinese in Massachusetts	8,884	10,475

Sources: For Chinese: U.S. Department of Commerce, Bureau of the Census, Subject Report, PC(2)1G (1970), Table 24; for
United States and states: U.S. Department of Commerce, Bureau of
the Census, Subject Report, PC(1)C1 (1970), Table 178.

these two states, the Chinese are predominantly service workers
and operatives; the rate of illiteracy is high, as is the proportion of
college graduates (see Tables 4.3 and 5.3). Obviously the main causal
factor in the much lower income seems to be the recentness of arrival
in this country.

How does the average Chinese family income compare with the
U.S. and state averages? Table 9.2 gives a comparison. In the
United States and in the states of California and Hawaii, the Chinese
median, as well as mean, income is higher. In New York, Illinois,
and Massachusetts, the figures are lower.

The mean is higher than the median in every instance, which
indicates that the Chinese in the upper-income bracket have a substantially higher income to pull up the average. In this way the Chinese
in Hawaii have pulled up the U.S. family income of the Chinese. Attention to regional or state differences must, therefore, be considered
in any social or economic planning.

MULTIEARNERS

Since the average income of the Chinese family exceeds in many instances that for the people of the nation and some states, can it be surmised that the Chinese are well paid and well off? On the surface, it may appear that way until we take a look at the number of earners in the Chinese family. The fact that half of the Chinese females 16 years and over are in the labor force is a telling clue that the family income for the Chinese comes from more than one source. The number of earners in Chinese families is given in Table 9.3. In the $10,000 to $14,999 bracket, just a bit over two out of five (43.1 percent) attained this family income with one earner; 31 percent had two earners; and as much as 9.4 percent of the families with this income had five earners. Obviously, then, the additional persons contributing to the family "kitty" will raise the total amount, but, when viewed in light of manpower expended and remuneration per unit of labor, the true picture begins to emerge.

The higher mean family income may come from the 16.1 percent of families with $15,000 to $19,999 and even the 10.0 percent with $20,000 to $29,999, but in these higher income brackets the increment invariably comes from a larger number of earners, rather than from increases in individual pay.

PER CAPITA INCOME

This fact is apparent when personal income is compared with family income. These figures are presented in Table 9.4 (see also Table 6.13). Personal income is that amount received per individual 16 years and over. When one examines this table, the seeming affluence of the Chinese fades. Only one-fourth of the Chinese males earned over $10,000, and less than 5 percent of the females did. If family members did not pool their incomes, the Chinese would be in a sorry economic shape.

ARE THE CHINESE POOR?

In 1970, for the first time in U.S. census history, a new economic characteristic was introduced into the census. It was the poverty level index. "The index provides a range of poverty income cutoffs adjusted by such factors as family size, sex of the family head, number of children under 18 years old, and farm and non-farm residence."[2]

TABLE 9.3

Family Income of Chinese in the United States, by Number of Earners, 1969
(in percent)

Income of Families with Earners (in dollars)	Total Families	Number of Earners					Percent of Families in Income Bracket (100.0 percent)
		One	Two	Three	Four	Five	
1-999 or less	100.0	58.8	35.3	5.9	0.0	0.0	1.5
1,000-1,999	100.0	47.8	43.5	0.0	4.3	4.3	2.0
2,000-2,999	100.0	42.4	45.5	6.1	3.0	3.0	2.9
3,000-3,999	100.0	43.4	43.4	5.7	1.9	5.7	4.6
4,000-4,999	100.0	40.4	46.8	8.5	0.0	4.3	4.1
5,000-6,999	100.0	43.9	30.9	11.4	5.7	8.1	10.8
7,000-9,999	100.0	37.0	35.9	13.8	7.2	6.1	15.9
10,000-14,999	100.0	43.1	31.0	12.8	3.7	9.4	26.0
15,000-19,999	100.0	33.2	37.0	14.1	8.7	7.1	16.1
20,000-29,999	100.0	25.4	31.6	18.4	6.1	18.4	10.0
30,000-49,999	100.0	20.4	16.7	14.8	9.3	38.9	4.7
50,000 and over	100.0	20.0	26.7	6.7	0.0	46.7	1.3
Median income (in dollars)	11,574	10,664	10,815	12,961	13,636	23,750	11,574
Mean income (in dollars)	13,577	11,857	12,411	15,073	15,363	24,722	13,577

Source: U.S. Department of Commerce, Bureau of the Census, Special Tabulation, Public Use Sample Data (1970).

TABLE 9.4

Comparison of Personal and Family Income of the Chinese in the United States, 1969

| | Personal Income | | | | Family Income | |
| | Male 16 and over | | Female 16 and over | | | |
Income (in dollars)	Number	Percent	Number	Percent	Number	Percent
Total persons or families	146,969	100.0	95,332	100.0	94,931	100.0
1–999 or less	17,799	12.1	23,744	24.9	2,378	2.5
1,000–1,999	17,286	11.8	16,209	17.0	2,449	2.6
2,000–2,999	12,707	8.7	11,237	11.8	3,021	3.2
3,000–3,999	12,332	8.4	10,304	10.8	4,037	4.3
4,000–4,999	11,216	7.6	8,654	9.1	4,737	5.0
5,000–5,999	9,619	6.5	7,057	7.4	5,393	5.7
6,000–6,999	8,821	6.0	5,216	5.5	5,543	5.8
7,000–7,999	8,215	5.6	3,748	4.0	5,638	5.9
8,000–8,999	7,491	5.1	2,933	3.1	5,413	5.7
9,000–9,999	6,247	4.3	1,687	1.8	5,494	5.8
10,000–14,999	21,419	14.6	3,478	3.6	23,869	25.1
15,000 or more	13,817	9.4	1,065	1.1	26,979	28.4
Median income (in dollars)	5,223		2,686		10,610	
Mean income (in dollars)	6,877		3,512		12,210	
Less than 5,000	71,340	48.5	70,148	73.6	16,622	17.5
5,000–10,000	40,393	27.5	20,641	21.7	27,481	28.9
10,000–15,000	21,419	14.6	3,478	3.6	23,869	25.1
15,000 or more	13,817	9.4	1,065	1.1	26,979	28.4

Source: U.S. Department of Commerce, Bureau of the Census, Subject Report, PC(2)1G (1970), Tables 19, 24.

In 1969, the poverty thresholds ranged from approximately $1,500 to $6,000. The average poverty threshold for a nonfarm family of four headed by a male was $3,745. The thresholds are computed on a national basis only and are not adjusted for local or state variations in the cost of living.

Table 9.5 shows the number of Chinese families with income less than poverty level. A substantial 9,753 families fall into this category, and the table gives a further breakdown by states. New York has a higher percentage of poverty level families, with 13.8 percent, compared to a Chinese national average of 10.3 percent. This proportion is just about the same as for the U.S. poverty level for whites (10.2 percent), but substantially below that for black families (29.9 percent). Again, the reader is reminded that Chinese families have multiearners. There also is a good deal of moonlighting and long hours so that the income figures are not exactly comparable.

PAY GOES UP WITH AGE

There is a definite correlation between income and age, except for those beyond age 65. The reason is apparent, and follows the normal course of events. The only remarkable factor about the pay-age correlation is the long period it takes for the Chinese to get started. By age 20 to 24, over three-quarters of the Chinese males earn less than $4,000, and it is not until the 25- to 34-year age category that the males begin to move into the higher income brackets. This is explained in large part by the fact that the Chinese are still going for their graduate degrees, and whatever earnings they make come from school-related or part-time work.

The 40.6 percent of male teenagers 16 to 19 years old who have no income (see Table 9.6) is a current and potentially explosive troublespot. Young fellows at this age need initiation into the work world. Their demands are great, fueled by the long hours spent in front of television. Teenagers should have more access to paying jobs, which would give them some sense of personal worth and would reduce the time spent watching the "boob tube" or hanging out with the gang. Teenage gangs and their violent behavior in San Francisco and New York's Chinatowns are now headline producers. The old adage still holds, "Idle hands are the devil's workshop."

Pay for Chinese females increases with age at a much slower pace than for males. The median pay is approximately one-half that of the males for all age brackets except the teens. At the height of their earning power (age 35 to 44) only 7.5 percent take in over $10,000 annually.

TABLE 9.5

Chinese Persons and Families with Income Less than Poverty Level, Total United States and Five Selected States, 1970

Income Less than Poverty Level	United States	California	New York	Hawaii	Illinois	Massachusetts
Families	9,753	3,694	2,560	676	301	371
Percent all families	10.3	9.9	13.8	5.5	10.3	12.7
Mean size of families	3.98	4.03	4.03	3.89	3.75	4.45
Mean income deficit (in dollars)	1,596	1,645	1,506	1,551	1,533	1,698
With related children under 18	6,302	2,344	1,716	397	152	284
Families with female heads	1,290	559	174	209	19	42
Unrelated Individuals 14 Years and over	17,867	6,983	3,344	958	625	578
Percent unrelated individuals 14 years and over	40.3	40.3	36.5	37.7	38.8	37.3
Mean income deficit (in dollars)	1,174	1,157	1,142	1,038	1,181	1,136
Percent 65 years and over	24.1	21.0	37.4	39.6	18.7	24.4
Persons Involved	55,748	21,668	13,188	3,566	1,718	2,150
Percent of all persons	13.3	13.0	16.3	6.9	12.9	16.1
Percent 65 years and over	13.4	13.1	16.4	18.9	12.7	9.1

Note: Based on a 20 percent sampling.

Source: U.S. Department of Commerce, Bureau of the Census, Subject Report, PC(2)1G (1970), Table 24.

144

TABLE 9.6

Personal Income of the Chinese in the United States, by Age Group and Sex, 1969

	Total 16 Years and over		16–19 Years		20–24 Years		25–34 Years		35–44 Years		45–64 Years		65 Years and over	
	Number	Per-cent	Number	Per-cent	Number	Per-cent	Number	Per-cent	Number	Per-cent	Number	Per-cent	Number	Per-cent
Male 16 Years and over	163,893		18,757		22,996		33,575		31,082		42,239		15,244	
Without income[a]	16,924	10.3	7,610	40.6	4,303	18.7	1,947	5.8	645	2.1	1,510	3.6	909	6.0
With income[b]	146,969	100.0	11,147	100.0	18,693	100.0	31,628	100.0	30,437	100.0	40,729	100.0	14,335	100.0
Under $2,000 or less	35,085	23.9	9,029	81.0	9,416	50.4	3,335	10.5	1,722	5.7	4,158	10.2	7,425	51.8
$2,000–3,999	25,039	17.0	1,586	14.2	5,266	28.2	5,347	16.9	3,143	10.3	6,068	14.9	3,647	25.4
$4,000–5,999	20,835	14.2	335	3.0	2,034	10.9	5,220	17.0	4,702	15.5	7,207	17.7	1,337	9.3
$6,000–7,999	17,036	11.6	147	1.3	1,104	5.9	4,631	14.6	4,343	14.3	6,114	15.0	697	4.9
$8,000–9,999	13,738	9.4	21	0.2	569	3.0	4,175	13.2	3,934	12.9	4,657	11.4	382	2.7
$10,000–14,999	21,419	14.6	18	0.2	259	1.4	6,439	20.4	7,450	24.5	6,791	16.7	462	3.2
$15,000 or more	13,817	9.4	11	0.1	45	0.2	2,481	7.8	5,161	17.0	5,734	14.1	385	2.7
Median income (in dollars)	5,223		916		1,985		6,887		8,643		6,904		1,943	
Mean income (in dollars)	6,877		1,277		2,650		7,458		9,951		8,842		3,348	
Female 16 Years and over	145,012		17,099		22,888		32,411		28,194		32,808		11,612	
Without income[a]	49,680	34.3	7,627	44.6	5,935	25.9	12,639	39.0	10,146	36.0	10,692	32.6	2,641	22.7
With income[b]	95,332	100.0	9,472	100.0	16,953	100.0	19,772	100.0	18,048	100.0	22,116	100.0	8,971	100.0
Under $2,000 or less	39,953	41.9	7,891	83.3	8,900	53.0	5,383	27.2	4,513	25.0	6,556	29.6	6,710	74.8
$2,000–3,999	21,541	22.6	1,227	13.0	3,908	23.1	4,315	21.8	4,541	25.2	6,192	28.0	1,358	15.1
$4,000–5,999	15,711	16.5	262	2.8	2,781	16.4	3,994	20.2	3,984	22.1	4,296	19.4	394	4.4
$6,000–7,999	8,964	9.4	46	0.5	1,081	6.4	3,130	15.8	2,402	13.3	2,120	9.6	185	2.1
$8,000–9,999	4,620	4.9	5	0.1	174	1.0	1,727	8.7	1,253	7.0	1,345	6.1	116	1.3
$10,000–14,999	3,478	3.7	29	0.3	86	1.0	1,043	5.3	1,080	6.0	1,121	5.1	119	1.3
$15,000 or more	1,065	1.1	12	0.1	23	0.1	180	1.0	275	1.5	486	2.2	89	1.0
Median income (in dollars)	2,686		856		1,889		4,090		3,988		3,464		1,188	
Mean income (in dollars)	3,512		1,154		2,486		4,472		4,493		4,294		1,918	

[a]Percentage based on all persons 16 years and over.
[b]Percentage based on persons with income.

Source: U.S. Department of Commerce, Bureau of the Census, Subject Report, PC(2)1G (1970), Table 21.

TABLE 9.7

Average Earnings of Employed Chinese Who Worked 50-52 Weeks in 1969, by Selected Occupation and Sex
(in dollars)

Occupation	Male Earnings		Female Earnings	
	Median	Mean	Median	Mean
Professional and Technical	11,049	11,445	6,076	6,591
Architects	11,000	11,167	6,000	6,625
Computer specialists	10,600	12,313	9,000	7,688
Engineers	13,062	13,541	9,000	7,000
Lawyers and judges	13,000	12,600	–	7,000
Librarians, archivists, and curators	8,500	13,900	7,000	17,500
Mathematical specialists	13,000	13,000	17,500	7,500
Life and physical scientists	13,000	13,075	9,500	15,750
Physicians, dentists, and related practitioners	14,000	14,719	15,000	7,900
Health workers, except practitioners	8,000	7,600	9,000	3,250
Social scientists	15,000	14,500	5,000	5,429
Teachers, college and university	10,750	10,597	2,500	6,530
Teachers, elementary and secondary	4,800	7,105	6,500	3,667
Technicians	8,000	7,986	4,000	4,417
Writers, artists, and entertainers	10,000	11,275	4,000	–
Research workers	6,000	6,000	–	5,917
Other professionals	4,777	7,732	5,000	–
Managers and Administrators	8,450	9,901	6,375	7,093
Salaried				
Manufacturing	25,000	23,125	–	–
Trade	7,750	8,913	6,000	6,000
Service industries	11,000	18,900	8,000	7,333
Other	12,000	11,591	8,500	13,667
Self-employed				
Manufacturing	6,000	6,667	–	–
Trade	7,833	9,667	5,750	6,545
Service industries	6,600	8,607	6,000	5,300
Other	5,000	7,417	6,000	6,000
Sales Workers	6,714	8,409	2,533	3,314
Insurance agents and brokers	10,000	10,250	11,000	7,500
Stock and bond salesmen	25,000	22,500	–	–
Sales clerks, retail trade	4,666	4,813	2,363	2,980
Other sales workers	7,250	8,786	3,000	3,313

Clerical and Kindred Workers	5,529	6,084	4,717	4,786
Bank tellers	6,666	8,200	4,200	4,400
Bookkeepers	7,666	7,300	5,416	4,889
File clerks	3,000	3,000	3,400	3,100
Office machine operators	5,000	5,667	5,000	5,111
Secretaries, stenographers, and typists	5,500	5,200	5,333	5,072
Telephone operators	—	—	3,000	3,125
Other clerical workers	4,923	5,978	3,916	4,773
Craftsmen and Kindred Workers	9,937	9,137	3,000	4,583
Mechanics and repairmen, including automobile	9,666	8,981	—	—
Printing trade craftsmen	8,333	9,583	—	—
Construction craftsmen	9,500	9,611		
Tailors	7,000	7,000	2,000	2,000
Other craftsmen	9,363	9,047	5,000	5,875
Operatives, Except Transport	5,562	6,379	3,095	3,438
Food industry	8,250	9,967	4,000	4,000
Apparel industry	2,125	3,767	2,818	3,290
Laundry and dry cleaning operatives	5,600	5,860	3,000	2,750
Other operatives	5,857	6,338	4,000	4,033
Transport Equipment Operatives	8,000	7,533	—	—
Laborers, Except Farm	3,500	4,661	3,000	3,125
Freight, stock, and material handlers	3,500	5,053	2,000	2,833
Other laborers	3,500	3,833	4,000	4,000
Farm Workers and Managers	8,000	9,444	5,000	4,625
Service Workers	4,555	4,886	2,619	3,000
Cleaning	3,666	4,500	3,000	3,333
Food	4,516	4,797	2,333	2,773
Health	7,000	4,250	5,000	5,000
Personal	7,000	4,625	3,000	3,667
Protective	8,000	8,500	—	—
Private Household Workers	5,000	4,625	2,000	2,130

Source: U.S. Department of Commerce, Bureau of the Census, Special Tabulation, Public Use Sample Data (1970).

INCOME BY OCCUPATION

Table 9.7 gives median earnings by selected occupations. Why is it that Chinese physicians' or dentists' earnings average out to between $14,000 and $15,000 annually, considerably below the average doctor's earning capacity? It is conjectured here that many have not fulfilled the licensing or citizenship requirements and are earning a small pittance in a hospital as a resident physician, whereas the established M.D.s may be doing quite well.

SAVINGS AS A SOURCE OF INCOME

In his study of ethnic enterprise, Ivan Light stated that the Oriental communities had decided economic advantages over the black communities in that they had ethnic institutions and, more important, capital.[3] With low-paying occupations, where did the Asians obtain capital? Only from savings and the pooling of resources.

The Chinese are a frugal people. Saving their pennies and nickels and dimes, they invest to earn dividends or interest. In Mountain of Gold, some of the simple methods contrived by the Chinese to save and obtain credit are described.[4] Ivan Light describes others.[5] With resource to capital, the Chinese could undertake ventures that would lift them out of the laboring class into the small entrepreneur class.

The ability of the Chinese to postpone demand and save capital for future utilization gives them building blocks upon which to expand their earning power. Many Chinese buy shares in going enterprises, like restaurants, where they may insure themselves of a job if they are a part-owner and at the same time collect dividends in addition to a wage and salary. When they are part-owner, they are more conscientious and less wasteful, so the benefits accrue all around.

Although the Chinese communities are going through a tremendous transition at this time, accommodating to the huge influx of immigrants, they are taking positive steps to pull themselves up by their own bootstraps. Just as they devised a simple credit system called the hui, literally a club whereby they pooled savings to make available capital, "minorities are banding together and pooling their resources to finance savings and loan associations that service their local communities. Federal and state authorities are approving these new associations in record numbers."[6]

Since January 1972, the Federal Home Loan Bank approved 15 new charters for mutually owned banks in the western region; three of these charters were granted to Chinese-oriented associations. The first to open its doors, in Los Angeles' Chinatown, had over $5 million in deposits by the end of the first year. The second to open, in San Francisco's Chinatown, had on deposit over $2.5 million in 1,250 accounts in just under four months of operation. The third and newest opened in San Francisco's Richmond area, and a fourth application is pending for Oakland's Chinatown. On the East Coast, the Chinese-American Bank in New York's Chinatown has been in existence for over a decade, and it has played an important role in the financial life of the community. In Washington, D.C., CBS television reporter Connie Chung is organizing an Asian-American Bank to serve minority communities.

This accrual of capital is one of the hidden economic strengths of the Chinese people. Along with education, it has been a prime factor in the maintenance of economic life in a hostile environment. Both education and capital resources are stepping stones to upward mobility for the Chinese in the United States.

SUMMARY OF FINDINGS

1. In interpreting the figures on income, one must be aware that the concept of income is not the same in the Chinese mind as it is in the American mind. Chinese employers are responsible for board, if not room, income taxes, Social Security payments, and, oftentimes, health insurance. Eighty dollars a week means $80 in the pay envelope. Net income is what the Chinese employee reports as income.

2. The Chinese-American family income shows wide disparity from state to state. New York is significantly poorer than Hawaii or California.

3. The national median income for Chinese families is slightly higher than for the United States as a whole, but this figure is somewhat deceptive. There are multiearners in the Chinese families who tend to boost the family income. Personal income is a more accurate reflection of what the Chinese make. These figures are comparatively low.

4. Are the Chinese poor? No, if the yardstick is family income upon which the poverty index is based. A more accurate measurement would be income per unit of work.

5. A good proportion of Chinese families have income from such other sources as dividends, interests, and return on investments. Capital accumulation has been one of the major sources of economic strength of the Chinese people.

6. Public assistance to the Chinese has been minimal. The younger generations of Chinese-Americans no longer view government assistance as dole. On the contrary, as taxpayers they are beginning to vie for their fair share of the government's revenues.

RECOMMENDATIONS

Too much credence should not be placed in the exact amount of census income figures. Even the Census Bureau concedes that the range of deviation on the question of income is plus or minus 10 percent. Nevertheless, the income data does reveal some glaring symptoms. Among them: the large number of earners in a family that inflates the family income; the depressed level of income of Chinese females; and the large proportion of teenagers who have no income at all. The latter two syndromes cannot be disputed. Both call for remedies that are beyond the scope of this book. They require attention not only from the ethnic community but from labor, government, and educational institutions as well. These problems are not just peculiar to the Chinese. They are also symptomatic of the employment situation as a whole.

A bright spot in the picture is the thrifty habits of the Chinese and their ability to accumulate capital as a stepping stone to a better life. Some of the credit facilities developed by the Chinese in the past may be fading away, and the more impersonal, complicated setups of the American banking system taking their place. But recent immigrants, who are coming from a rural or less developed economy, are not familiar with the sophisticated procedures of applying for credit from banks. The more personal and simple credit facilities within the ethnic community should be revived for those who feel that they can deal more comfortably with a familiar setup. For example, the Lee Family Association Credit Union is a very successful model to follow. It operates like any other credit union, but its membership is based upon the extended kinship family. The special features of a credit institution like this are the primary relationship of its members, the elimination of the language barrier, and the less stringent procedures governing its operations because the members are known to one another.

NOTES

1. U.S. Department of Commerce, Bureau of the Census, The Methods and Materials of Demography, vol. 1 (1971), p. 365.

2. U.S. Department of Commerce, Bureau of the Census, General Social and Economic Characteristics, U.S. Summary (1970), App. 30.

3. Ivan H. Light, Ethnic Enterprise in America (Los Angeles and Berkeley: University of California Press, 1972), p. 87.

4. Betty Lee Sung, Mountain of Gold (New York: Macmillan Co., 1967), pp. 140-42.

5. Light, op. cit., pp. 23-27.

6. Richard Springer, "Minority-Based Savings and Loans on the Upsurge," East/West, August 21, 1974.

10

UNEMPLOYMENT
AND UNDEREMPLOYMENT

In 1970, a year of relative prosperity, the unemployment rate for white males was 3.6 percent; for black males, 6.3 percent; for the Chinese male, only 3.0 percent. The female unemployment rates ran to 4.7 percent for whites, 7.7 percent for blacks, and 3.7 percent for the Chinese.[1]

In some states, the unemployment rates for the Chinese were even lower. Table 5.2 shows the labor force and employment status of the Chinese for three states and ten SMSAs. For males, the unemployment rate sank to 1.4 percent in Washington, D.C., and in most other eastern states it was but a little higher than 2 percent. The unemployment rate in the western states ran higher, and it was highest in the San Francisco-Oakland area. Nevertheless, when compared city by city with the urban area rate for all persons, the Chinese unemployment rate falls far below that of the general area. More important, the disparity is frequently a large one (see Table 10.1). From these figures, one could simply surmise that, for the Chinese, jobs are easy to come by.

Perhaps. One must admit that the Chinese have benefited tremendously from the assertion of minority groups for their legitimate rights over the past two decades, and they owe a great debt to the civil rights movement, which initiated this drive. But within the Chinese context there are other factors that mask the low rate of unemployment. The reasons are many and varied.

JOBS IN SEARCH OF PEOPLE

There are always jobs in search of people. Many such jobs, however, are the more undesirable ones that are low in status, un-

TABLE 10.1

Unemployment Rate for Males in the Civilian Labor Force
in Ten SMSAs, 1970
(in percent)

SMSAs	All Persons	Chinese
Boston	3.5	2.8
Chicago	3.5	2.5
Honolulu	3.0	2.1
Los Angeles-Long Beach	6.2	3.9
New York	3.8	2.4
Sacramento	7.2	2.1
San Francisco-Oakland	5.8	4.4
San Jose	5.8	3.6
Seattle-Everett	8.2	3.8
Washington, D.C.-Maryland-Virginia	2.7	1.4

Sources: U.S. Department of Commerce, Bureau of the Census, U.S. Summary, PC(1)C1 (1970), Table 184; and Subject Report, PC(2)1G (1970), Table 28.

pleasant in nature, low in pay, and paid by the piece. Other drawbacks are long working hours, poor working conditions, off hours, repetitive and unimaginative work, dead-end jobs, and other unattractive conditions. It traditionally has been the lot of the newest wave of immigrants to assume these positions until they or their children could move up and out. In a highly mobile society like that of the United States, the lower echelon occupations always have a high turnover rate. People who are willing to accept employment in these jobs have no problem finding work, and if an employer can find a steady reliable source of labor for such positions, he is more than elated.

The garment industry is a good example. It is extremely easy to get a job as a seamstress. The usual procedure is for a friend or relative to take the applicant down in person and introduce her to the owner or boss. The boss says, "Try it out." The applicant sits down at a machine and the friend explains to her what is to be done. They work at first with some scraps, and then the applicant is given a garment. She takes her time and may finish it with the help of her friend in three or four hours or as long as is needed. The boss does not care. He pays by the piece. The pay is something like 60 cents a skirt.

Even at 20 cents a piece, the women grasp the job eagerly. It is a job they can handle. They do not have to go far beyond Chinatown; and, once they get the knack of finishing a garment, they can find ready employment in another factory. There are over 230 garment factories in and around New York's Chinatown, and others are being attracted to Chinatown to tap the reservoir of high-quality Chinese female labor at cheap prices.

Kitchen duties are a large area of employment for Chinese males. The hours are long, the temperature in the kitchen is always hot, the duties are not the most pleasant, the status is low. Restaurants always have openings for dishwashers, in spite of the installation of dishwashing machines and other mechanical devices. One of the biggest headaches of a restaurant manager is to find a person to scrape the dishes and put them into the dishwashing machine. Few people want the job. They may take it for three months or half a year, but they do not stay long. A dishwasher's position is very easy to come by.

In cities like New York, San Francisco, Los Angeles, and Boston, many jobs held by the Chinese are ingrown occupations servicing the Chinese community itself. Chinatowns may be the fastest growing sectors in many large cities where urban decline is the general trend. The huge influx of recent immigrants has created a demand for goods and services within the community. Almost any business opening up in New York's Chinatown seems to be making money. The local economy relies not so much on the tourist trade today as on local consumption. The newcomers are buying furniture, clothes, appliances, and food. They need the services of barbers, doctors, dentists, bankers, lawyers, and accountants. Any discrimination resulting from a recession in the larger American economy will be buffered by the fact that the Chinese in Chinatowns are consumers as well as workers, and their demand for goods and services have created many jobs.

BUSINESS BAD—UNEMPLOYMENT DOWN

When business is bad the unemployment rate among the Chinese may decrease rather than increase. In years past, it generally did. The population was fairly homogeneous and oftentimes related. If a person lost his job, a relative would take him into his restaurant or laundry or grocery store until the fellow landed another. Strongly inherent in the Chinese culture is an emphasis on family and social obligations. This is in contrast to the practice in times of adverse business conditions when American business management efficiency calls immediately for a cut in personnel.

American businessmen were surprised to learn of some of these traditional Oriental practices while doing business in Japan. They discovered that once a Japanese worker is hired he considers his employment a lifelong relationship, except under unusual circumstances. When sales fell off for Toyota, the workers in Japan were furloughed at 90 percent pay. At the same time, General Motors in Detroit laid off 12,000 workers, leaving them to unemployment insurance and their own resources until such time as the cost accountants could justify their return to the plant.

Today's circumstances among the Chinese-Americans are somewhat different. There are fewer self-owned and -operated enterprises to permit this method of mutual aid; the population is more diverse and people are more impersonal; family ties are not as strong; there is unemployment insurance. Furthermore, American society and culture tend to deprive the worker of his sense of duty, security, and belonging.

ESCALATOR PROFITS

Along the same lines of reasoning, the Chinese small businessmen can survive and surmount business adversity a little better when he has more flexibility. Take the average Chinese restaurant. It is seldom owned by one man any more. The usual procedure is to pool the capital resources and manpower of a small group that sets up a joint venture, either in a partnership or a corporation. The partners are both employers and employees. Each one insures for himself a job and a salary. When business is good, they give themselves a raise. When business is bad, they look at the receipts and say, "We'll have to take less this month." The employers/employees are not out of work. They try to pull through the bad times together.

These are some of the techniques and responses that the Chinese have developed to live and survive in the United States. The problem is that, as the employment horizons are broadened and the Chinese must compete in the larger society in an alien setting, they are going to encounter situations in which responses have not been tried and developed. Each man or woman is going to be on his own to meet the problems, not as a group, but as an individual. The nature of the transition period is conjectural. No one can predict which way the wind will blow, and the generation of the 1970s will be in the vanguard. Will the Chinese fall back upon the traditional responses? Should they crawl back into their shells and insulate themselves by self-isolation as they did in the past? Or will they devise new ways to deal collectively with the specter of unemployment?

WHO ARE THE UNEMPLOYED?

Recent Immigrants

The unemployed are the recent immigrants. In fact, the statistics covering them may not even be in the 1970 census. Had they been included, the unemployment rates would have been much higher. The reasons are inherent in their migration. They gave up whatever occupation or status or income they had in their homeland to begin life anew in this country. When they got here, they immediately joined the ranks of those looking for jobs. The problem lies in how to help these newcomers smooth over their period of transition.

Approximately two-thirds of the total immigrants coming into this country fall within the 20- to 60-year age bracket. Three out of four able-bodied adult males join the ranks of those looking for employment. About half of the women will join the labor force. The most urgent employment needs of the Chinese lie with the new immigrants. Their greatest obstacle is unfamiliarity with the English language and American customs. They do not know how or where to turn for help except to their immediate relatives or friends, whose own knowledge of the employment field may be equally limited.

Refugees in Limbo

The unemployed are the refugees. Generally, employers shy away from hiring anyone who does not have a green card testifying to the fact that he or she is lawfully admitted as a permanent resident and is permitted to seek employment in this country. Nonimmigrants, such as visitors, students, businessmen, and tourists, are not allowed to work. Refugees are a special case. They are permitted to work, but they are not issued a green card until they have a record of two years of good conduct in this country. Most employers do not know of this technicality, however, and will only accept the green card as proof of eligibility. Furthermore, a great deal of publicity has been given to a bill sponsored by Congressman Peter W. Rodino that would severely penalize the employer of an alien who is not entitled to work here, thereby creating more uncertainty and fear.

Not Female Operatives

The unemployed are not the women in operative jobs. For example, in New York, San Francisco, Chicago, and Boston, where the garment industry is strong, the unemployment rate is very low. In New York City, the proportion of the total Chinese female labor force in operative jobs is 43.7 percent and the unemployment rate for Chinese females is 2.8 percent (see Tables 5.2 and 5.4). In Sacramento, 43.6 percent are in the clerical field and the unemployment rate is 11.1 percent. These unemployment figures reinforce this author's contention that some jobs are easy to come by when no one else wants them. The figures also support the argument that as the Chinese leave their community and reach out into the larger society, they will become highly vulnerable to the ups and downs of the larger economy.

Young or Old

There is no distinct pattern to unemployment by age group. Table 10.2 shows a comparison of the Chinese in the labor force with those unemployed by age group, for the United States and five states. For females, the proportions are almost identical: they are found in the labor force more or less proportionate to their rate of unemployment. But the percentages for the males present some disturbing dislocations.

In the national figures, the rate of unemployment for young men from 16 to 24 years is double that of their proportion in the labor force. In the state of Hawaii, the rate is triple or higher. In other words, Chinese males in the 20- to 24-year age bracket are 11 percent of the labor force, yet they make up 31 percent of the unemployed. This may explain why Hawaii's young men are leaving the islands.

In New York, the dislocation is at the other end of the age spectrum. Chinese males are 35 percent of the labor force in the 45- to 64-year age bracket, but they constitute 44 percent of the unemployed.

The problem is worse in Massachusetts. The greatest proportion of unemployed is found in the 25- to 34-year age bracket. These age brackets are generally the ones in which the full potential of the male workers is achieved. They have finished their education; they are most likely married and have families to support; and they have had time to gain some experience and an opportunity to establish themselves. If they are unemployed at this stage in their lives, the problem is doubly acute.

TEENAGE AND YOUTH UNEMPLOYMENT

According to Table 10.3, teenage and youth unemployment is not much of a problem, except in New York City and, to a lesser degree, San Francisco. This table gives the number of Chinese males who are

TABLE 10.2

Comparison of Employment Status with Labor Force of the Chinese in the United States, by Age Group and Sex, for Total United States and Five Selected States, 1970

(in percent)

Age Group and Sex	U.S. Total		California		New York		Hawaii		Illinois		Massachusetts	
	Labor Force	Unemployed	Labor Force	Unemployed	Labor Force	Unemployed	Labor Force	Unemployed	Labor Force	Unemployed	Labor Force	Unemployed
Male 16 years and over	100	100	100	100	100	100	100	100	100	100	100	100
16–19 years	6	12	7	12	4	8	6	30	5	7	6	4
20–24 years	11	22	12	22	9	14	11	31	11	23	12	20
25–34 years	24	16	22	12	23	13	19	6	31	23	28	43
35–44 years	25	14	26	15	26	13	24	10	24	11	22	13
45–64 years	31	30	31	34	35	44	37	22	25	23	28	21
65 years and over	3	5	3	5	3	7	4	2	3	12	3	—
Female 16 years and over	100	100	100	100	100	100	100	100	100	100	100	100
16–19 years	8	12	9	11	7	11	7	22	9	9	12	12
20–24 years	18	20	18	20	17	17	14	22	20	20	19	19
25–34 years	23	22	21	16	22	30	19	26	26	25	24	24
35–44 years	23	20	24	20	25	19	23	16	23	23	19	19
45–64 years	26	23	25	30	28	18	35	15	20	20	25	24
65 years and over	2	4	2	8	2	5	1	—	2	2	3	3

Source: U.S. Department of Commerce, Bureau of the Census, Subject Report, PC(2)1G (1970), Table 21.

157

TABLE 10.3

Education and Employment Status of Chinese Males 16 to 21 Years Old, for Ten SMSAs, 1970

Male 16–21 Years Old	Total Number (100 percent)	Not Enrolled in School		Not High School Graduate		Unemployed or Not in Labor Force	
		Number	Percent	Number	Percent	Number	Percent
U.S. total	31,297	5,347	17	1,584	5	784	3
Boston	1,082	259	24	68	6	34	3
Chicago	797	102	13	42	5	21	3
Honolulu	2,728	725	26	154	6	110	4
Los Angeles–Long Beach	2,901	379	13	41	1	17	1
New York City	5,217	1,099	21	491	9	245	5
Sacramento	908	116	13	33	4	6	1
San Francisco–Oakland	6,532	960	15	259	4	157	2
San Jose	650	57	8	8	1	8	1
Seattle	606	109	18	34	6	10	2
Washington, D.C.–Maryland–Virginia	385	46	12	14	4	—	0
Total ten SMSAs	21,806	3,852	18	1,144	5	608	3

Source: U.S. Department of Commerce, Bureau of the Census, Subject Report, PC(2)1G (1970), Tables 19, 28.

16 to 21 years of age for ten SMSAs in the United States with sizable
Chinese populations. The columns show the number of youths in each
SMSA and the percentages who are not enrolled in school, who are
not high school graduates, and who are unemployed. Of the 608 who
fit all these labels, 245 are found in New York City and 157 are in
the San Francisco area. Again, New York seems to be the problem
area. Perhaps these idle youths are the cause of the recent waves of
crime plaguing New York's Chinatown.

UNDEREMPLOYMENT

The problem of underemployment is greater than that of unemployment for the Chinese. There are always some jobs available to
serve immediate needs if one is willing to do the work. When it comes
to dire necessity, one accepts such work, even though the position
may be far beneath the worker's qualifications.

Contributing to the underemployment syndrome is the U.S. government immigration policy of giving preference to persons with good
skills and education. When highly educated and skilled persons are
admitted to this country but are hampered at every turn to practice
their trade or profession, underemployment inevitably results. The
former Shanghai plastics manufacturer is working as a waiter. The
former accountant from Hong Kong is the salad-and-dessert man in
a kitchen. The former principal of a normal school sells groceries
in a Chinese food store. Instances like these are all too common.
To get a general idea of how pervasive underemployment is, the first
20 names were taken off the roster of trainees who had completed
their 12-week course at the Chinatown Manpower Project in Chinatown
and were listed by education, former positions in Hong Kong or Taiwan, and present positions (see Table 10.4).

Some people will say, "So what? It happens to all immigrant
groups who first come here. The setback is an inevitable part of
the transitional process. Given time, they will catch up." Some do,
but the majority will not. This is evident from the information given
in Tables 10.5 and 10.6). The Chinese simply do not readily move
from one line of work to another. If they accept employment at a
lower level, the tendency is that they will stay there for some time,
unless helped to move out of the rut or given a strong impetus to do
so on their own.

Stuck at Entry Level

Underemployment is also prevalent among the U.S.-born Chinese-
American who does not face the same problem of transition as his

TABLE 10.4

Underemployment of the Chinese as Reflected in Chinatown Manpower Roster, 1972

Case Number	Education	Past Experience	Present Position
1	College student	Teacher in Hong Kong	Embroidery work
2	High school graduate	Nurse	Maintenance work
3	Normal school graduate	Teacher	Cashier
4	High School graduate	Self-employed business	Manager—small business
5	College graduate (economics)	Teacher in Hong Kong	Assembler, office supplies
6	College graduate (economics)	Teacher in Hong Kong	Cashier
7	College graduate (business)	Teacher in Hong Kong	Clerk, service agency
8	College graduate (education)	Teacher in Hong Kong	Secretary—Chinese agency
9	College graduate	Government service, Taiwan	Assistant manager—restaurant
10	Nursing school graduate	Nurse, Taiwan	Nurse's aide, nursing home
11	College graduate	Herb doctor	Nurse's trainee
12	College graduate	Nurse	Nurse's aide, hospital
13	College graduate	Medical doctor	Teacher, advanced ESL class
14	College graduate	Minister, Hong Kong	Examiner in bank
15	College graduate (law)	Teacher in Taiwan	Bank clerk
16	Nursing school graduate	Registered nurse in Hong Kong	Preparing for nurse's license
17	College graduate	High school teacher in Hong Kong	Restaurant manager
18	High school graduate	Manager, rubber factory	Student, advanced ESL class
19	High school graduate	Teacher in Hong Kong	Restaurant cashier
20	College graduate (law)	Lawyer in Taiwan	Bank, examining clerk

ESL: English as a second language
<u>Source</u>: Chinatown Manpower Project (1972).

160

TABLE 10.5

Current Occupation and Occupation Five Years Ago of the Chinese 16 Years and over, 1970
(in hundreds)

Current Occupation	Total	Occupation Five Years Ago									
		Professional, Technical	Managers, Administrators	Sale Workers	Cleri-cal	Crafts-men	Oper-atives	Labor-ers	Farm-ers	Service Workers	Private Household
Male 16 years and over	1,125	230	104	26	48	65	83	20	2	164	2
Professional, technical	359	212	5	1	5	3	2	2	0	1	0
Managers, administrators	120	6	79	3	2	0	8	3	0	7	0
Sales workers	47	1	4	16	0	1	0	2	0	3	0
Clerical	94	5	2	3	35	0	0	4	0	5	0
Craftsmen	98	2	3	0	0	55	6	1	0	3	0
Operatives	113	2	6	0	1	2	58	1	0	4	0
Laborers	31	0	0	0	0	1	1	6	0	1	0
Farmers	2	0	0	0	0	0	0	0	2	0	0
Service workers	257	2	5	3	5	3	8	1	0	140	0
Private household	4	0	0	0	0	0	0	0	0	0	2
Female 16 years and over	732	79	20	15	100	5	91	4	0	51	3
Professional, technical	155	67	2	0	7	0	1	0	0	1	0
Managers, administrators	27	1	12	1	1	0	0	0	0	0	0
Sales workers	39	2	1	12	0	1	0	0	0	0	0
Clerical workers	220	6	2	2	87	4	2	0	0	4	0
Craftsmen	14	0	0	0	1	0	1	0	0	0	0
Operatives	151	2	2	0	2	0	91	0	0	0	0
Laborers	7	0	0	0	0	0	0	4	0	0	0
Farmers	2	0	0	0	0	0	0	0	0	0	0
Service workers	105	0	1	0	2	0	2	0	0	46	0
Private household	12	0	0	0	0	0	0	0	0	0	3

Note: Based on a 5 percent sampling.

Source: U.S. Department of Commerce, Bureau of the Census, Special Tabulation, Public Use Sample Data (1970).

TABLE 10.6

Current Industry and Industry Five Years Ago of the Chinese 16 Years and over, 1970
(in hundreds)

Current Industry*	1970 Total	Industry Five Years Ago										
		Manu-facturing	Trans-portation	Com-muni-cations	Trade: Gro-cery Stores	Trade: Eat, Drink Places	Finance, Insurance, Real Estate	Business and Repair Service	Per-sonal Ser-vice	Entertain-ment and Recreational Service	Profes-sional Ser-vice	Public Admin-istra-tion
Male 16 years and over	1,125	103	29	14	51	168	17	22	58	5	116	7
Manufacturing	142	81	0	1	0	4	0	0	0	0	4	1
Transportation	28	0	21	0	0	2	0	0	0	0	2	1
Communications	22	1	1	9	0	0	1	1	0	0	0	0
Trade												
Grocery stores	53	1	0	0	36	3	0	0	0	0	0	0
Eat, drink places	241	6	2	2	5	147	0	4	6	0	2	2
Finance, insurance, real estate	39	3	0	0	2	2	15	1	0	0	1	0
Business and repair service	41	1	1	1	0	1	0	15	2	0	4	0
Personal services	70	0	0	0	2	1	0	0	48	0	3	0
Entertainment, recreational service	12	1	0	0	0	2	0	0	0	4	0	0
Professional service	213	4	0	0	1	1	1	0	0	1	95	4
Public administration	96	0	4	0	1	1	1	0	1	0	2	59
Female 16 years and over	732	89	4	4	15	43	23	4	25	3	89	30
Manufacturing	161	81	1	1	0	0	1	0	1	0	4	1
Transportation	8	0	2	0	0	0	1	0	0	1	0	0
Communications	9	0	0	3	0	0	0	0	0	0	0	0
Trade												
Grocery stores	18	0	0	0	12	0	0	0	0	0	0	0
Eat, drink places	70	2	0	0	0	35	0	0	1	0	0	0
Finance, insurance, real estate	54	1	1	0	0	0	18	0	0	0	5	0
Business and repair service	10	0	0	0	0	0	0	1	2	0	2	0
Personal services	50	0	0	0	1	0	0	2	22	0	1	0
Entertainment, recreational service	5	0	0	0	0	0	0	0	0	2	0	0
Professional service	200	4	0	0	0	5	2	0	0	0	74	3
Public administration	45	1	0	0	0	2	1	0	1	0	0	23

*Omitted because numbers were insignificant: agriculture, construction, mining, utilities, and sanitation services.

Note: Based on a 5 percent sampling.

Source: U.S. Department of Commerce, Bureau of the Census, Special Tabulation, Public Use Sample Data (1970).

foreign-born counterpart. Since he has little problem with the English language and the likelihood is that he is highly educated, he will encounter little difficulty finding employment at the entry level of professional careers. He usually performs competently and logs considerable years of experience, but fellow workers who came in at the same time he did will have gone on to bigger and better positions while he still plugs away in the same position year after year.

These Chinese are the engineers who draft the plans, the architects who do the renderings, the teachers who have the same grades every year, the lab technicians who do the tests, the librarians who catalog the books, and so on. They are the unsung workers who do their daily chores quietly and efficiently, and then are overlooked at promotion time. They have professional positions, but they are drones.

Because the drones are the workers, there is a tendency on the part of employers to retain such people in their positions as long as possible. All too often, the Chinese-American never voices dissatisfaction with his position. He is quiet, reliable, docile; in effect, he is penalized for his performance, rather than rewarded. Tragically few people are aware of the extent to which many Chinese-Americans are underemployed because they remain so quiet.

Worse yet is when deliberate attempts are made to keep highly qualified personnel from moving ahead for indefensible motives. At the Civil Rights Commission Hearings on Equal Opportunity for Asian-Americans in the New York area in 1974, Dr. John S. Hong revealed some of the tactics employed to keep Asian doctors, educated and trained abroad, from advancing in their professions.

> From the economic point of view, the new wave of Asian immigrants represents some form of net gain to the U.S. They are some of the best minds in Asia. They are highly skilled and established professionals in their countries.
>
> In 1972, a very conservative estimate of $50,000 is the face value of the foreign medical graduate at the time he enters the country. . . .
>
> Foreign medical graduates have contributed very much to the health care of this country, yet among those I interviewed, there was a mixed feeling of gratitude and dissatisfaction. . . . The competence of a foreign medical graduate is disregarded simply because he does not have the Standard Certificate issued by the ECFMG [Educational Council for Foreign Medical Graduates]. Instances were cited wherein some residents were nominated for senior

or chief positions but were turned down for the same
reason.

There seems to be an intentional scoring to see
to it that there are not enough passing prospective
interns to fill up completely all internship positions
available. A shortage of interns produces a shortage
of physicians. The lesser the supply, the greater
the demand, the higher the medical costs.

Dr. Hong said that doctors often are given visas because they
have an M.D. after their names, "but once they enter the country,
without the ECFMG they will never have an opportunity to be employees or intern residents in the so-called approved training hospitals.
. . . Often they are used as technicians or nurse's aides or in almost
any capacity."[2]

The implication here was that these doctors are paid less than
a doctor but are used to do medical work. In fact, such foreign medical graduates can be hired cheaper than the going rate for a nurse.

Dr. Chungik Rhee also testified before the same commission
hearings and his reference pertained to nurses, nutritionists, pharmacists, and X-ray and lab technicians. It was again pointed out that
such professionals are granted visas from Asian countries simply
because they are skilled technicians and professionals, but once they
come to this country they cannot find a job because of the constraints
of professional associations, which take the position that unless you
go through the same kind of internship and the same kind of licensing,
a permit cannot be issued.

Rhee gave an example of how Asian pharmacists are being exploited, and Albert J. Sica, executive secretary of the State Board of
Pharmacy in New York, confirmed it. Their testimonies brought out
the fact that pharmacists are given preference in applying for an immigrant visa, but 48 states and the District of Columbia bar graduates
of foreign pharmacy schools from applying for licenses to practice.

In New York and Illinois, applications are accepted, but the
foreign pharmacists must serve a period of internship before they
can take the regular licensing examination. Since there are only two
states in the country that will accept pharmacists educated and/or
trained abroad, prospective interns gravitate to these two states, and
the supply exceeds the demand to such a degree that pharmacists in
these states must offer their services free for a one- or two-year period in order to have the opportunity to work as an intern to qualify
for the licensing examination. If one refuses to work without pay
(the euphemism is "volunteer their services"), someone else will.
The economic hardships borne by the families of these men or women
are devastating during the time that these pharmacists are serving

out their internships. At the same time, one might say these people are not just underemployed or underpaid, they are undergoing compulsory servitude.[3]

Female Underemployment

The most flagrantly underemployed are the Chinese females. Their plight already has been touched upon in many instances in this study, and Chapter 6 is devoted exclusively to Chinese female employment. In spite of the high educational attainment (approximately one out of three has some college education or is a college graduate), the positions they occupy are lowly and the income they receive is deplorable (see also Chapters 4 and 9). At the risk of being repetitive, the grossly inequitable situation of the Chinese female cannot be overemphasized.

SUMMARY OF FINDINGS

1. In 1970 the unemployment rate for the Chinese in the United States was noticeably lower than that for whites or blacks.

2. The low unemployment rate may be attributed to the following:

   a. Because of the compelling urgency to earn a livelihood and because there is little choice, the Chinese are willing to take certain jobs that no one else wants. Such jobs are easy to come by.
   b. Many jobs held by the Chinese are generated by the community and are community-related.
   c. Employment is oftentimes artificially shored up when times are bad. The unemployed are squeezed into going concerns until better times.
   d. In Chinese enterprises, the partners are generally both employers and employees. In bad times, the partners tighten their belts, and in good times, they work a little harder.

3. The recent immigrants pose the most urgent unemployment problems. Their need for jobs is immediate. They have no Social Security or unemployment compensation cushion to fall back on. They have problems of language and adjustment. The recent immigrants are the priority group for employment attention.

4. Political refugees are suspended in a peculiar limbo because employers think they do not have the right to seek employment in this country.

5. Women operatives have little difficulty finding employment.

6. In Hawaii, the young from age 16 to 24 are the most likely candidates for the ranks of the unemployed. In New York, the age range is 45 to 64. In Massachusetts, it shifts to 25 to 34—the worst possible age range for being unemployed.

7. In absolute numbers, New York City has the largest number of idle youth not enrolled in school, not high school graduates, and not employed. The number is 245 out of a national total of 608.

8. For the Chinese, the underemployment problem is greater than that of unemployment.

9. Under the Immigration Act of 1965 immigrants are granted preferential visas if they are highly educated or possess skills in short supply in this country, but doe to the recentness of their arrival and their language difficulties they invariably take low-paying and low-status jobs to meet their immediate economic needs.

10. The census shows that, once in a job, few Chinese move out of their occupations.

11. The U.S.-born Chinese-American encounters different problems of underemployment. He is generally stuck at the entry level of professional positions.

12. Sometimes deliberate attempts are made to keep highly qualified personnel from attaining professional status in order to obtain their services cheaply or without pay.

13. Attention is again called to the gross underemployment of Chinese females whose educational attainment is fairly high, but whose occupational status and income are very low.

RECOMMENDATIONS

Judging from the unemployment rates for the Chinese according to the 1970 census, the Chinese situation in comparison to other minority groups or to the national average looks impressive—on the surface. Most economists or manpower administrators would conclude that the Chinese are a model minority, a hard-working people, a group that takes care of its own, and, hence, no further attention need be directed toward them.

This viewpoint is fairly prevalent throughout American officialdom, and it explains why so few programs with such meager funding have been set up for the Chinese. In fact, most of the uplift projects initiated under the "Great Society" and "War on Poverty" programs are based on the prevalence of pathological conditions in the commu-

nities involved. If a group can show that it has three times the national unemployment rate, five times the crime rate, two times the
broken family rate, one and a half times the school dropout rate, ad
nauseam, the chances for obtaining governmental funding are excellent. And the opposite holds true. If a people try to be self-sustaining,
self-reliant, industrious—even to the extent of lowering their sights
considerably and accepting work far beneath their qualifications so
that they need not be unemployed or apply for welfare—they are by-
passed.

From rather cursory deduction of the overall census figures
and from superficial studies of social scientists who are not familiar
with the customs, the ways, the thinking, and the history of the Chinese in the United States, it seems that another statistical study of
the census would only reinforce the belief that the Chinese have no
problems.

A New Policy

The first recommendation, therefore, is to look beyond the unemployment figures and interpret them in conjunction with the cultural
background and special characteristics of the group involved. If the
criteria for government funding, revenue sharing, or awarding of
grants continue to be based exclusively upon pathology, then the
desperate may feel that they have to adopt the tactics of the pathological in order to be heard. If the payoff comes from demonstrations,
protests, rioting, violence, and such, the new breed of Chinese-
Americans, who are imbued with the American outlook in many respects, may feel that this is the only way to attract attention and to
get anything done. The fact that the government came running with
fistfuls of money into Watts and Detroit and Bedford-Stuyvesant in the
late 1960s has not been lost upon the youth of Chinatowns. Such tactics have been increasingly employed or advocated to bring about some
amelioration of the intolerable conditions in the Chinatowns of San
Francisco and New York. At the same time, it does seem ironic
that present-day government policy for service to its people operates
on the basis of a reverse reward system.

Job Referrals

The second recommendation would be to provide more and better job referral services to the Chinese community. Specifically, in
the larger Chinatowns, a branch of the federal or state Employment
Service should be set up with bilingual personnel who are fully cogni-

zant of the language problems and special circumstances of the Chinese. These career counselors should make every effort to help the Chinese diversify into as many areas of employment as possible.

A good model for this type of branch office is the State Employment Service in San Francisco's Chinatown, under the directorship of Steve Lee, who has a staff of approximately 25 employment interviewers. Each month he receives an average of about 500 applications for jobs and manages to fill about 150 of these. Lee feels that job placement of the recent immigrants is especially difficult for several reasons. One is that the Chinese applicants need a great deal of hand-holding. They are timid, fearful, and wary of going beyond the borders of Chinatown. A second reason is, of course, the language, and a third reason is the nontransferability of former skills. For example, a skilled midwife has no market for her services in the United States. A subsistence rice farmer from southern China would be totally lost on a mechanized farm where rice planting is done by airplanes.

Lee also operates a chef training program under a government Economics Development Administration (EDA) grant, at which each trainee is charged $50 to attend school for a five and a half month period. These chefs are not trained to make chop suey and chow mein; rather, they are taught the continental cuisine. After graduation, they are placed in hotels and name restaurants. "Good chefs can earn up to $20,000 per year," said Lee, "and our trainees are accepted into the unions readily." Lee feels that his training program has been highly successful.

In New York, where the number of immigrants coming into that city exceeds that of San Francisco by more than three times, there is no similar employment service branch in Chinatown. Outside of a few private employment agencies that handle restaurant personnel only, there are two agencies partially funded by the government. These are the Chinatown Planning Council, which is a multiservice agency that deals only peripherally with job referral, and the Chinatown Manpower Project, which is geared more to job training than to job referral.

Both agencies are funded by private sources, contributions, and the government on a year-to-year basis. Some of the personnel are volunteers. Those who are salaried cannot commit themselves to any kind of continuity or look upon their service as a career. There is no question that service and morale could be greatly improved if the personnel could look upon their jobs as something more than a transient position, dependent upon the yearly renewal of the grant or the operating funds. That is why such an important service as job referrals for the Chinese should have some permanence and continuity. Incorporating it into the state or federal Employment Service and extending it to a group sorely in need of its services would have that effect. After all, that is the raison d'etre of the employment services in the first place.

Job applicants at the Chinatown Manpower Project in New York run to about 125 per week, but placements average only about 15. The personnel in that office number one full-time and one part-time placement counselor, one job developer, and one full-time and one part-time vocational counselor. "The problem," says the director, "is that four people can only accomplish so much within a certain period of time." Certainly, more attention should be devoted to job referrals.

The Chinatown Manpower Project in New York offers clerical training classes. It is only two years old, but it already has graduated about ten classes. Under the stipulations of government funding, the project must place 50 percent (the requirement now is 75 percent) of its trainees in jobs. This project has the proud record of 95 percent placement in such nontraditional Chinese institutions as banks, insurance companies, the telephone company, computer centers, and the like. These graduates no longer need to compete for the limited job opportunities within the Chinatown community.

For this quality manpower training center, the project received from government sources a mere $133,440 for the fiscal year 1973. Of course, the Chinese community is grateful that it has the center, and it can be proud of the fact that it has successfully solicited private sources of funding, but government funding has been token at best.

Therefore, the third recommendation is addressed to the Department of Labor. It should underwrite broader-based training programs for the Chinese on a performance basis. If the community or director can come up with support from private sources, the government should reward such effort by coupling it to effort expended and results obtained. The worst possible policy would be to say, "The Chinese are doing a good job by themselves. We need not bother with them. Yes, they have an enormous problem of adjustment and transition, but they'll take care of their own." This attitude can only invite the type of protest and resentment that will manifest itself in undesirable ways.

A fourth suggestion would be to rectify the glaring omission of training programs geared more for the Chinese male. The subjects currently taught in the Chinatown Manpower Training Program are entirely in the clerical field. They should be expanded to include training in the trades or crafts.

Remediation of Underemployment

To repeat: For the Chinese underemployment is a greater problem than unemployment. For example, political refugees are invariably persons with impressive backgrounds. The American people should try to utilize the services of these people to the fullest extent. Take the example of the foreign-trained pharmacists. New York and Illinois are the only two states where their credentials are accepted for internship. Can the other 48 states justify their refusal to accept these skilled professionals trained abroad?

A talent bank or directory of qualified Chinese-Americans, set up according to their specialty or experience, should be compiled, so that employers may be made aware of their caliber and availability.

The underemployment of the U.S.-born Chinese-American or those who have penetrated the higher occupational groups, but are stuck at the entry level, poses a different set of problems altogether. Theirs is a matter of more aggressive effort to push ahead, to throw off the burden of past discrimination and stereotypes. Both these topics will be dealt with in greater length in Chapter 14.

NOTES

1. Figures for blacks and whites: U.S. Department of Commerce, Bureau of the Census, Subject Report, PC(1)C1 (1970); for Chinese: U.S. Department of Commerce, Bureau of the Census, Subject Report, PC(2)1G (1970).

2. Testimony given before U.S. Civil Rights Commission, Hearings on Equal Opportunity for Asian-Americans, New York, July 12, 1974, II, pp. 203-04.

3. Ibid., pp. 200 ff.

CHAPTER

11

THE CHINESE
WORK ETHIC

LONG HOURS

The kind of work that the Chinese do predisposes them to long, hard hours. An overwhelming proportion work 40 hours a week or more, and a considerable proportion of both males and females work 60 or more hours a week (see Table 11.1). Those who put in the longest hours are the self-employed managers and laundry operatives. The proportion of males who work less than 35 hours per week is less than one in six; for females, about one in four. Obviously, not too many are part-time workers. Nor does it look as if the women work much fewer hours at their jobs than do the men. About two out of five males who are self-employed put in more than 60 hours per week. The fact that up to one-half of the laundrymen still work over 60 hours testifies to their lives as continuous toil.

Ten thousand female operatives work for the garment industry. One would suspect that these women work to supplement their family incomes and that they would put in less hours than the usual 40. However, 67 percent stated that they work the full work week or more. Restaurants try to abide by the eight-hour regulations, but most employees in this line of work must put in six days a week with one day off taken during the week. That already makes the restaurant worker's week a 48-hour one, but, unless the business attracts a continuous clientele, it cannot afford two shifts of workers to cover luncheon and dinner. As a result, restaurant workers get what is known in the trade as a short-off—the worker's day is cut into two segments. He goes to work from eleven to two o'clock, takes off for three hours, and resumes work at five in the afternoon to cover the dinner hours. This makes the restaurant worker's day a very long one.

In view of the long hours, the personal and family income of the Chinese must be reconsidered. If the totals seem higher than the

TABLE 11.1

Employed Chinese Who Worked 40 or More Hours per Week in 1969, by Sex
(in percent)

	Male		Female	
	40 Hours or More	60 Hours or More*	40 Hours or More	60 Hours or More*
Employed Persons 16 Years and over	80	12	62	6
Professional and technical	73	5	57	1
Managers and administrators	93	2	82	25
Salaried	91	7	70	0
Self-employed	94	40	88	35
Sales workers	78	11	52	10
Clerical workers	71	4	57	3
Craftsmen	88	6	71	0
Operatives	85	17	72	8
Food industry	87	28	67	0
Apparel industry	82	13	67	3
Laundry and dry cleaning	92	42	91	50
Laborers	60	4	60	0
Service workers	81	17	62	13
Food service	82	19	60	16
Private household	85	0	58	4

*Subdivision of the 40-hours-or-more category.

Note: Based on a 1 percent sampling.

Source: U.S. Department of Commerce, Bureau of the Census, Special Tabulation, Public Use Sample Data (1970).

national averages, one must keep in mind that they are attained by a
longer work week.

WEEKS WORKED PER YEAR

In 1969, 61 percent of the Chinese males worked the full 52-
week year. This percentage is much lower than the 68 percent for
white males and 71 percent for Japanese males (see Table 11.2) and
appears somewhat out of character. Since the number of weeks worked
includes paid vacations, we can interpret these figures to mean that
the Chinese are not fully employed throughout the year. If this conclusion is not ruled out, we see here a symptom of employment malaise.

Occupation and Weeks Worked

Is full-year employment more common with certain occupations?
We know that laborers, salespersons, operatives, clerical workers,
and service workers are more likely to have a shorter work year.
Positions in these job categories traditionally have been more unsta-
ble with a higher rate of part-time work and turnover.

A pattern appears when we scrutinize the weeks worked for
selected cities of Chinese concentration. The SMSAs with the larger
proportion of recent Chinese immigrants, such as Boston and New
York City, find that their employed labor force works a shorter work
year than more established communities like Honolulu and Washington,
D.C. (see Table 11.3).

How do we reconcile the long work week and the short work year
for the Chinese? Reviewing the situation in light of the general economic conditions for 1969, we must take into account that the year
preceding the 1970 census was a recession year. However, if employees are eager to work long hard hours when they are holding a job
but are not sure of having year-round employment, then we have uncovered another symptom of employment ills.

ATTITUDE OF CHINESE TOWARD WORK

The stereotype of the Chinese is that he is a hard worker; he
is a reliable worker; and he works long hours without letup or com-
plaint. Our census data tend to bear this out. For this group, the
conditioning from the old country still prevails. For most, economic
survival or security is their uppermost concern. They have little
choice. They must compensate for their disadvantaged position by

TABLE 11.2

Comparison of Weeks Worked in 1969 by Ethnic Group and Sex

	Chinese	Japanese	White	Black	Spanish Surname
Males 16 years and over					
50–52 weeks	61	71	68	58	62
27–49 weeks	22	16	19	27	24
26 weeks or less	17	13	13	15	14
Females 16 years and over					
50–52 weeks	42	52	44	43	39
27–49 weeks	30	25	27	32	29
26 weeks or less	28	22	29	26	32

Source: U.S. Department of Commerce, Bureau of the Census, U.S. Summary, PC(1)C1, Table 93; and Subject Report, PC(2)1G.

having more people in the family work, by working longer hours, and by working at more than one job.

Industry is a commendable trait, and it is fast becoming a scarce one. But even good things can be overdone, and the Chinese tend to overdo. In a visit to a Chinatown garment factory, this author saw the women sitting on the edge of their seats, waiting to get back to their sewing machines, although they were still on their lunch hour. Union regulations decree that no one may work during the lunch period and all machines must be closed. But instead of utilizing the lunch hour to get away from their work, to eat a leisurely meal, or to relax a bit, a number of women used this time to ready their garments in preparation for the clock to strike one, when they could open their machines again. They were paid by the piece and they were racing against themselves like horses straining at the starting gate.

A Chinese neighbor used to be a designer for one of the largest department stores in the country. By profession, he is also an architect. During the weekdays, he works full time as a designer. At night, he works on commissions as an architect. In payment for redecorating it, he acquired shares in a restaurant at which he works as a maitre d' on weekends. Actually, one income would have sufficed for this gentleman's family expenses, but he chose to have his time totally taken up by work, leaving very little time for him to spend with his wife and children.

TABLE 11.3

Weeks Worked in 1969 by the Chinese in the United States for Selected SMSAs, by Sex

SMSA	Total 16 and over	50-52 Weeks		27-49 Weeks		26 Weeks or Less	
		Number	Percent	Number	Percent	Number	Percent
Male 16 years and over							
Boston	3,929	2,014	51.3	988	25.1	927	23.6
Chicago	3,828	2,396	62.6	863	22.5	569	14.9
Honolulu	14,065	10,726	76.3	1,606	11.4	1,733	12.3
Los Angeles-Long Beach	12,759	7,954	62.3	2,777	21.8	2,028	15.9
New York City	23,405	13,181	56.3	6,602	28.2	3,622	15.5
Sacramento	2,948	1,955	66.3	488	16.6	505	17.1
San Francisco-Oakland	25,891	15,698	60.6	5,859	22.6	4,334	16.7
San Jose	2,704	1,741	64.4	495	18.3	468	17.3
Seattle-Everett	2,327	1,379	59.3	601	25.8	347	14.9
Washington, D.C.-Maryland-Virginia	2,387	1,717	71.9	352	14.7	318	13.3
Female 16 years and over							
Boston	2,510	836	33.3	922	36.7	752	30.0
Chicago	2,284	883	38.7	828	36.3	573	25.1
Honolulu	10,399	6,163	59.3	1,941	18.7	2,295	22.1
Los Angeles-Long Beach	8,305	3,284	39.5	2,731	32.9	2,290	27.6
New York City	14,096	5,675	40.3	5,256	37.3	3,165	22.5
Sacramento	2,118	721	34.0	449	21.2	948	44.8
San Francisco-Oakland	19,213	8,018	41.7	6,296	32.8	4,899	25.5
San Jose	1,480	548	37.0	415	28.0	517	34.9
Seattle-Everett	1,449	568	39.2	493	34.0	388	26.8
Washington, D.C.-Maryland-Virginia	1,642	722	44.0	425	25.9	495	30.1

Note: Based on a 20 percent sampling.

Source: U.S. Department of Commerce, Bureau of the Census, Subject Report, PC(2)1G (1970).

It is not just that the Chinese equate industry and hard work with saintliness, it is also that they cannot afford to be mediocre or to let their guard down. They must uphold the good image of family and national group, for one bad egg spoils the broth for all Chinese. Combined, these psychological burdens constitute a heavy yoke to bear.

Insecurity

The Chinese also are driven by fear of losing their jobs. When they work, they work long, hard hours. But for one-sixth of the Chinese males who work 26 weeks or less per year, it may be a feast-or-famine situation. The census data are not detailed enough to support this conclusion, but this clue may be symptomatic. It is recommended that further inquiry or a closer look be taken at the extent of and reason for the part-time employment of the Chinese.

THE PAST IS PAST

Formerly, the Chinese in the United States was a sojourner. He planned for his eventual return to a land where his status was more assured. Today's Chinese are transplants. They have cast their future in the United States, where the rewards are more uncertain; the prospects more illusory.

Our Chinese forebears were haunted by the specter of economic insecurity and bound by the strong sense of duty. The upcoming generations of Chinese-Americans are being brought up in a climate that takes affluence for granted. Even some of the young Chinese immigrants whose fathers came to this country ahead of their families feel this way. The children did not see their fathers toil and sweat at their labors. They simply cashed the remittance checks sent back to Hong Kong, which with a favorable rate of exchange afforded the overseas Chinese families a relative degree of affluence.

The difference between the old work ethic and the new stems from the change in our economic circumstances and our outlook on life. In former days, work was looked upon as an end in itself. Today, work is the means to an end and is not the sole pursuit in life. This is a societal change that the younger generations are grappling with and trying to bring about.

Can the Chinese youth help but be affected by the social milieu in which they live? As they are removed in time from the immigrant generation, they too will take on American values and will exhibit a lower intensity of work effort.

SUMMARY OF FINDINGS

1. The Chinese were conditioned by economic necessity in their homeland to hard work and long hours. More than 60-hour weeks were quite common in the traditional occupations of laundries, restaurants, and small business enterprises. Long hours are still the rule, rather than the exception, among the Chinese today. Moonlighting is fairly common also.

2. When calculated in terms of hours worked, the hourly income rate of the Chinese appears less favorable than the total income figures would indicate.

3. The work year is shorter for the Chinese in comparison with other ethnic groups. Only 61 percent worked the 50- to 52-week years. Even worse, one out of six males worked 26 hours per week or less. This is a rather large percentage who worked only half the time during the year 1969.

4. The attitude toward hard work and long hours is changing, especially among the younger generations, who view work in a different light from their parents. The heavy influx of immigrants from China will sustain the reputation of the Chinese as a hard-working group, but the longer they are here in this country, the more likelihood of their adopting the prevailing American values toward work.

RECOMMENDATIONS

There are some jobs that no one likes to do: for example, stoop labor, cleaning public toilets, filing cards day after day. Who is going to do the menial work? In the past, those who could afford it hired others to do the jobs they did not want to do. Conquerors enslaved the conquered for these tasks. The white Europeans subjugated the colored races on their own soil and relegated them to the lowly tasks. Slavery in the South was a manifestation of the white man's distaste for the back-breaking work of growing cotton and tobacco. He sought some method to get out of it and slavery was his answer. The whole history of Asian immigrants to the American West is but another manifestation of the white man's disdain for such menial work as cultivation of crops, ditch digging to reclaim tidelands, laying railroad tracks, cooking meals, and washing clothes. The white man was caught on the horns of a dilemma: he did not want the yellow or brown man around, yet he could not do without him because of the many chores that he performed.

With the rise of the masses and the rising consciousness of the black, yellow, brown, and red men, the distasteful jobs can no longer be pushed on to the shoulders of the colored races. But the question remains: Who is going to do the unpleasant jobs? Perhaps the Chinese on the mainland have found some answers. Here are some of the methods they use:

1. Ascribe new status to manual work. The laborer, the farmer, the working man are glorified. The parasite is not allowed to exist. The position of being a former landowner or progeny of the leisure class is now an onus that is borne heavily.

2. Rotate work. Every worker must leave his regular job for a specified time and either work on the farm, work in a factory, or do his daily stint in an unpleasant but necessary task. For instance, doctors, professors, storekeepers, or nurses may be assigned to bring in their quota of cow dung or horse manure from the droppings on the streets. The streets are cleaned and the droppings are added to the fertilizer stocks.

3. The existence of an intellectual elite or any other privileged class is being nullified by such policies as decreeing that all students must, after graduation from high school, put in a two-year tour of duty on the farm or in a factory. By being in the shoes of these people, the learned come to appreciate firsthand the problems of the laboring people.

4. Work in teams. When a project needs to be done, large groups of people are mobilized at once and the task is attacked in full force. If an irrigation ditch must be dug, a date is set, the people informed, the gong sounded, and everyone is mobilized for the job at hand. This generates a cooperative spirit and because everyone else is working, an individual is less apt to shirk his duty.

5. Give purpose and direction to work. There must be dedication to a cause. The cause may be for God, for country, for mankind, to make the world safe for democracy, to rid the country of imperialists, to give our children the privileges we never had—the list is endless. Let us recall that doing something worthwhile is one of the strongest work motivations.

6. Encourage self-criticism and group struggle. Work groups meet periodically to review performance. Each person assesses his own contribution to see if he has done his best. Then his peers judge and criticize him. By these cathartic and scrutinizing routines the individual is goaded on to better performance.

These are some of the methods used in China, where distinction between classes is being reduced to ensure that one group does not use or exploit another and that the pleasant and unpleasant tasks are shared. Many of these methods are not applicable to conditions in this country, because we emphasize individualism over the social group or community. However, some are worth study and consideration.

12

SELF-EMPLOYMENT
AND SMALL BUSINESS

Until very recently, white firms simply did not hire Chinese employees. There was no choice for the Chinese but to create their own jobs by setting up small service or business enterprises. Small business has been the rule, rather than the exception, in the employment pattern of the Chinese in the United States.

ECONOMIC INDEPENDENCE

The private enterprise pattern of employment made the Chinese different from other ethnic or minority groups who relied more heavily upon working for others for a living. Ling Liu has estimated that there were 10,000 laundries, 4,300 restaurants, and 2,000 groceries operated by the Chinese in continental United States.[1] These were the three main occupations of the Chinese, and they took the form of self-owned and -operated private businesses, generally run as individual or family enterprises.

In Mountain of Gold, the experiences of the Yugoslav immigrants and the blacks have been compared with that of the Chinese.[2] The former sold their labor to the construction and mining companies in Pennsylvania, and employment depended upon seasonal fluctuation and the whims of the construction bosses. Strikes and layoffs meant uncertainty of income, insecurity of job tenure, hunger, and want. Black ownership of private businesses was almost nil, even in their own ghettos. This total economic dependence upon the white man held the black man down and perpetuated his inferior status. Not that laundry or restaurant work is less menial than that of janitor, ditch digger, field hand, miner, or construction worker; it was simply that the Chinese were independent and self-sufficient. They were spared the indignation, abuse, and hurt that came from groveling for a job.

FAMILY BUSINESSES

By and large, the Chinese enterprises had the following characteristics:

1. Contrary to popular belief, they were fairly widely scattered
in large urban centers along the East and West Coasts and were not
concentrated entirely in Chinatowns.

2. They catered more to non-Chinese clientele. Therefore,
the economic base was broad.

3. They were very small in capitalization. Equity capital came
primarily from pooled savings. Little or none came from non-Chinese
financial sources.

4. They were set up along a kinship basis. Laundries and groceries were generally "mom-and-pop" stores. In such businesses,
the family was a work unit that lived together (usually above or behind
the store), and everyone worked. Father and mother were always
present, and the children grew up seeing their parents work and having responsibility for the performance of chores. This work experience has had tremendous impact upon the second-generation Chinese-
American, shaping his work attitude and character.[3]

5. Restaurants required more capital investment and, therefore, were usually cooperative ventures based upon a larger kinship
group. For example, several brothers would form a partnership, or
uncles and cousins would hold shares in an incorporated restaurant.

6. The operation of these enterprises was fairly simple. Although few had previous experience in their type of work, the owners
could swap stories about their experiences or call upon a compatriot
for information about suppliers and problem solving.

7. Earnings were marginal or low by American standards.
Nevertheless, these enterprises provided employment and income in a
hostile land.

REVOLUTION IN CHINESE EMPLOYMENT PATTERN

Since 1950, a quiet revolution has taken place in the employment
pattern of the Chinese. They have abandoned their private businesses
in droves and prefer working for wages and salaries. Two main factors are responsible for this upheaval. First, obstacles to finding a
job were lowered; and, second, recent generations disdain the long
hours, hard work, and marginal nature of small business or service
enterprises. They prefer a 9-to-5 schedule, no risk, and a no-head-
aches-after-hours job.

Table 12.1 shows Chinese employed in 1970 by class of worker.
Those who earn a wage and salary far exceed those who are self-em-

TABLE 12.1

Wage and Salary of Self-Employed Chinese in the United States, for Selected SMSAs, 1970

SMSA	Total Employed 16 Years and over (100 percent)	Wage and Salary		Self-Employed	
		Number	Percent	Number	Percent
United States	183,562	163,009	88.8	20,553	11.2
Boston	5,391	4,991	92.6	400	7.4
Chicago	5,305	4,780	90.1	525	9.9
Honolulu	21,538	20,287	94.2	1,251	5.8
Los Angeles–Long Beach	18,315	16,103	87.9	2,212	12.1
New York	33,400	30,330	90.8	3,070	9.2
Sacramento	3,911	3,357	85.8	554	14.2
San Francisco–Oakland	38,727	34,502	89.1	4,225	10.9
San Jose	3,346	2,839	84.9	507	15.2
Seattle–Everett	3,122	2,726	87.3	396	12.7
Washington, D.C.,–Maryland–Virginia	3,358	3,028	90.2	330	9.8

Note: Based on a 20 percent sampling.

Source: U.S. Department of Commerce, Bureau of the Census, Subject Report, PC(2)1G (1970), Tables 19, 28.

TABLE 12.2

Class of Worker, by Age Group of the Chinese in the United States,
1970

Age Group	Wage and Salary	Self-Employed	Ratio, Column 1:Column 2
16-24 years	53,600	600	89:1
25-34 years	48,100	3,400	14:1
35-44 years	42,700	6,500	7:1
45-54 years	31,400	6,900	5:1
55-64 years	17,800	3,600	5:1
65 years and over	6,100	2,000	3:1

Note: Based on a 1 percent sampling.

Source: U.S. Department of Commerce, Bureau of the Census,
Special Tabulation, Public Use Sample Data (1970).

ployed. The national ratio is about 8:1. Broken down by cities, the
percentages reveal that the Chinese on the West Coast are more likely
to be self-employed than those on the East Coast. Why? The reason
may be that the Chinese on the East Coast are more recent immigrants
and may not yet have sufficient capital to embark on any private venture. Another reason may be that there are more professional people
who are self-employed on the West Coast.

The young definitely prefer being employed to self-employment.
This fact is quite obvious from Table 12.2, which shows the ratio,
by age group, of wage and salary workers to the self-employed. The
older generation still clings to small businesses because there is no
alternative. The younger generations are primarily in the professions
and evidently prefer working for others.

A word of caution, however, about accepting at face value these
figures compiled from the census: The category "wage and salary"
includes all persons who work for any incorporated firm. Many private enterprises incorporate to limit their liability, although they may
be one-man or family-operated setups. In Chinese restaurants, particularly when the venture is a cooperative one, the restaurant is owned
collectively and the shareowners are both employers and employees.
These people have invested capital in a small, private enterprise, but
they are salaried employees of their own businesses. Since restaurant

work is the single leading area of employment for the Chinese in the United States, the actual importance of small business enterprises has not diminished to the extent indicated by the census.

CHINATOWN ENTERPRISES

In their own ghettos, or Chinatowns, the Chinese are definitely proprietors of their own businesses. Tables 12.3 and 12.4 show the type of services and commercial establishments in which the Chinese are engaged in New York and San Francisco. The figures are outdated, but the type of enterprise gives us an inkling of the characteristics of these small businesses.

1. They cater to Chinese clientele.
2. They seek to capitalize on the tourist trade.
3. They offer essential services.
4. Garment or sewing factories are the only manufacturing enterprises shown where the market is with non-Chinese clientele. Recently, light industries, such as electronic components and frozen foods, have been introduced.
5. They are operated by a group limited in education, language, and financial resources.

The small size and lack of variety of the Chinatown enterprises are just as revealing as the existing types. The Chinatown Chinese are still small-time operators. The florist shop may be a husband-and-wife store. The accountant may operate from his desk space with a limited Chinese clientele. Here is a symptom that warrants closer scrutiny. Can the Chinese aim for bigger and better enterprises? Do they have the resources and capability to try? Is private enterprise an answer to the employment problem of immigrants who cannot meet the job specification of language proficiency? There is a great need for exploring this avenue of inquiry.

BEYOND CHINATOWN BORDERS

Private enterprises outside Chinatown are more varied and operate on a larger scale. No systematic study of these businesses has been undertaken, but they are much more sophisticated and efficient. Offhand, a few come to mind whose capitalization could easily exceed a million dollars, and they are not within the traditional restaurant, supermarket, or garment factory categories.

TABLE 12.3

Private Enterprises in New York's Chinatown (Core Area), 1973

Type of Business	Number of Establishments	Type of Business	Number of Establishments
Restaurants	77	Dentists	6
Exporters and importers	72	Furniture	6
Garment factories	60	Theaters	6
Groceries	52	Florists	6
Doctors (physicians and surgeons)	46	Bakeries	6
Insurance, real estate, and stockbrokers	35	Clothing stores	6
Gift shops	30	Employment agencies	6
Coffee shops	25	Carpenters, painters, and plumbers	5
Lawyers	22	Drug stores	5
Chinese newspapers, news agencies, publications	15	Jewelers	4
Meat and poultry	15	Liquor stores	4
Accountants	13	Photo studios	4
Barber shops	13	China, cookery, and glass wares	4
Banks	12	Tailors	4
Printers	12	Department stores	3
Beauty salons	10	Advertising and art design	3
Herbalists	10	Funeral parlors	3
Book stores	9	Candy stores	2
Laundry supply and appliance	9	Fish markets	2
Radio, television, and recorded music	8	Cigars and cigarettes	1
Dry cleaning and laundries	8	Transportation company	1
Noodle manufacturers	7		

Note: These figures are quite outdated but are given to show types of enterprises Chinese in Chinatown are engaged in. For example, garment factories have swelled to over 230 as of 1975.

Source: Chinese Trading Journal, New York Chinese Import and Export Association, 1973.

TABLE 12.4

Private Enterprises in San Francisco's Chinatown (Core Area), 1969

Type of Business	Number of Establishments
Markets and grocery stores	162
Dry goods and fine arts (curio shops)	136
Sewing factories	120
Restaurants	67
Insurance offices	41
Pharmacies	29
Laundries	29
Bakeries	18
Clothing shops	18
Hotels and motels	15
Beauty salons	15
Banks	13
Jewelry shops	12
Barber shops	10
Studios	9
Travel agencies	9
Schools	9
Noodle factories	6
Painter and carpenter shops	6
Theaters	5
Book stores	5
Printing shops	5
Architects	4
Shoe stores	3
Total	747

Note: These figures are quite outdated but are given to show types of enterprises Chinese in Chinatown are engaged in.

Source: San Francisco Chinese Community Citizens Survey and Fact Finding Committee Report (1969).

Case One—ETEC: One of the most impressive undertakings is the ETEC corporation in Hayward, California, which makes an electron microscope called Autoscan. James Dao, the president, and Nelson Yu, the technical manager, are young men in their mid-30s. They are the founders, the owners, and the driving force behind this most unusual venture. According to Dao, there are only six companies in the entire world, three of them in the United States, that manufacture electron microscopes.

During a visit to the plant in 1973, the company had been in business for only two and a half years. Since its inception, the staff had grown to 126, most of them highly educated and highly paid scientists and technicians. The company was doing about $500,000 in business a month. The scanning electron microscopes sold from $50,000 to $250,000 each. The Autoscan is one of the latest developments in electron-optical instrumentation. It can produce three-dimensional images in which all details are in sharp focus. The features of the Autoscan are astounding, and the possibilities that this microscope has for medical and physical research are boundless.

Nelson Yu has the technical know-how. He was an assistant to the professor at Stanford who developed the electron microscope. James Dao runs the business end. He is a graduate of the University of California at Berkeley with a degree in electrical engineering. He came to the United States at the age of 13, working at jobs ranging from milking cows to waiting on tables to electrical engineering for the city government.

The following three case histories were compiled by Ernest D. Chu, senior vice-president of an investment banking house off Wall Street, and are excellent examples of small business successes pioneered or led by Chinese-Americans.

Case Two—Wangco Inc.: This company designs and produces magnetic tape-drive systems (electronic devices that record, store, and reproduce data on computer tapes) and sells them to original equipment manufacturers mainly for use in minicomputers and related systems. In fiscal 1973, the company broadened its product line by the introduction of a fixed-head disc drive.

The company chairman is Dr. Ben C. Wang, who immigrated from China 25 years ago. When he arrived in this country, he had $100 in his pocket and a conviction that as long as he could find a job —any kind of a job—he "would never starve in the United States." Today, Wangco Inc. is the nation's second largest producer of tape drives for the minicomputer industry, and Wang himself is worth more than $3 million in company stock and other interests.

After working his way through the University of California at Berkeley and the Illinois Institute of Technology, engineer Wang went to work for IBM and "drifted into computer peripherals." Later, lured to Ampex, he developed direct-driven, single-capstan tape drive, which is still a standard in the industry. Attracted by Wang's growing reputation, Scientific Data Systems hired him to start up a new computer peripherals operation in 1964. Five years later, Wang was ready to go into the peripherals business for himself. Catching the first wave of growth in the new minicomputer business, his little company expanded rapidly to $10.7 million volume and $1.2 million net in fiscal 1973. The company employs over 400 people. In 1970 the company's sales were $23,000. By 1974 they had shot up to $18,260,000.

Case Three—Macrodata Corporation: Macrodata Corporation makes and designs equipment for testing small- and large-scale integrated semiconductor circuits that perform specialized memory and logic functions, such as data storage, counting, timing, and mathematical computation. It also makes computer-controlled design systems and offers design consulting services. Its chairman and president is Dr. William C. W. Mow; its vice-president, Stuart Liu. In 1969, this company's sales were $18,000. By 1973 they had escalated to $8,609,000.

Case Four—Finnegan Corporation: This company was founded by Robert Finnegan, but ran into serious financial difficulties. After the appointment of T. Z. Chu as president and chief operating officer, the company has shown an impressive growth record.

Finnegan Corporation develops, manufactures, and sells spectrometer systems. These systems are used to detect, identify, and quantify the constituents of gases, liquids, and solids. The company's systems are in use in the fields of biomedicine, for the analysis of drugs and drug metabolites in toxicology and pharmacology applications; analytical chemistry, for quantitative and qualitative analysis of compounds in research and industrial setting; environmental research and pollution control, for identification of chemical contaminants in water, soil, foodstuffs, and air; and forensic science, for positive identification of various types of physical evidence used in criminal justice proceedings.

The company employs about 300 people. After a steady financial loss since its founding in 1969, recovery was brought about by Chu in 1974. That year the company grossed $10,500,000.

EXPORT AND IMPORT

International trade, an important area of employment and income source for the Chinese in the United States, will inevitably grow. Formerly, it was confined to importation of foodstuffs and art goods— the former for the Chinese population, the latter for the tourist trade.

The market for today's imports is entirely different. Textiles, electron products, and wool products lead the list of imports from Taiwan, and exports to that island consist of agricultural products (wheat, cotton, soybeans, and tobacco), machinery tools, and vehicles and vessels. According to the Chinese Information Service, the volume of trade runs to about $4 billion annually.

Trade with the People's Republic of China was forbidden by the Trading with the Enemy Act, passed in 1950 during the Korean War, and did not resume until shortly before President Nixon's visit to Peking in 1972. Both countries are proceeding cautiously, so the volume of trade is not significant at the moment. China's trading policy will be dictated more by politics than by economics. Those who wish to trade with China must have her permission or sanction. They are invited to the Trade Fair in Canton, which is held each spring and fall. At the fair, contacts are established with the Foreign Trading Corporations, which are legally responsible for negotiating all China's trade contracts.

American firms wishing to do business with China will have a great need for personnel familiar with the language, the culture, and the channels of doing business with the People's Republic. Interpreters of the culture, as well as the language, will be in great demand. The Chinese will not cater to Americans by conducting their business entirely in English, as was done in the past. Americans expecting to do business in volume would be advised to take a Chinese interpreter with them to the Canton Trade Fairs.

The subtleties of Chinese etiquette also warrant extra attention. American businessmen are accustomed to snapping their fingers and expecting quick results. The Chinese place great store on personal contact and person-to-person relationships. Their sales contract may be sparsely expressed, including only the most basic elements of the transaction, such as a concise description of the goods and their specifications, delivery date, type of packing, unit price, total price, and method of payment. American businessmen may insist on detailed and exact terms couched in highly legalistic wording that may prove offensive to Chinese sensitivity. These differences require the services of middlemen versed in the ways of both countries.

China must also be apprised of American regulations governing import-export trade. Stipulations, such as place-of-origin labeling, reporting of end-use of the product, declaration of trade volume to the American government, and so on, are procedures that must be explained to Chinese officials who do not encounter such red tape in trade with Southeast Asian or African countries.

Acting as intermediaries who can provide such services for companies dealing in trade with the People's Republic of China is a potential field of private enterprise for refugees and immigrants who may have rich experience in international trade in China or Southeast Asia. There is no reason why such persons cannot eventually deal directly in importing and exporting on a larger scale than do the small firms that now operate out of Chinatowns.

MANAGEMENT CONSULTANT FIRMS

Engineering is a favorite profession of Chinese males. How engineering skills can be utilized in a private venture is shown by a management consulting firm in Long Island, New York. The firm specializes in troubleshooting. It packages a group of highly specialized engineers and sends them in under contract for a specific job and specific period of time. The engineers are on the payroll of the consulting firm. The advantages to the contracting clients are that they can get competent and skilled personnel quickly without having to recruit and put extra people on the payroll and then lay them off upon completion of the task at hand. The function of this consulting firm is parallel to that of office temporaries, except that the latter handles secretarial and clerical help while the former handles engineers and technicians. The owner of this service enterprise is a second-generation Chinese and a product of New York's Chinatown. He has about 50 engineers on his payroll.

Private ventures of the Chinese outside Chinatowns are many and varied. Others that quickly come to mind are a manufacturer of plastic boats, a home-cleaning service, a computer sales agency, a tin-and-gold foil mill, and a sailboat chartering company.

From a one-man laundry to ETEC, the Chinese have shown that they can work for themselves, that they have the enterprising traits to succeed at it, and that they are willing to work hard and persevere toward their goals. They also have had a few other factors in their favor, not the least of which is their ability to garner equity capital.

AVAILABILITY OF CREDIT

Through their kinship organizations, such as the family associations, the Chinese devised credit facilities so that they could save and have access to funds in the event of emergency or sudden need. Some of these rotating credit clubs are described in detail in Ivan Light's Ethnic Enterprise in America. Light attributes the Chinese and Japanese ownership of small business in no small measure to these facilities for capital accumulation.[4]

Such money pools were adequate for the simpler Chinese communities of yesteryear, but they can no longer serve the larger Chinese population in the United States today. Some of these savings clubs still exist, but they cannot provide the services offered by credit institutions like banks.

Banks

One would presume that a bank could provide more sophisticated and satisfactory service than the rotating credit associations. However, the first Chinese-American Bank, founded in California during the early 1900s, closed its doors in 1926. The bulk of its services was in the remittance of foreign exchange to China and its impact upon the commercial life of the Chinese in the United States was nil. Known as the Canton Bank, it was suspended for mismanagement.[5]

Not until 1962 did another Chinese-owned bank appear on the American scene. It was the state-chartered Cathay Bank of Los Angeles.[6] Chinese-owned banks in the United States can still be counted on the fingers of one hand, but the Chinese have availed themselves of the services of American banks. For instance, 12 banks (none owned by Chinese-Americans)* have offices or branches in New York's Chinatown, and their business is brisk. Services are no longer limited to remittances, but cover the full range of banking services.

The Bank of North America is one of the largest banks in New York's Chinatown. It is not Chinese-owned, although when one walks into the bank one may think so. Its staff is 100 percent Chinese, as are almost all its patrons. The branch located in Chinatown about ten years ago, nosing out other giants, like Chase Manhattan and the Chemical Bank, which only recently recognized the potentialities of the Chinese community.

The Bank of North America is a commercial bank, not a savings bank. Its loans are made primarily to restaurateurs, importer-exporters, and gift shop owners. The average loan is for about $10,000. At this bank, the Chinese borrower generally has little difficulty obtaining credit. According to the manager, the rate of delinquent payment is "very, very small."

Conversation with the bank manager revealed both signs of strength and symptoms of malaise in the Chinese entrepreneur in Chinatown. The strengths are that he encounters little problem in obtaining credit, and his credit rating is excellent. This intangible

---

*The Chinese American Bank of New York is the former Bank of China and is foreign-owned.

asset has stood the Chinese businessman in good stead. Wherever
he has gone and wherever he has traded, he has built up a solid reputation of honesty and integrity. "His word is as good as his bond," is
a generally held opinion of the Chinese. In some parts of the world,
Southeast Asia in particular, the Chinese operate vast trading empires,
and much of the business is done by verbal agreement. The Chinese
guard this reputation of honesty and integrity carefully, for to them
this intangible asset is worth more than gold or silver. If any Chinese
in the United States is tempted to sell this reputation short he will
harm both himself and his compatriots.

The symptoms of malaise are revealed by the limited type of
borrowers and by the size of the loans. It evidences small-scale and
perhaps marginal businesses employing few people and handling a
small volume. It is hoped that the Chinatown entrepreneurs will dream
of bigger and more venturesome undertakings and that they will launch
into more efficient and optimum use of capital and manpower. But to
climb out of the "Little League" may take more capital and know-how
than the Chinatown businessman can muster.

GOVERNMENT RESOURCES

Office of Minority Business Enterprise

There are many federal resources available to minority entrepreneurs that will provide them with funds, with counsel and advice,
and with technical assistance. To coordinate these activities, the Office of Minority Business Enterprise (OMBE) was created on March
15, 1969, by President Nixon's Executive Order No. 11458. In an-
nouncing the creation of OMBE,

> The President indicated that there were 116 federal
> programs, administered by twenty or more federal
> agencies, that might help minorities go into business
> for themselves or that could help to develop existing
> businesses. OMBE's job would be to coordinate the
> government's efforts and keep track of all workable
> programs.[7]

The main focus of OMBE is to get private corporations, commercial banks, and the government itself to speed the development of
minority businesses. The device to be used is the Minority Enterprise Small Business Investment Company (MESBIC).

Actually, MESBIC is no more than a revised version of the Small Business Investment Company (SBIC), authorized by the Small Business Investment Act of 1958. An SBIC is a company chartered under state law and licensed and regulated by the Small Business Administration (SBA) to make investments in small businesses. A minimum of $300,000 was required as minimum capitalization of the parent company. This money is then invested in small business of the SBIC's choice. As the SBIC invests its money, it is allowed to draw additional funds from the federal government for more investments, up to a maximum of twice its own capitalization. Thus $300,000 could grow to $900,000. This sum could be further pyramided, since the small businesses in which SBIC made an investment could then turn to the SBA and receive additional assistance in loans or guarantee of loans. The MESBIC differs essentially from the SBIC only in the fact that it seeks out minority small businesses and the minimum capitalization is reduced to $150,000 instead of $300,000. [8] Experience has shown, however, that an optimum capitalization is in the range of $1 million to $2 million. A central feature of each MESBIC is the continuing management assistance it provides without charge to the enterprises in which it invests or to which it lends money. The assistance is designed to ensure their successful and competitive operation.

Of the 66 MESBICs now licensed to operate in 1974, only one was started by a Chinese-American—Rose Leong, a Los Angeles building developer and construction contractor. Mrs. Leong arrived in the United States in 1948. She obtained a Master's Degree in education from the University of Southern California and, in 1955, started a real estate investment company. Later, when she announced that she wanted to be a construction contractor, everyone laughed. She started in business by building structures that were leased to the Post Office as branches. She went on to build apartments and office buildings for some of the nation's best-known corporate tenants. She admits that when she first started she did not even know what a two-by-four was.

In March 1974, with $300,000 of her own money, Mrs. Leong put up the capital for her own MESBIC, the Chinese Investment Company of California. This is the first federally licensed minority venture capital company to be formed and the only one wholly capitalized by a woman. Mrs. Leong now feels that she would like to share her talents and help others get started. [9]

SBA Section 8(a)—Procurement Program

A presidential directive in 1969 requested all federal agencies and departments to provide procurement opportunities for minority businessmen by exempting them from competitive bidding and allowing a cost differential. These dispensations were carried out under Section 8(a) of the Small Business Act. This is how the 8(a) program operates:

> The minority businessman contacts his local SBA office and tells the procurement specialist about the products he can produce. SBA specialists then visit the businessman's company and make an on-site field survey and evaluation of the company's capability. If the business has the capability, SBA then locates and identifies the products it needs and contacts a federal agency that wants to buy. SBA negotiates the contract.[10]

The General Services Administration Purchasing Agency for the federal government is further permitted to set aside 10 to 15 percent of its total purchases for minority businesses and contractors on a permanent basis. These provisos now guarantee a substantial market for many businesses now unable to compete with larger companies.[11]

OMBE-Funded Asian Programs

There are a number of OMBE-funded programs initiated by Asians in California. Among them are the Asian American National Business Alliance, Inc. in Los Angeles; Asians, Inc. in San Francisco; and Arcata Management in Palo Alto. All these firms act as management consultants to Asian-Americans.

The director of Arcata is Buck Wong, an MBA graduate from Stanford. In his words,

> We are attempting to help those minority businessmen who have a better opportunity for success. We are trying to get away from the marginal operations that have in the past been supported. We offer free consultation. We will train a staff member of the minority enterprise in accounting. We will help establish a business plan. We will try to line up capital to get a company started. The time we stay with a company varies from three weeks to eighteen months. On the average we devote 165 man-hours to a company, usually spread over a long period. Our client load ranges from 50 to 60.[12]

Among the companies helped by Arcata was Lee Engineering of Palo Alto. It now has an annual business of over $1 million, including a contract in 1974 for a nuclear power plant and a sewage disposal piping system.[13]

There is no question that the government has established a policy and has embarked on programs designed to aid the minority business-man in breaking into private enterprise. This policy was instituted in recognition of the fact that minorities comprise 17 percent of the American population, but own from 1-3 percent of all businesses and do only 1 percent of the business volume. For further information about federal resources for minority businessmen, OMBE puts out a number of booklets of which minorities should avail themselves:

1. "Special Catalog of Federal Programs Assisting Minority Enterprise" (1971). Description of 85 federal programs specifically designed to aid minority business enterprise and an additional 175 programs that offer potential business opportunities to minorities.

2. "Minority Business Opportunity Committee Handbook, Guidance and Procedures" (July 1974).

3. "Franchise Opportunities Handbook" (September 1973).

Other Government Resources

To mention a few of the other governmental resources available to the minority businessman, the National Minority Purchasing Council works to increase corporate purchases from minority firms. The General Services Administration offers counseling on doing business with the government by assisting minority businessmen to develop a government market for their products and services and to obtain contract opportunities. The Economic Development Corporation of the Department of Commerce is not usually aimed at the small minority entrepreneur, but it can provide technical and management assistance.

Although many of these programs have been operative in the black and Spanish-speaking communities for a number of years, few Chinese seem to be aware of the resources available to them. With the tradition of small private enterprise that the Chinese in this country have, it is time for them to move on to bigger and more diversified ventures.

SUMMARY OF FINDINGS

1. Traditionally, small business has been the rule, rather than the exception, for the Chinese in the United States because (a) the Chinese could not meet standards set up by American firms for jobs; (b) the temperament and background of the Chinese immigrant was more suited to self-enterprise; and (c) American firms simply did not hire Chinese.

2. Self-employment spared the Chinese some of the demeaning treatment meted out to minority groups who depended totally upon others for jobs.

3. As the social climate and attitude toward the Chinese improved, the predominant pattern of self-employment has changed to one in which wage-and-salary workers exceed the self-employed.

4. Contrary to popular belief, Chinese enterprises were located primarily outside Chinatowns and most catered to non-Chinese clientele. These businesses were set up on a family basis. They operated on a marginal level and managed to stay afloat primarily because of perseverance, long hours, and unpaid help available from family members.

5. Chinatown enterprises, especially those inside the ghetto, catered to a Chinese clientele and were very limited in scale, size, and variety.

6. The hand laundry, once overwhelmingly the most common type of self-owned and -operated type of enterprise up to 20 years ago, is now on the verge of extinction.

7. Chinese ventures outside Chinatown's borders today are more varied and operate on a larger scale.

8. Foreign trade is an important area of potential for Chinese-American businessmen.

9. A valuable, intangible asset that the Chinese have is their reputation for honesty and integrity in business dealings.

10. The Chinese have traditionally created their own sources of capital and credit to launch them into private enterprise on a small scale. Today, capital needs are greater than the local community can provide.

11. The Office of Minority Business Enterprise was set up in 1969 to coordinate and facilitate government efforts to help minority entrepreneurs with loans, counsel, and technical assistance.

RECOMMENDATIONS

The drastic reversal of the Chinese employment pattern, from private entrepreneur (albeit on a small scale) to wage or salary worker, can be viewed from two angles.

On the plus side, the Chinese now do have an entree into the mainstream job market. Many are fully qualified to compete at all levels. They need no longer create their own jobs to eke out a marginal livelihood by putting in long hours and hard work. In working for others their responsibility usually ends when they leave their place of employment, and they need not risk their capital and savings.

With the decline of small self-owned and -operated businesses, there arise a number of likely minuses. What is considered negative may be more sociological or psychological than occupational or economic; but these aspects are related to economics, and the well-being or malaise in one affects the other.

By being self-employed, the Chinese insulated themselves, or were at least one step removed, from occupational discrimination. They never put themselves in a position to be last hired and first fired. The usual response to bad times of the Chinese self-employed was to tighten the belt and expect less, which is better than being outright unemployed. Being one's own boss also added to self-image and dignity, especially when such dignity was constantly undercut and trampled.

The Chinese also found collective security in the way they set up their private businesses. The family was the working unit. Economic dependence held the family members together and generated jobs for the close of kin. All these factors were important to the survival of the Chinese in the past.

What may be considered the saving grace of the Chinese, however, the younger generation Chinese-Americans look upon as an albatross. They do not care to continue in the family businesses. They view their parents' work with distaste and disdain. They would prefer getting a job and working for others to being self-employed. To them the traits of industry and thrift are old-fashioned and even stupid. These are the attitudes that replaced those of self-help, family solidarity, and mutual aid and they are reflected in the high ratio (8:1) of employed to self-employed.

Vulnerability to Economic Reverses

Times have changed. Attitudes have changed. The nature of small business has changed. The Chinese population has changed increasingly to a first-generation immigrant group that lacks familiarity with American ways and the English language. Therefore, it is first recommended that a strong backward look at self-employment and small business ventures be made. This does not mean a return to the restaurants, laundries, grocery stores, gift shops, one-man stands, or family-run operations that characterized Chinese entrepreneurship in the past. More sophisticated lines and a somewhat larger scale are suggested.

In fact, the risks of going into business for oneself are extremely high. One out of every three businesses fails within a year. The rate of failure decreases as net worth increases,[14] which is why it is vitally important to be adequately capitalized.

The Chinese do have access to limited capital, but big money is a different story. Commercial banks trust the Chinese, but, as a rule,

they do not provide entrepreneurs with risk capital. Access to venture capital is what the Chinese need, and taking advantage of govern-
ment-proffered assistances such as MESBICs may be one answer.
The mechanism whereby MESBICs make available venture capital
was touched upon earlier. They are set up to involve private investors
and to provide risk capital to minority enterprises. MESBICs provide
counseling and technical assistance as well.

MESBICs have been available for several years, and in only one
instance have the Chinese taken advantage of this opportunity. Because the Chinese have not availed themselves of the many opportunities set up for minority enterprise, it is surmised that they simply
do not know about them. A second recommendation, therefore, is to
create better channels of information to ethnic communities besides
the black and Spanish-speaking ones. This recommendation applies
also to government programs other than MESBIC that help minority
businesses find needed resources, and managerial, technical, and
marketing assistance.

The third recommendation is to invite Asian-American members
to serve on the private sector Minority Advisory Council. These people would convey the pulse and economic conditions of the Asian communities to the Executive Office of the President through OMBE. An
Asian-American should be included in the Public Sector Interagency
Committee. This person's responsibility would be to make sure that
Asian-Americans are apprised of the help available from the government and that they are fairly represented for their share of programs
awarded. Hopefully, Asian representation will ensure better channels
of information in both directions: from the government to the Chinese
community, and from the Chinese community to the government.

Chinese Do Meet Criteria

The Chinese make good candidates for assistance under the
minority business enterprise program. They have had a long tradition
of self-employment, and cultural tradition has equipped them with the
temperament, the industry, the credit concepts, and the kinship support to operate on a minuscule scale. Now it is time for them to expand their vision and move up in scale—not out of small business and
self-employment entirely.

What Kinds of Business?

The type of business ventures that the Chinese should consider
ought to have some of the following characteristics:

1. They should utilize the talents of a highly educated population for its managerial and technical ability, and should complement it with a group that can provide a steady source of labor. The purpose of the latter, of course, is to accommodate the recent immigrants who must find employment quickly, but do not have the English facility that would enable them to compete in the labor market. In effect, an attempt should be made to create jobs for other Chinese, if possible.

2. They should diversify into other occupations and industries, to broaden the economic base beyond the existing narrow ones of retail trade and service enterprises. Areas for widening should include professional services, manufacturing, foreign trade, the crafts, and even agriculture.

3. They should encourage dispersion of the heavy population concentrated in Chinatowns. One can see immediately the differences in the types of enterprise that exist in Chinatowns and those that are no longer tied to the ghetto. In other words, locating outside Chinatowns would enrich and expand not only the employment opportunities but the living environment of the Chinese as well.

These characteristics are not all inclusive. Perhaps it is too immense a task to add the difficult dimension of social consciousness and responsibility to the already difficult task of setting up a successful private enterprise. But, if government is seriously trying to address itself to social problems, the private sector must not evade the issues entirely.

NOTES

1. Ling Lui, Chinese in North America (privately published in Chinese, 1949).

2. Betty Lee Sung, Mountain of Gold (New York: Macmillan Co., 1967).

3. Lin Yutang, Chinatown Family (New York: John Day Co., 1948); Jade Snow Wong, Fifth Chinese Daughter (New York: Harper Bros., 1950).

4. Ivan Light, Ethnic Enterprise in America (Los Angeles and Berkeley: University of California Press, 1972), pp. 45-61.

5. Ibid., p. 47.

6. Ibid.

7. Edward H. Jones, Blacks in Business (New York: Grosset & Dunlap, 1971), p. 132.

8. Ibid., pp. 132-34.

9. "From China with Skill," Commerce Today, April 1, 1974, p. 7.

10. Jones, op. cit., p. 138.

11. Ibid.

12. Chinatown News (Vancouver, Canada), August 18, 1974, pp. 15-16.

13. Ibid.

14. Joseph D. Phillips, Little Business in the American Economy (Urbana: University of Illinois Press, 1958), p. 55.

CHAPTER 13

Bicultural conflicts pose formidable obstacles to the Chinese looking for jobs—especially those in the higher echelons. For example, the American approach is "to get out there and sell yourself." To do that, one must boast about or even exaggerate one's educational background, personal qualities, experience, responsibilities, and abilities. The applicant must demonstrate that he stands heads above many other applicants and prove that he is best qualified for the job. Such tactics call for aggressiveness and assertiveness, which go strongly against the grain of the Chinese character. To pursue a job in this fashion in China would lower inestimably the employer's opinion of the applicant and mark him as one of uncouth and coarse manners. Humbleness and humility are prized virtues in China, but they are cultural yokes when it comes to looking for a job in the United States.

CULTURAL DISSIMILARITIES

According to Francis L. K. Hsu, the noted anthropologist, the American culture is individual-centered; the Chinese culture, situation-centered. The former calls for self-reliance and rugged individualism; the latter, for mutual dependence and accommodation. Hsu points out these cultural dissimilarities by showing how Americans and Chinese view the plot and drama of the movie version of Marcia Davenport's novel, Valley of Decision. [1]

The plot involves a wealthy industrialist whose son is unhappily married to a woman who sides with her father-in-law in a labor dispute. The son is sympathetic toward the workers, and he falls in love with the family maid. When violence erupts in a labor strike, the industrialist is killed. When order is restored, the son takes over man-

200

agement of the plant and institutes liberalized factory policies. He divorces his wife and marries the family maid.

Hsu wrote:

> To the American audience this was good drama, since every conflict was resolved in a way that is desirable from an American point of view. The production conflict was resolved in favor of new views on manufacturing methods over the old-fashioned ones; liberal attitudes toward labor won out in the social conflict with hard-fisted attempts to suppress the working-men [and the son and maid were married].[2]

To a Chinese audience, however, the son was shamefully unfilial. "A son in conflict with his father was a bad son, and a maid who would help such a son in his ventures was a bad woman. Through the same Chinese lens, the daughter-in-law was regarded as an extremely virtuous woman who suffered in malicious hands."[3]

Hsu gives another example of how cultural baggage interferes with the Chinese in the United States when they need to speak up for their rights.

> The pattern of mutual dependence directs all men— laborer and businessman, tenant farmer and landowner—to seek their security and advancement through persons, through the alliance of superior and subordinate. This means that when there is conflict, the tendency is to compromise rather than to adopt a unilateral position.
>
> It is for these reasons that Chinese workers have never been militant supporters of large-scale labor movements and have not, in the Western sense of the term, proved to be good or persevering fighters in an economic struggle. The individual does not fight with the owner and managers for higher wages or better working conditions, but tries to achieve these goals by joining their ranks or influencing them through family connections, friendship, and neighborhood or communal ties.[4]

These tried and tested tactics evolved from an overpopulated society where accommodation oiled the gears of daily life and whose goals were to reduce conflict to a minimum. Taken from its native setting, this reluctance to challenge the status quo can place the Chinese at a disadvantage.

PERSONALITY TESTS

Many American corporations use personality tests to screen job applicants. These tests are designed to probe the inner recesses of a person's psyche, and they include such devices as the Rorschach Inkblot Test and the Thematic Apperception Test (TAT). These tests are not only given as standard procedure to job applicants but also are used to weed out personnel and to check up on people already on the work force.

No matter what tests are given, the interpretation of them is surcharged with dominant American values. For example, Burleigh Gardner, of Social Research Inc., a giant testing outfit in Chicago, claims to have distilled (from the TAT) the 12 factors that make a good business leader. "The men who still feel strong emotional ties —far more than mere affection—to the mother have systematically had difficulty in the business situation," warns Gardner. Such men are not executive timber. [5] Gardner probably has not read the family history of the Rothchilds, nor a biography of Franklin D. Roosevelt; in both cases, strong-willed mothers ruled the family roosts. The Chinese in Southeast Asia operate huge business enterprises, yet they cling to the kinship family of their motherland.

The American standard of emotional maturity, however, is to cut parental ties as soon as possible. Against these yardsticks, how can a Chinese pass the personality tests and be considered for an executive position when he has been taught since infancy that there is no greater virtue than to honor, respect, love, and obey one's parents? In all probability, the values he prizes may work against his interest in getting beyond the personnel officer. He will not climb too high on the corporation's ladder unless he forsakes his Chinese upbringing and becomes an unfilial son, or is aware of these cultural discrepancies as they are applied in the United States and takes measures to protect himself.

PROCLIVITY OR DISDAIN FOR AN OCCUPATION

In every society, there is a social ranking of occupations independent of monetary rewards. For centuries, in Europe, the clergy was the highest calling. In Asia, the monk occupies a very lowly status. In eighteenth-century England, the man of means wore white gloves to show that he did not have to dirty his hands, and he was looked up to and envied. In other societies, he would be considered a useless parasite.

Movie, stage, and television stars enjoy fame and command astronomical salaries in the United States; actors and actresses are placed near the bottom of the occupational totem pole in China. The samurai, or warrior class, stood directly below royalty and nobility in Japan; the military was at the bottom of the entire heap in China. And so it goes. Each culture judges its occupations according to its own scale of values, but, in moving from one country to the other, the immigrant finds that the yardstick has changed on him. What he once considered lowly or prestigious positions may be completely reversed, and he might have to revise his attitudes and thinking.

From time immemorial, the philosopher and scholar stood at the apex of the occupational scale in China. Then came farmers, the laboring class, the tradesmen, and, last of all, the military men. The cultural holdover is quite evident in the high educational attainment of the Chinese in the United States and in the heavy concentration of the labor force in the teaching profession. However, if the declining birthrate foreshadows a shrunken student population with less employment opportunities in the educational field, Chinese-Americans will be disproportionately and adversely affected.

What is more difficult for many Chinese to overcome is their attitude toward certain lines of work. There seems to be a considerable amount of disdain among the foreign-born Chinese for such occupations as religious work, acting, heavy labor, and soldiering.

PARTICIPATION IN THE MILITARY

The census of 1970 shows only 2,098 males of Chinese ancestry in the armed forces of the United States, and these few may have been the result of the draft, rather than voluntary enlistment. Now that the draft has ended, the numbers may be fewer yet. It was with some hesitation, then, that the military was included as an employment possibility for the Chinese. However, an interview with Air Force Major Jung K. Chung has altered that view, and a few of his comments are worth mentioning here.

Major Chung feels that the armed forces at the officer's level today offer more of an opportunity to break into the management level and administrative work than does private industry. Having been employed in private industry in a technical capacity and having gone as high as he could in that respect, he found himself up against a stone wall in trying to get into management. As an officer in the air force, Major Chung, who is still a young man, will gain invaluable administrative and leadership experience that will stand him in good stead should he go back into private industry.

The branch of the armed forces that he knows best, the air force, is a highly technical outfit. Men and women trained in the air force have marketable skills for the private sector. When these people return to civilian life, they enhance the economic strength of the nation. According to the Department of Labor, one out of every six civilian craftsmen or technicians received his initial technical training in some military school.

The air force is the first branch of the armed services to promote a person of Chinese descent to the rank of brigadier general. General Dewey Dwoc Kung Lowe graduated from the University of California at Berkeley and has a law degree from the San Francisco Law School. The general is a much-decorated command pilot with the Legion of Merit and the Distinguished Flying Cross among his many awards and honors.

Although the military is a conduit for training and experience, it may hold little appeal for the Chinese. Soldiering has been a much-despised occupation for the Chinese for too long.

These few examples of cultural divergence give some inkling of the tremendous adjustment that the Chinese undergo and that affects, directly or indirectly, their employment situation. There are innumerable other instances that would take too long to recount here. We must repeat, however, that the language barrier is the greatest cultural hurdle that the immigrant Chinese must scale. Even though he may master the written language, he may never speak without an accent, and this will inevitably be a handicap to him in all of his dealings, both economic and social.

SUMMARY OF FINDINGS

1. Oftentimes, the widely disparate cultural values of two strong civilizations create bicultural conflicts that the Chinese must resolve. Examples of these are the competitiveness and aggressiveness of the West in contrast to the humbleness and accommodation of the East. Another is the strong emphasis on parental ties, which is valued in China, but looked upon as a weakness in the United States.

2. Psychological tests, commonly used today in hiring, retaining, and promoting, are highly value-oriented against the Chinese.

3. Cultural attitudes in favor of or against certain lines of work limit the occupational options for many Chinese.

4. Language remains the most difficult barrier that challenges the Chinese immigrant.

RECOMMENDATIONS

The melting pot theory in this nation of immigrants already has been debunked. Lip service has been paid to cultural pluralism, but it is not yet a reality. In fact, the West could take a few lessons from the East in the sphere of societal precepts. Take American competitiveness, which is so highly valued and is the key to upward mobility in the United States. Again, to quote Hsu:

> American competitiveness . . . never brings men together because its basis is "each for himself." One individual's gain invariably means some degree of loss to others. . . . The more successful need the inferiority of the less successful to make their triumph more absolute.[6]

As for untying the parental apron strings, an achievement so highly touted as a special characteristic of a top executive, Hsu has this to say: To the Chinese, "the parent-child ties are permanent rather than transitory. It is taken for granted that they are immutable, and so are not subject to individual acceptance or rejection."[7] It is precisely in the primordial relations of the family that the Chinese find continuity, permanence, and personal security. That is why some values cannot be compromised. They cannot and should not be given up for a bowl of porridge.

Nevertheless, the cultural values of China's great heritage are loosening their hold on Chinese-Americans. The fallacy of this line of thinking is that to adjust to living in the United States, one must embrace the American way in toto and cast off the American heritage like an outgrown garment. This tendency is becoming increasingly prevalent, at great psychological damage to those who are the farthest removed from their ancestral culture. I recommend that all Chinese-Americans pause in their tracks toward Americanization, and be a little more selective about what is accepted. At the same time, let us study our cultural heritage to see what can be retained. This way, there will be give and take of the best from both civilizations.

Technological Aids for Language Learning

American technology could be put to good use in the area of language learning. Since Chinese is so radically different from those languages based upon a Roman alphabet, greater time and effort must be devoted to its mastery. Since most immigrants come to the United States full grown and after their formal education has been completed, attending classes poses a formidable hurdle, especially if there are family responsibilities that take priority.

In Chapter 2, it was recommended that more English language classes be established for adults. In addition to the classes, which in

all likelihood can only be established where there are large concentrations of Chinese, it is recommended that the state education departments or the federal Office of Education fund the preparation and re-
cording of cassette tapes in English language instruction for Chinese.
These tapes should be prepared by linguists versed in the teaching of
English as a second language. The Chinese dialect should be used to
explain the terms and the lesson should be in Cantonese, rather than
Mandarin. There are a number of records and tapes now available for
the Mandarin-speaking person, but little for the Cantonese speakers.
Yet it is the latter who make up the bulk of the Chinese population in
the United States.

These tapes should be made widely available on loan through the
public library system to those who do not have time to attend classes.
This method of distribution of educational materials does not depart
from usual library practice. Currently, many libraries provide books
in Braille for the blind, large-print books for the elderly, and even
music records and works of art for music and art lovers.

Ample publicity must be given through the Chinese press and
radio to the availability of such tapes. Unless prospective users are
informed of the existence and easy accessibility of such tapes, few
people will benefit from them. It is just as important to publicize the
tapes as to create them.

NOTES

1. Francis L. K. Hsu, Americans and Chinese: Reflections
on Two Cultures and Their People (New York: Doubleday Natural History Press, 1972).
2. Ibid., p. 3.
3. Ibid.
4. Ibid., p. 309.
5. Quoted in Martin L. Gross, The Brain Watchers (New York:
Random House, 1962), p. 61.
6. Hsu, op. cit., p. 305.
7. Ibid., p. 111.

14

STEREOTYPING THE CHINESE

As a highly visible and distinct ethnic group, the Chinese in the United States are subject to a number of factors that are not applicable to most other groups looking for jobs or being considered for promotion. One such factor is stereotyping. Stereotypes are legitimatized as representing classifications of people based on distinctive, easily recognized, and easily articulated criteria shared by members of society. Such attributes, as assigned to a group, may however, be based upon a false impression, a misinterpretation, an outdated characteristic, or a deliberate attempt to disparage a group and relegate it to a disadvantaged social status.

Tied to the Apron Strings of the Mother Country

When will the Chinese-Americans be considered apart from the mother country? Invariably the first question to which any Chinese-American will have to respond when he sits across the desk from an interviewer is, "How long have you been in this country?" Even when the reply is, "I was born here. I've lived here all my life," the presumption is that an ethnic Chinese is a Chinese national forever. He is tied in with the ups and downs of Sino-American relations.

In fact, favorable or ill treatment of the Chinese in the United States seems to correspond to the rise and fall of China's international status and her relationship with the United States. Prior to World War II, the Chinese were aliens, ineligible for citizenship. During World War II, they were an ally-in-arms, and the Chinese Exclusion Acts were repealed. The Chinese wore buttons proclaiming, "I am Chinese" to differentiate themselves from the Japanese. To have proclaimed, "I am American" would not have served the purpose at all. During the Korean War, Chinese businesses had to exhibit signs stating, "I am Nationalist Chinese" to disassociate themselves from the Communist Chinese; and J. Edgar Hoover, former director of the FBI, publicly stated that he suspected the entire Chinese-American populace of being potential Communist agents. In 1972, President Nixon's visit to Peking heralded an aura of elevated status and prestige for the Chinese in the United States.

Few other national groups are so irrevocably tied to the apron strings of the mother country. The Italian did not have to answer for the deeds of Mussolini. German-Americans were not incarcerated in concentration camps during World War II. A Russian immigrant is not automatically labeled a Communist. White ethnics were not labeled the "enemy" or "gook," even as they were serving on the front line in the U.S. Army in Vietnam, as were Asian-Americans.

An American-born Jew is not asked, "How long have you been in this country?" Nor is he complimented on how well he speaks English without an accent. An American black is not associated with any of the African nations. On the contrary, Nigerian blacks and West Indian blacks made special efforts to separate themselves from American blacks so that they will be associated with their motherland, but, if they do not wear their native dress and headdress, they are taken for native-born Americans. An ethnic Chinese, however, is taken for a foreigner forever.

"A Foreigner Has No Right to a Job"

When there are many applicants for a job or when a number of aspirants are vying for a promotion, the competition gets keen, and stereotyping serves a very useful purpose for disqualifying potential competitors. If all Chinese-Americans are considered foreign, then patriotism or nationalism can be invoked to place the Chinese-American at a disadvantage: "What right have those foreigners got to take a job away from a full-blooded American?" becomes the rallying cry. In an era of declining employment, even third- or fourth-generation Chinese-Americans may be subjected to unpleasantries and hostile stares suggesting that they have deprived "Americans" of their jobs.

Cheap Labor, Hard-Working

The first wave of Chinese immigrants to hit the Western shores over a hundred years ago came as coolies. Coolie literally means bitter strength, and it is true these men had nothing more to offer than their muscles and their labor. They were willing to work at jobs the white man scorned, and they were willing to do it for less. As a result, the Chinese came to be associated with cheap labor.

Stereotypes die hard. More than a century later, the Chinese employee is expected to work for less, and he is offered less than the going rate. Worse yet, it is presumed that Chinese are content with less. The fact that he is earning less than persons with comparable education is documented in Table 9.7. Some employers may even consider it an affront if a Chinese-American asks for the same salary and working conditions as others of his caliber are commanding.

At the same time, the prevailing belief that all Chinese are hard workers exacts from the Chinese-American an extra toll. If a Chinese person departs from the stereotyped image of being hard-working, noncomplaining, docile, and quiet, he is told, "You're Chinese, but you don't act Chinese," as if all Chinese were alike.

Laundryman, Restaurant Worker

It is difficult to get people in this country to accept the fact that there are Chinese bankers, outstanding Chinese scientists and architects, Chinese presidents of colleges, and Chinese presidents of large corporations. Somehow the American mind cannot erase the image of the Chinese as mere laundrymen and restaurateurs. In the experience of almost every adult Chinese-American, he has been taken at least three times for one or the other or both. Sometimes it is even hard for the Chinese themselves to accept the fact that some of their kind have penetrated the upper echelon.

Favorable Labels

Some stereotypes attributed to the Chinese have been laudatory, rather than derogatory. Such favorable labels tacked on to the group as a whole are industrious, honest, dependable, intelligent, efficient, and strongly familial. Such blanket labels have aided the Chinese in finding employment. In fact, when business firms are under compulsion to upgrade their minority representation, the Chinese are actively sought by personnel officers who earnestly believe that all Chinese possess these qualities.

As mechanisms for the reinforcement of prejudice, stereotypes can be irrational and contradictory. The Chinese are at once honest and sneaky; they are cunning and mysterious. They are artistic, but not creative. They are immoral, yet highly civilized. They are good businessmen, and they are Communists. Stereotypes, whether good or bad, are not applicable to every member in the group. The determinants of stereotypes are to be found, not in the target group, but in the social setting and the economy of the United States. They change both with the international climate and with the economic situation. They are applied to the group without allowing for individual differences.

DOES BELIEF LEAD TO ACTION?

Stereotypes are a set of beliefs about a group. Prejudice is a negative attitude, but discrimination is overt action—prejudice acted out. Today's practitioners of discrimination are no longer openly crude. No one will put a want ad in the newspaper saying, "Chinese need not apply." Laws could never pass legislative bodies today in the out-and-out racist language commonly found in the anti-Chinese statutes of the 1880s. Federal government policy is no longer officially racist. There are even watchdogs in government and private agencies who seek to guard the interests of racial minorities. But that does not mean that prejudice and discrimination no longer exist. Some of it is rerouted; some is given respectable euphemisms; some is hung on institutional hooks. When accomplished through these diversionary tactics, it is no longer recognizable.

For example, the first Chinese Exclusion Act of 1882 did not have any qualms about naming the Chinese specifically. By 1924, racism had put on silk gloves, and the yellow and brown peoples were redefined as "aliens ineligible to citizenship." The end result was the same.

"Local experience" is a new term that is frequently encountered by Chinese immigrants looking for employment outside of the Chinatown community. For example, a reservation agent who worked for an international airline for five years in Hong Kong may apply for a similar job in New York. Her experience is discounted, or not counted at all, because she does not have local experience, meaning experience in the United States. In some instances, local experience is important to job performance, but, in most instances, the skills and experience are readily transferable, given a short period of reorientation. Therefore local experience translates into a "no" that is difficult for an immigrant to overcome.

INEQUITIES AND DISADVANTAGES

To what extent is employment discrimination practiced against the Chinese and what form does it take? We have touched upon this topic in almost every chapter of this book. It would be redundant to repeat everything here. Discrimination against the Chinese is no longer expressed in outright hostility but is grounded more along the lines of inequities and disadvantages stemming from their immigration status or cultural conflicts and dissimilarities.

Unfortunately, some of these inequities pose employment barriers that are impossible for large numbers of Chinese to overcome through personal effort. Examples of these are such legal roadblocks as citizenship requirements—minimum waiting period of five years— or probationary periods for refugees—minimum waiting period, two years. Another solid wall against an ethnic group, which has so recently been admitted to these shores after nearly a century of exclusion, is state-prohibited employment of foreign-trained professionals. The father-son tradition of gaining admittance to the trade union is an area where the Chinese find it almost impossible to effect a breakthrough.

The disadvantages shouldered by the Chinese, which are inherent in their cultural differences, can be moderated somewhat through personal effort. How? By attending English language classes, by persevering through the period of cultural shock and transition, and by being more competitive. There is no question that the Chinese have to try harder to obtain the same or lesser results, and no one can or will dispute the fact that gross inequality exists.

UPWARD MOBILITY

Let us recognize, however, that there has been substantial progress in economic opportunities for minorities within the past several decades. The facts and figures bear this out.[1] The progress has not been uniformly distributed nor equally applied, but significant changes for the better have come about.

Some indication of occupational mobility for the Chinese can be gleaned from Table 14.1. Immigrants who came to the United States prior to 1945 have, by and large, remained in the operatives and service workers category. Keeping in mind that the type of Chinese immigrants changed drastically after 1949, we can see that those who came to the United States during 1955-60 managed to move up into the professional category to the extent of 39.5 percent. At the same time, the service workers category shrank to 13.5 percent.

A smaller percentage of the more recent immigrants in the 1965-70 column are in the professional group (30 percent), and more are in the service workers category (23 percent). It seems that given time—and the span may be a 20-year period or an entire generation— upward mobility does occur. The first generation may not see the

TABLE 14.1

Major Occupations of the Foreign-Born Chinese, by Year of Immigration, 1970

	Year of Immigration																		Total Foreign-Born	
	1965-70		1960-64		1955-60		1950-54		1945-49		1935-44		1925-34		1915-24		Before 1915			
	Number	Percent	Number	Percent	Number	Percent	Number	Percent	Number	Percent	Number	Percent	Number	Percent	Number	Percent	Number	Percent	Number	Percent
Professionals	14,700	30.0	9,500	35.8	7,300	39.5	4,000	29.0	3,800	30.2	1,300	12.5	300	3.9	100	1.5	0	0.0	41,700	33.0
Managers	1,300	2.6	800	3.0	1,000	5.4	1,400	10.1	600	4.8	2,400	23.1	1,000	13.2	1,300	19.7	400	30.8	10,300	8.2
Sales workers	2,700	5.5	1,100	4.2	800	4.3	200	1.4	500	4.0	400	3.8	700	9.2	100	1.5	100	7.7	6,600	5.2
Clerical workers	8,700	17.7	5,200	19.6	3,000	16.2	800	5.8	1,300	10.3	300	2.9	800	10.5	500	7.6	0	0.0	20,600	16.3
Craftsmen	1,400	2.8	700	2.6	700	3.8	700	5.1	300	2.4	600	5.8	200	2.6	200	3.0	0	0.0	5,200	4.1
Operatives	7,200	14.6	4,500	17.0	3,100	16.8	2,300	16.7	2,600	20.6	2,400	23.1	1,500	19.7	1,000	15.2	200	15.4	2,500	2.0
Laborers	800	1.6	500	1.9	100	0.5	100	0.7	400	3.2	100	1.0	200	2.6	200	3.0	0	0.0	2,500	2.0
Farm workers	200	0.4	100	0.4	0	0.0	100	0.7	0	0.0	100	1.0	0	0.0	100	1.5	0	0.0	600	0.5
Service workers	11,300	23.0	3,800	14.3	2,500	13.5	4,200	30.4	3,100	24.6	2,800	26.9	2,500	32.9	2,900	43.9	400	30.8	34,200	27.1
Private household	900	1.8	300	1.1	0	0.0	0	0.0	0	0.0	0	0.0	400	5.3	200	3.0	200	15.4	2,000	1.6
Total (100 percent)	49,200		26,500		18,500		13,800		12,600		10,400		7,600		6,600		1,300		126,200	

Source: U.S. Department of Commerce, Bureau of the Census, Special Tabulation, Public Use Sample Data (1970).

fruits of its labor and its struggles, but at least the second generation
may reap or harvest what their parents sowed.

However, upward occupational mobility does become a reality
for the second generation, if a small sample of the alumni of City
College of New York is representative of the lower socioeconomic
class of Chinese in the United States. CCNY is a municipal, tuition-
free institution of higher learning that traditionally has attracted the
sons and daughters of immigrant families in this gateway metropolis.
From 1960 to 1972, CCNY graduated 400 students of Chinese ancestry.
A questionnaire sent to these alumni netted 80 replies. The occupation
of the father was compared to that of the graduate. This information
is tabulated in Table 14.2. Of the total respondents 35 gave their
fathers' occupation as laundryman or restaurant worker. Others included seamen, clerk, house-boy, warehouse worker, and a scattered few as businessmen or professionals. In general, the fathers
held low-level, low-paying jobs. The column to the right gives the
occupations of the CCNY graduates. The job titles show that most
are in the professions, in business, in technical work, or in administration. The four in clerical work are females. In general the income of these graduates is higher than the median U.S. family income
for 1969.

1975—RECESSION GOING INTO DEPRESSION

The acid test comes when economic conditions are bad. It is
easy to be tolerant and magnanimous when there is prosperity and full
employment. And that is what this country has enjoyed, except for
minor dips, since World War II. In this favorable economic climate,
minorities in the United States were able to push for betterment of
their status. In 1975, dark clouds shrouded the economic horizon.
Creeping anxiety and insecurity gripped the nation. Opportunist poli-
ticians called for a crackdown on aliens. Gains from the Civil Rights
Movement, Equal Employment Opportunity, Affirmative Action, and
Contract Compliance were being eroded. The black unemployment
rate was twice that of the whites. The Bureau of Labor Statistics did
not issue separate figures for Asians, so we had no way of knowing
how the Chinese had fared. Heated debates ensued over whether
seniority provisions were to be modified in favor of minorities. Strong
voices were raised against the goals and timetables of the Affirmative
Action plans. Would the government ease its pressure on employers
to comply with the law on minority hiring if the economic situation
worsened?

TABLE 14.2

Occupational Mobility as Reflected in Two Generations of Chinese CCNY Graduates' Families

Number of Students	Father's Occupation	CCNY Alumni's Present Occupation
20	Laundrymen	6 teachers, 2 engineers, 1 accountant, 1 manager, 1 scientist, 2 executives, 1 actuary-trainee, 1 computer programmer, 2 clerks, 3 no responses
15	Restaurant workers	2 teachers, 2 engineers, 2 managers, 1 executive, 1 computer programmer, 1 hospital investigator, 1 supervisor, 1 field assistant, 2 unemployed, 2 no responses
3	Engineers	2 engineers, 1 intern
2	Teachers	1 engineer, 1 scientist
1	Accountant	consultant
1	Statistician	engineer
6	Businessmen	2 teachers, 1 junior executive, 1 actuary/trainee, 1 research assistant, 1 UN worker
2	Clerks	1 patent attorney, 1 clerk
1	Seaman	engineer
1	Clergyman	teacher
1	Houseboy	junior executive
1	Warehouse worker	engineer
1	Adult education aide	armed forces
1	Manager	no response
1	Officer	engineer
1	Chinese Association President	teacher
7	Retired	3 teachers, 2 lab technicians, 1 businessman, 1 student
3	Unemployed	1 teacher, 1 research assistant, 1 supervisor
5	Deceased	1 teacher, 1 junior executive, 1 lab technician, 1 businessman, 1 technician
7	No response	3 engineers, 1 computer programmer, 1 consultant, 1 technician, 1 clerk

Source: Survey of City College New York Chinese Alumni (1972).

214

SENIORITY AS DISCRIMINATION

A seniority clause is contained in virtually all collective bargaining contracts. But minorities charge that seniority perpetuates
discrimination because those that are last hired are first in line to be
fired. Companies caught between the collective bargaining agreements
and contracts signed with the Equal Employment Opportunity Commission asked the courts for a decision. In the Jersey Central Power &
Light Company case, the judge ordered the company and union "to
work something out consistent with both contracts."[2] The solution
was to set up three seniority lists: one for minorities, one for females, and one for all others. Layoffs would come from the bottom
of the lists rotating from Column A to Column B to Column C, thereby
preserving some of the gains made by minorities and women.

QUOTAS VERSUS GOALS

In another case, Charles Watkins et al. v. the Continental Can
Company and the Steelworkers Union, the judge ordered the reinstate-
ment of seven blacks according to a formula that would help maintain
their steady percentage in the work force. Out of a work force of
400, there were originally 50 blacks. In a drastic cutback, the company
retained only 149 whites and 2 blacks. The judge held that the blacks'
low seniority and the disparate effect the layoffs had on them stemmed
from the company's racially discriminatory hiring policies before 1965.

Appeal on the Watkins case is being watched very closely. Many
legal minds contend that it cannot be upheld. William J. Kilberg,
Solicitor of Labor at the Labor Department, said,

> It's one thing when people are laid off and there are
> other jobs in the community. But when you compound
> layoffs with the knowledge that there are no other jobs
> and you add to that a racial overtone, you have a seri-
> ous problem. It shouldn't be handled cavalierly by
> middle-class white lawyers who are in no danger of
> losing their jobs.[3]

Making a distinction between quotas and goals is very difficult.
Both are based on percentages, but quotas are fixed, whereas goals
are flexible objectives to aim for within a certain time limit.

REVERSE DISCRIMINATION

Are minorities getting priority consideration for the scarce
jobs? Are they being hired over the better qualified white males?

"Definitely," assert the whites, and the number of complaints charging reverse discrimination are rising rapidly. Some indication of the courts' stance was expected from the Defunis case, in which a white male said he was discriminated against by the University of Washington Law School because other candidates with lower test scores and lower grades were admitted whereas he was not. By the time the courts came around to hearing the case, the issue was a moot one, and they said as much. Defunis had been belatedly admitted and had already earned his law degree.

On charges of reverse discrimination, John Powell, former chairman of the Federal EEOC, said, "There might be cases where the expectations of the white majority might have to be modified." Robert D. Lilley, president of ATT, expanded on this viewpoint by saying, "What the white male is losing is not opportunity itself but the favored place he's held over the years in relation to that opportunity."[4]

It does seem that some effort is being made to hold onto some of the gains made by minorities over the past two decades. Civil Rights, Equal Employment Opportunity, Affirmative Action were not completely abandoned at the first sign of economic setback. However, the decision in the cases cited above were handed down toward the latter part of 1974, just when the recession was beginning to be felt. As the recession deepened and unemployment climbed, Affirmative Action plans came under stronger attacks. Selective hiring giving an edge to minorities was expressly forbidden, and, in the case of the appointment of a school principal in New York's school district No. 4, the job was taken away from a woman of Puerto Rican extraction and given to a white male because of the latter's higher qualifications.

ANTIDISCRIMINATION LEGISLATION

There is no question that antidiscrimination legislation has been a strong lever in raising the status of minorities, and the Chinese have benefited as much as other ethnics. These laws were strong levers and they were strong crutches. But as Bayard Rustin said, "An affirmative action program cannot find jobs for the unemployed or help the underemployed into better jobs if those jobs do not exist."[5] Racism and discrimination cannot be dealt with outside the context of the U.S. economy.

LACK OF SOCIAL CONTACTS

A main reason given by CCNY Chinese alumni as the determining factors of occupational mobility was lack of social contacts. In a speech presented before the Asian-American Conference at Princeton in 1974, Professor James Wei gave a bird's-eye view of where the Chinese engineers and scientists are today.

Pointing out that engineering is one of the major occupations of the Chinese male professional, he said that the diversity of jobs held by Chinese engineers today was simply beyond the imagination back in 1950. Chinese engineers tend to go into fields where the technology is changing rapidly, such as electronics, aeronautics, petroleum, and chemistry. These fields are challenging and demanding. Not too many Chinese engineers are in highway construction or the building of schools or public housing. Wei gave a very plausible reason for their absence:

> You need political connections for these projects. If
> I were to grade the past 25 years, I think I would give
> them a B in terms of prestige, in terms of numbers
> in the field, and in terms of income. But in positions
> of responsibility, they are conspicuously absent. At
> the management level, you are no longer dealing with
> concepts or things, you are dealing with people, and
> upward mobility is determined by socializing and so-
> cial amenities.

This is precisely the area to which the Chinese must pay attention. They are going to have to attack the bulwarks of private clubs and elitist organizations, and they are going to encounter resistance. As the Chinese reach beyond the middle level, the ascent becomes steeper, the competition keener, and the going rougher. All things being equal, racism may rear its ugly head and reinject itself at the higher levels just as it is being reduced at the lower ones.

Will efforts toward meeting the standards set by the dominant groups eliminate the boundaries between the races? The theory has been advanced that cleavages between the races can never be bridged. Once a group in the lower stratum attains the culture, the speech, the values, and the way of life of the upper stratum, the standards will be changed or revised and other impediments put in their path so that the lower stratum will never come up to the expectations of the upper. Hence one group will always feel superior to the other by some imposed criteria.

There is some validity to this line of reasoning, but it is a defeatist and pessimistic attitude. Without hope, there is no incentive. There are remedies or, at least, improvements to problems. Knowledge and understanding of the differences between peoples and the underlying causes of their friction can pave the way toward solutions.

This research and report on the occupational status and economic characteristics of the Chinese in the United States is a means to that end. By looking at their special circumstances and conditions, by finding out where they are at, by assessing the impact of their history in this country, by pointing out the divergence of their culture from American expectations, and by bringing out the inequities and disadvantages shouldered by the Chinese, we obtain the facts with which to come to workable solutions.

SUMMARY OF FINDINGS

1. The Chinese are hindered by stereotypes applied to the group. Some stereotypes of the Chinese are laudatory and some are contradictory, which goes to show how illogical they can be.

2. No matter how far back the roots of a Chinese-American go in this country, he is always looked upon as a foreigner, an alien, and a usurper of what rightfully belongs to "Americans."

3. Attitudes toward Chinese-Americans ride up and down from goodwill to hostility, depending upon the foreign relations of the United States and China.

4. It is hard to rid employers of the notion that all Chinese will work harder for less. It is also difficult to shed the laundryman-restaurant worker image.

5. Discrimination is no longer blatant. Some of it is rerouted; some is masked; and some is hung on institutional hooks. One must look more carefully to unmask the disguises.

6. Substantial progress has been effected in economic opportunities for the Chinese. Upward mobility is not generally experienced by the first generation. It is the second generation that reaps the harvest of the hardships and toil of the first.

7. With the country facing economic adversity, the gains of the minorities over the past two decades may be eroded. Questions of seniority, quotas versus affirmative action plans, and charges of reverse discrimination are being tested in the courts. In the first round, minorities seemed to have held onto some of their gains, but the final round may tell a different story. The economic health of the nation determines to a large extent the race relations.

8. Lack of social contacts is one of the main roadblocks to upward mobility for the Chinese.

9. Research and reports like this one provide the background and the facts for workable solutions to the problems of the Chinese-Americans.

RECOMMENDATIONS

Stereotypes and prejudices are shaped primarily by three dominant influences in a person's life—the family, the school, and the media.

Family influence is the strongest and the most lasting, but insofar
as the government is concerned, the family cannot be the starting point
in any attempt to dispel stereotypes and reduce prejudice because it is
difficult to reach into individual homes. The variables are too great
and the target too dispersed.

The Schools

That leaves the school and the media, both of which are highly
concentrated and centrally controlled. Choice of school curriculum,
textbooks, and educational materials are matters of board policies
or decisions made by a few school administrators. Over two-thirds
of the American population live in metropolitan areas where a few
school boards wield tremendous influence over the educational content
of our public schools. These people have the power to influence, for
better or worse, the attitudes, the thinking, and even the actions of
our future citizens. With compulsory education, all our children are
processed, for six hours a day, for ten to twelve years of their forma-
tive years, through the schools. This is the vital area in any attempt
to ameliorate the pervasive racism that afflicts our nation.

It is recommended that a special commission be appointed on the
national level to review the curriculum and the content of our educational matter for intentional ethnic slurs and stereotyping, not just
for Chinese-Americans, but for all ethnic groups. The commission
would make recommendations to the secretary of health, education
and welfare for the introduction of a more balanced curriculum and
for a more diverse study of the peoples and areas of the world. Currently, the course of study in our schools is predominantly European-
centered, but our dealings with the world are not. Today's newspaper
headlines are focused more on Asia, Africa, the Middle East, and
Latin America than on Europe. The United States handicaps itself
by remaining uninformed about these vast continents and their peoples.
For our own sake and for the sake of the future course of American
history, American children must be exposed to and led to appreciate
the differences in the varied races, cultures, and languages. If their
entire education is lacking in any exposure to these places, people,
and things, later contact will only render them suspicious and super-
cilious toward these strangers. The schools, therefore, are the ap-
propriate place and the most powerful force toward effecting any modi-
fication of stereotypes and prejudice.

The Media

At prime time on any given day, 50 million people may be sitting
in front of their television sets. In 1969, 95 percent of the households

reported that they had a television set, and a third of these reported that they had two sets or more. Radios are even more commonplace, being found not only in the home but in almost every automobile on the street. Only three television networks and seven radio networks control the airwaves. With such awesome power concentrated in a few hands, television and radio can shape the minds of the American people. The medium of print is no less influential in whatever form: books, periodicals, newspapers, advertisements, and the comics. Now can we omit the movies and records. The media already stand indicted for a host of past sins. The stamp of Fu Manchu, the Dragon Lady, Chop-Chop, the pidgin-English-speaking domestic are still with us.

Can we expect some reform in the future? At the Civil Rights Commission Hearings in New York City in July 1974, representatives from the media all admitted that their consciousness was raised by the testimony presented before the panel. Television and radio stations, advertisement agencies, and representatives from a number of the major newspapers in New York testified that they had review boards to screen for offensive ethnic slurs or material of questionable taste. Yet, when confronted with examples of offensive characterization or commercials, most of the representatives confessed that they had not thought of these commercials as such, which supports the contention that non-Asians are not tuned in to Asian sensitivity.

A recommendation to the media, therefore, is to open their ranks to Asian writers, reporters, editors, producers, cameramen, performers, and actors. In 1974, a landmark decision was handed down against the Repertory Theatre of Lincoln Center in New York, finding it guilty of discrimination because "it systematically failed or refused to give equal opportunity to Asian-American actors, particularly as evidenced by the regular awarding of Oriental parts to non-Oriental actors."

Those Chinese-Americans who have entered the media have done great credit to themselves. Connie Chung, who has international exposure on WCBS-TV, is a prime example. In 1971, she was named Outstanding Young Woman of America, and the American Association of University Women awarded her the Metro Area Mass Media citation for outstanding excellence in the field of news reporting. However, the Connie Chungs are rare.

The last recommendation is directed at the Chinese themselves. They have the privilege, the duty, and the obligation to protect their interests and their image from false or offensive representation. That is why organizations such as the Chinese for Affirmative Action in San Francisco are to be commended for their efforts. This organization works actively for the eradication of stereotypes and the expansion of employment opportunities for Asians. Join such organizations or lend them your support. If you cannot be involved directly, contribute to their operating expenses. Inform yourselves of the levers of control in the American system. For example, every three years the radio and television stations come up for review of station performance in the renewal of their licenses. Leverage can be exerted at this time, if not sooner, for some accountability by the stations. "Eternal vigilance is the price of liberty," is a statement attributed to Thomas Jefferson. If the white forefathers had to pay that price in the founding of this nation, it is no less true now in its preservation.

NOTES

1. Bayard Rustin, "Affirmative Action in an Economy of Scarcity," New York Teacher, November 3, 1974.
2. Marilyn Bender, "Job Discrimination 10 Years After the Ban," New York Times, November 10, 1974.
3. Ibid.
4. Quoted in ibid.
5. Rustin, op. cit.

CHAPTER 15

The purpose of this study and research was fourfold:

1. To generate a basic statistical body of data from reliable sources about the Chinese in the United States;
2. To document Chinese-American manpower and employment characteristics;
3. To point out areas of cultural difference and divergence that affect the attitude, behavior, and performance of the Chinese in this country in their quest for a meaningful livelihood;
4. To make concrete suggestions for expanding, both vertically and horizontally, the occupational horizon of the Chinese-Americans.

BASIC STATISTICAL BODY OF DATA

The data came primarily from the 1970 census. Its limitations already have been stated, but the data did reflect a wide sample at a certain time. Since there is no other comparable data bank as comprehensive as the 1970 census, it was used primarily as a jumping-off place. It provided some facts where none existed before, and in years to come the data will be part of the history of the Chinese in the United States.

In a desire to take every advantage of the special opportunity afforded under the Manpower Administration grant to undertake a special tabulation, an attempt was made to extract only as much information as could be reasonably handled without straying too far from the main topic of occupation and employment. Although some of the data may not have been used for this volume, the statistics were tabulated nevertheless.

Examples of this are three separate monographs put out under the imprimatur of the Asian Studies Department at City College of New York on ethnic population by census tracts for 11 major SMSAs. These tables provide a detailed breakdown of minority populations in the major urban centers of the United States. It is hoped that demographers, social scientists, school boards, and government agencies will find these tabulations useful for their particular purposes. Copies were made available to the Manpower Administration, the Census Bureau, and research libraries.

The Census Bureau tabulated and published some data on Chinese-Americans for only five states. I was able to obtain comparable data for the remaining 45 states. When the tabulations are published, Chinese in all 50 states may obtain figures pertaining to their own area.

Even in the tables used and reproduced in this report, an attempt was made to be more inclusive and detailed rather than abbreviated or concise. This tends to make the tables cumbersome and difficult to read, but, for the sake of those who need a detailed breakdown, the information will be available. It is possible to add up the parts to arrive at the whole, but the process is not reversible.

There are rich diggings in the statistical information from the tables in this report for other researchers, students, academicians, social scientists, urban planners, community workers, and others. The findings and analyses here only grazed the surface. Perhaps others will find different interpretations from the same figures. Maybe the figures will spark other ideas that can be pursued further.

The 1970 census was not the only statistical source utilized. State and municipal government publications were consulted wherever and whenever possible, and these yielded unexpected findings for our purposes. Once uncovered as sources of information, they can be tapped again and again.

To relate governmental statistics to what is actually happening in the communities takes a thorough familiarity with the Chinese communities and their leaders in a number of cities spanning the American continent. Through the medium of this report, I have tried to express some of the thoughts, the anxieties, and the suggestions of many working in the field who are concerned and who are ethnically conscious about their place in the larger American scheme. These feelings were garnered through interviews, through correspondence, or expressed at conferences. I hope that I have accurately conveyed these thoughts.

One area that was not touched upon at all was housing. This was covered by a separate census and is somewhat removed from occupation and employment. Since time was limited, no attempt was made to deal with this subject, but it deserves priority attention as an area of major concern.

SUMMARY OF FINDINGS

Occupation is livelihood that translates into income, food, and survival. Since it is a basic determinant of our daily existence—how we live, our social status, and how we spend the major portion of our waking hours—it is the most logical area with which to begin any study of the Chinese in the United States. The thrust of this report is aimed at the economic characteristics and occupational status of the Chinese with a view toward finding out where and how they stand and to make suggestions for improvement where necessary and feasible.

At the end of every chapter in this book can be found a listing of the findings that had a bearing on employment aspects of the Chinese. To recapitulate briefly, the more significant factors are set down below:

1. The history of the Chinese in the United States goes back for more than 100 years, but the Chinese have perpetually remained an ' immigrant group due to the past exclusionary policies of this country.

2. Immigration has increased spectacularly since 1965, when the immigration laws were revised. The new law favors the professional and skilled. Consequently, there has been a shift in the type of Chinese immigrants coming in. The new immigrants are heading eastward—especially to New York City.

3. The 1970 census data do not reflect from one-fifth to one-fourth of the Chinese who have entered the country since that time. This vast increase in immigrants has once again tilted the Chinese population in this country toward a foreign-born one. The foreign-born are handicapped by the tremendous adjustment they have to make, by the language barrier, and by their lack of citizenship.

4. The Chinese population is concentrated along three vertical strips in the United States: the East and West Coasts and the Hawaiian Islands. An impressive 97 percent of the Chinese are found in large urban cities, primarily New York, San Francisco, Honolulu, and Los Angeles.

5. The new immigrants need the security of Chinatowns to help them in their transition. In those cities with large immigrant populations, the Chinatowns are expanding and the problems are more acute. These are the areas of greatest need.

6. As presently constituted, the Chinese population is one of extremes with concentrations at opposite ends of the educational and occupational poles. They tend to be either college graduates or illiterates, and they are in the professions or service work.

7. The Chinese labor force in 1970 was but 190,000.

8. A very narrow range of jobs, such as restaurant work, engineering, and college teaching, are the most prevalent occupations

for Chinese males. A phenomenal increase toward the professions is especially evident among the younger generation Chinese-Americans.

9. One-third of the Chinese females have some college education, but they are concentrated in two areas of employment—garment work and clerical work. The proportion of Chinese females in the labor force is greater than that for black or white females. The Chinese female is pitifully underemployed and underpaid compared to either her white or black sisters.

10. The effect of employment on the Chinese-American females has been postponement of marriage and postponement of children, resulting in a birthrate below replacement level.

11. Close to one out of five Chinese in the labor force is in government service. In government, the Chinese are primarily professionals or technicians, and they have attained the middle ranks. In state and local government, they are almost totally absent from such agencies as the sanitation, fire, or police departments.

12. In the construction industry, where the unions control the hiring and firing, the Chinese are conspicuously absent. The union stronghold has been assaulted but not penetrated as yet.

13. The Chinese family median income is higher than the national average, but the figures in themselves are deceptive. The higher income may be the result of more people in the family working, having more than one job, working longer hours or a longer work week. The substantially lower personal income figures reveal a more accurate measure. Furthermore, the Chinese concept of income differs from the American, so dollars and cents may not represent a true income picture.

14. In Hawaii, where the Chinese have experienced less discrimination, the median family income is close to $6,000 higher than that of the Chinese in New York. Substantial differences such as these reveal where the troubled areas are.

15. The unemployment rate for the Chinese labor force is comparatively low. One explanation may be that the Chinese would rather work at jobs beneath their ability and qualifications than be unemployed. Hence, underemployment is fairly widespread.

16. A disquieting factor seems to be the erratic work year; the Chinese are not employed the year round.

17. Whereas the Chinese used to compensate for their disadvantaged position in the labor market by hard work, there is a decided shift in this attitude among the younger generations growing up in the United States.

18. Self-employment or small business enterprises, once the predominant mode of employment for the Chinese, has declined precipitiously. In 1970, the ratio of salaried and wage workers to the self-employed was 8:1.

19. The traditional family-operated enterprises, such as laundries, gift shops, grocery stores, and restaurants, are losing ground to occupations in the professions and incorporated businesses.

20. The Chinese have the temperament and background for successful entrepreneurship. At the same time, they have access to limited capital through their habit of thrift and their community credit facilities.

CULTURAL ANCHORS AND DIFFERENCES

More than for most other ethnic groups in the United States, the employment pattern of the Chinese is a product of their culture. Their cuisine created for them a field of employment in restaurants and food service that has lasted for more than a hundred years. Their esteem for the scholar and for learning prodded them on to high educational attainment, even when college degrees brought no prospect of occupational rewards. The status of a government official was prestigious enough to lure one-fifth of the Chinese-American labor force into government. Kinship bonds were so strong that it enabled the Chinese to survive in this country against exceedingly difficult odds. Unemployment never meant being cold and hungry and out on the streets as long as the doors of the family association headquarters were open. Yet, what the Chinese considered virtues, such as humility and willingness to accommodate, have worked against their interest in upward mobility.

The instances of culturally based aspects of employment are too numerous to repeat. Why has the culture maintained such a hold on the Chinese when other groups gave up the ways of the motherland soon after they arrived in this country? The main reasons are:

1. American immigration laws compelled the Chinese to remain a first-generation immigrant people with no roots in the United States.

2. Rejected by the larger society, the Chinese turned inward and perpetuated their own ways.

3. The Chinese culture was strong enough to compete effectively against Americanization.

4. The Chinese are physically distinct and easily identifiable as different from the majority white stock in the United States.

Only within recent years have many of the discriminatory laws against the Chinese been repealed, thereby modifying some of the effects of the above factors. For the first time, we now have a substantial native-born college-age group in the population. The Chinese

need no longer live in constant fear of the immigration inspectors.
Civil Rights legislation has pierced some of the barriers erected
against minority groups in the past. As evidenced by the statistics in
this report based upon the 1970 census, the Chinese have moved forward dramatically. As a result, the hold of Chinese culture is also
loosening.

Many Chinese are now experiencing a two-way tug, an identity
crisis. Are they Americans or are they Chinese? Are they to give
up their Chinese ways and values completely if such are inoperative
in the competitive American society? Are they to discard their
language and turn their backs on the teachings of their parents and
ancestors? How can they reconcile the conflict when the values are
diametrically opposite?

Even when they become totally American in speech, thought,
and action, what happens when they are still looked upon as foreign
or alien because their physical features are different? What effect
do these new factors have on Chinese-Americans in relation to their
occupational choices and the opportunities open to them?

What chances are there that the gains so recently won by the
Chinese will continue on an upward course or be consolidated? There
is the ever-present possibility that under adverse economic conditions
there may be a backslide and a reversion to racial intolerance and
prejudice.

SUMMARY OF RECOMMENDATIONS

Today, we are increasingly accepting the fact that the power of
government can be exerted for desirable social change or for the
remediation of society's ills. If any doubt lingers that government
policy can totally alter and shape the course of our lives, we have only
to look back at how American immigration laws dominated and shaped
the lives of the Chinese in the United States for nearly a century. Government decreed whether the immigrant population was to be male or
female, young or old, rich or poor, skilled or otherwise, educated or
illiterate, cultured or uncouth. Indirectly, it shaped the family structure and the personalities of the Chinese, and the heavy hand of the
laws could be felt in every sphere of activity.

At the outset of this study, it was mentioned that the 1970s will
be the decade of redress following a decade of protest. It is earnestly
hoped that the findings from this study can be used as guideposts to
show the way toward the prospect of better hopes and a better life for
a long-suffering people.

If the record of the Chinese in the United States appears bright
from this study, then it is all to their credit that they were able to sur-

mount insuperable barriers and handicaps, not merely to survive, but to try to forge ahead. If they have accomplished, let it be proof that they constitute a valuable human resource that will add to, not detract from, the national store. But those encountering difficulty in making the transition as a result of their uprooting deserve assistance to help them in their resettlement; for the more rapid their adjustment, the more quickly they will become useful members of society.

Therefore, to sum up briefly the main recommendations, not only to the government but also to all Americans and to the Chinese-Americans themselves:

1. Keep in mind that the people whose needs are greatest were not counted in the 1970 census. Additional and on-going studies need to be undertaken to bring the findings up to date.

2. Provide the Chinese with the maximum opportunity to learn the English language.

3. Give the Chinese the same considerations accorded other minorities under the special provisions of the Civil Rights Acts, the Equal Employment Opportunity Act, Affirmative Action Plans, Contract Compliance, and so on. All too often the Chinese are not considered minorities and are excluded from the provisions and benefits of minority programs.

4. Pass the "Gateway Bill" sponsored by Congresswoman Patsy Mink.

5. Reconsider all laws that purposely or inadvertently shut out large segments of the Chinese work force, either citizenship requirements or licensing stipulations that have no bearing on the ability to perform the job.

6. Encourage dispersion of the Chinese away from the ghettos and large urban centers like New York and San Francisco. Employers in other areas may well consider the desirability and feasibility of hiring Chinese personnel.

7. Give special consideration to the highly disadvantaged position of the Chinese female, who is either highly educated or illiterate but poorly paid, and who is in special need of facilities, such as day-care centers, and special consideration, such as part-time work.

8. Provide opportunities for Chinese females to break out of the molds of garment worker and clerical worker.

9. Expand the occupational horizon of Chinese professionals, who are too highly concentrated in the fields of teaching and engineering.

10. Review obstacles, such as subjective oral examinations or personality tests, that effectively bar the Chinese from upward mobility into the executive ranks or managerial positions.

11. Increase government and private commitment to more manpower retraining and job referral service to the Chinese. Currently,
government-funded programs at any level and in any area for the
Chinese have been minimal and token, at best.

12. Develop alternatives to hiring and firing in the construction
industry if the unions persist in discriminating against minorities.

13. Make more effective use of the federal Office of Minority
Business Enterprise to encourage a backward look at the advantages
of self-employment that has stood the Chinese in good stead over the
years.

14. Draw upon the reservoir of Chinese-Americans who are familiar with both China and the United States to bridge the chasm that
has separated the nations for a quarter of a century. Use their talents
also as middlemen to expand commerce and trade.

15. Restore the facts of the true role and the contributions of
the early Chinese to the history and development of this country. It
is the task of educators in ethnic studies courses, of publishers of
history books, and of the media to correct the mistaken and stereotyped images generally held about the Chinese.

16. Learn to accept the Chinese-American and other national
groups with identifiable physical differences as people who have legitimate rights in this country to earn a livelihood and to enjoy equal
privileges and protection under the law.

17. Seek to identify and groom leaders or potential leaders in
the communities. Support further research on the Chinese, so the
true facts will be available to enable the government and the leaders
to make rational and constructive decisions.

18. Do not disparage the cultural traits or differences of the
Chinese. The American way is not always the best, and the Chinese
way is not always to be discarded. This point is especially directed
at those Chinese-Americans who go through a period of self-hatred in
their quest to belong and get ahead in American society.

For the Chinese specifically:

19. The best employment insurance for the Chinese is to create
a work force or a bank of skills and talents that is not easily replace-
able. When accomplished individually, however, as the Chinese have
been wont to do in the past, it never can be an effective and collective
force.

20. Organize and develop a national organization, comparable
to the NAACP or Anti-Defamation League or Japanese-American Citizen's League, that will work for the welfare of the Chinese, serve as
a watchdog to guard their interests, and bring strength and solidarity
to the group.

21. Join with other Asian groups that share similar experiences and problems and broaden this base with other minority groups to form a coalition for more effective leverage.

22. Become more politicized and tuned in to what is happening on the local and national scene. A democratic form of government demands citizen involvement and participation. If involvement is not part of the Chinese heritage, then special civics classes or literature should be provided to help the Chinese bridge this cultural chasm.

These suggestions or recommendations have not been confined solely to what the government can do to help a minority or minorities during this period of tremendous upheaval brought on by the upsurge in immigration and by a heightened ethnic consciousness. But the government has the resources and mechanism by which it can facilitate an easier adjustment for the group. If it has extended such assistance to other immigrant groups and minorities, then surely the Chinese are no less deserving. It is hoped that this study is but the first link in further government attention to Chinese-Americans.

Hopefully, also, some of these findings will enable the Chinese people to better understand themselves and to act upon any pertinent data from this research to expand their employment opportunities. To all Americans, whether black, white, brown, red, or yellow, let us be mindful that we are a nation of immigrants. We rose to our position as leader of the world of nations through the invigorating mixture of diverse cultures and peoples. It is the constant infusion of new blood that is this country's source of greatness and wealth.

TABLE A.1

Chinese Population in the United States, by Decades, 1860–1970

Decade	Number
1860	34,933
1870	63,199
1880	105,465
1890	107,488
1900	89,863
1910	71,531
1920	61,639
1930	74,954
1940	77,504
1950	117,629
1960	237,292
1970	435,062

Source: U.S. Department of Commerce, Bureau of the Census, Census of Population, 1860–1970.

TABLE A.2

Age Distribution of the Chinese in the United States for Selected SMSAs, by Sex, 1970
(in percent)

Age Group	Boston	Chicago	Honolulu	Los Angeles-Long Beach	New York	Sacramento	San Francisco-Oakland	San Jose	Seattle-Everett	Washington, D.C.-Maryland-Virginia
Total number male	6,585	6,449	24,533	21,840	41,486	5,307	45,393	4,182	4,030	3,910
Under 5	8.1	9.4	7.8	9.2	7.5	6.5	7.1	8.8	7.0	8.1
5-14	17.5	16.3	20.9	18.6	17.3	21.5	18.5	19.7	19.8	17.3
15-19	10.6	9.4	10.1	9.3	9.9	14.0	10.9	8.2	10.5	8.7
20-24	11.6	9.2	7.7	10.0	8.2	9.4	9.6	15.1	9.7	6.1
25-29	8.6	8.4	5.8	7.5	5.2	4.0	5.2	7.6	6.7	7.1
30-44	20.0	24.1	18.0	24.5	21.4	19.8	19.9	26.3	21.3	23.1
45-64	17.0	16.9	21.8	16.4	21.9	17.9	20.8	12.6	17.8	22.3
65 and over	6.6	6.2	7.9	4.5	8.6	6.8	8.1	1.7	7.2	7.2
Total number female	5,572	5,546	24,364	19,660	35,613	5,150	43,009	3,837	3,671	3,948
Under 5	9.1	9.3	7.1	8.2	8.4	8.3	6.9	10.8	9.3	9.3
5-14	19.8	18.9	20.7	19.1	18.6	20.2	18.2	20.1	22.1	20.4
15-19	11.4	10.8	9.6	9.6	9.8	13.8	11.0	8.6	10.4	7.2
20-24	11.7	11.1	8.8	12.0	10.7	11.0	11.1	14.1	10.0	9.5
25-29	8.8	9.5	5.4	9.0	7.5	5.7	5.6	11.7	8.7	10.4
30-44	19.2	22.8	18.7	23.7	22.3	20.8	22.0	20.3	19.8	23.5
45-64	15.1	12.8	21.7	13.7	17.4	14.5	18.1	11.5	14.4	14.6
65 and over	4.9	4.8	7.9	4.7	5.3	5.6	7.0	2.9	5.3	5.2

Source: U.S. Department of Commerce, Bureau of the Census, Subject Report, PC(2)1G (1970), Table 27.

TABLE A.3

Selected Industry of the Chinese in the United States, by Sex and Percent of Total, 1970

Selected Industry	Male	Female	Total	Percent of Total
Total, 16 years and over	113,929	67,261	181,190	100.0
Agriculture, forestries, fisheries	1,069	393	1,462	0.8
Mining	277	65	342	0.1
Construction	3,753	388	4,141	2.2
Manufacturing	16,038	15,731	31,769	17.5
Durable goods	9,907	1,989	11,896	6.5
Metal industries	663	166	829	0.4
Machinery, excluding electrical	1,526	236	1,762	0.9
Electrical machinery, equipment, and supplies	2,259	369	2,628	1.4
Transportation equipment	2,944	227	3,171	1.7
Nondurable goods	6,075	13,519	19,594	10.8
Food and kindred products	1,039	878	1,917	1.0
Canning and preservation of fruit, vegetables, and seafood	246	564	810	0.4
Textile mill products	170	377	547	0.3
Yarn, thread, and fabric mills	101	276	377	0.2
Apparel and other fabric and textile products	952	10,176	11,128	6.1
Printing, publishing, and allied industries	1,370	594	1,964	1.0
Chemical and allied products	1,275	427	1,702	0.9
Transportation, communication, and other public utilities	5,367	2,155	7,522	4.1
Transportation	2,889	1,195	4,084	2.2
Water transportation	693	79	772	0.4
Air transportation	804	611	1,415	0.7
Communications	852	581	1,433	0.7
Telephones (wire and radio)	643	502	1,145	0.6
Utilities and sanitary services	713	182	895	0.4
Wholesale and retail trade				
Wholesale trade	3,451	1,648	5,099	2.8
Food and related products	748	422	1,170	0.6
Retail trade	38,973	14,848	53,821	29.7
General merchandise stores	1,142	2,460	3,602	1.9
Food stores	7,668	2,728	10,396	5.7
Grocery stores	6,581	2,359	8,940	4.9
Gasoline service station	961	21	982	0.5
Apparel and accessories stores, excluding shoe stores	343	546	889	0.4
Eating and drinking places	24,436	6,356	30,792	16.9
Drug stores	655	334	989	0.5

(continued)

TABLE A.3 (continued)

Selected Industry	Male	Female	Total	Percent of Total
Finance, insurance, and real estate	4,185	4,685	8,870	4.8
Banking	1,266	2,137	3,403	1.8
Security, commodity brokerage, and investment companies	842	340	1,182	0.6
Insurance	934	1,556	2,490	1.3
Real estate, including real estate insurance law offices	765	226	991	0.5
Business and repair services	3,260	1,177	4,437	2.4
Business services	1,829	924	2,753	1.5
Commercial research, development and testing laboratories	507	0	507	0.2
Computer programming services	272	141	413	0.2
Repair services	976	140	1,116	0.6
Personal services	7,350	4,596	11,946	6.5
Private households	366	714	1,080	0.5
Hotels and motels	1,667	732	2,390	1.3
Laundering, cleaning, and other garment services	4,582	1,817	6,399	3.5
Beauty shops	27	397	424	0.2
Entertainment and recreation services	765	489	1,254	0.6
Professional and related services	21,449	17,482	38,931	21.4
Health services	4,624	4,608	9,232	5.0
Offices of physicians	804	411	1,215	0.6
Offices of dentists	381	245	626	0.3
Hospitals	2,791	3,222	6,013	3.3
Legal services	258	359	617	0.3
Educational services	10,811	9,083	19,894	10.9
Elementary and secondary schools	1,629	3,577	5,206	2.8
Colleges and universities	8,871	4,746	13,617	7.5
Libraries	183	433	616	0.3
Welfare services	290	417	707	0.3
Nonprofit membership organizations	341	415	756	0.4
Engineering and architectural services	2,565	310	2,875	1.5
Accounting, auditing, and bookkeeping services	485	386	871	0.4
Public administration	7,992	3,601	11,593	6.3
Postal services	1,607	355	1,962	1.0
Federal public administration	3,780	2,034	5,814	3.2
State public administration	919	729	1,648	0.9
Local public administration	1,171	373	1,544	0.8

Source: U.S. Department of Commerce, Bureau of the Census, Subject Report, PC(2)7C (1970).

234

ARTICLES

Bender, Marilyn. "Job Discrimination 10 Years after the Ban."
New York Times, November 10, 1974.

Benzin, Peter. "Who Gets Laid Off First?: Seniority vs. Minorities."
Long Island Press, November 24, 1974.

Berger, Peter L. "A Lot of Beautiful People. No One Left to Do
the Chores." U.S. News & World Report, December 4, 1972,
p. 564.

Chang, Shu Yuan. "China or Taiwan: The Political Crisis of the
Chinese Intellectual." Amerasia Journal 2 (Fall 1973): 47-81.

"From China with Skill." Commerce Today, April 1, 1974.

Hsu, Francis L. K. "Rugged Individualism Reconsidered." Colorado
Quarterly, vol. 9, no. 2 (Autumn 1960).

Oh, Tai K. "New Estimate of the Student Brain Drain from Asia."
International Migration Review 7 (1972): 449-56.

"Orientals Find Bias Is Down Sharply in U.S." New York Times,
December 13, 1970.

Rustin, Bayard. "Affirmative Action in an Economy of Scarcity."
New York Teacher, November 3, 1974.

Shabecoff, Philip. "HEW Study Finds Job Discontent Is Hurting Nation." New York Times, December 22, 1972.

Smothers, Ronald. "Polarization over Hiring Minorities in Building Trade." New York Times, March 17, 1975.

Sneeling, Robert O. "Are There Jobs Enough for All of Us?" U.S. News & World Report, October 30, 1972.

Stern, Michael. "Job Decline Threatens City's Economy." New York Times, July 21, 1974.

Yuan, D. Y. "Chinatown and Beyond: The Chinese Population in Metropolitan New York." Phylon 27, no. 4: 321-32.

BOOKS

Allport, Gordon W. The Nature of Prejudice. Reading, Mass.: Addison-Wesley, 1954.

Alterman, Hyman. Counting People: The Census in History. New York: Harcourt & Brace, 1969.

Bogue, Donald J. Principles of Demography. New York: John Wiley, 1968.

Chinn, Thomas, ed. A History of the Chinese in California: A Syllabus. San Francisco: Chinese Historical Society of America, 1969.

Daniel, Roger, and Harry Kitano. American Racism: Exploration of the Nature of Prejudice. Englewood Cliffs, N.J.: Prentice-Hall, 1970.

Ford, Thomas R., and Gordon F. DeJong, eds. Social Demography. Englewood Cliffs, N.J.: Prentice-Hall, 1970.

Ginzberg, Eli. Middle Class Negro in the White Man's World. New York: Columbia University Press, 1967.

Goodwin, Leonard. Do the Poor Want to Work? Washington, D.C.: Brookings Institution, 1972.

Hansen, Gladys C. The Chinese in California: A Brief Bibliographic
    History. Portland, Ore.: Richard Abel, 1970.

Hiestand, Dale. Discrimination in Employment. Ann Arbor, Mich.:
    The Institute of Labor and Industrial Relations, University of
    Michigan, Wayne State University, and National Manpower Pol-
    icy Task Force, 1970.

Hsu, Francis L. K. Americans and Chinese—Two Ways of Life.
    New York: Henry Schuman, 1953.

_____. The Challenge of the American Dream: The Chinese in Amer-
    ica. Belmont, Calif.: Wadsworth, 1971.

Jones, Edward H. Blacks in Business. New York: Grosset and Dun-
    lap, 1971.

Light, Ivan H. Ethnic Enterprise in America. Los Angeles and
    Berkeley: University of California Press, 1972.

Lin, Yutang. Chinatown Family. New York: John Day, 1948.

Lind, Andrew. Hawaii's People. Honolulu: University Press of
    Hawaii, 1955.

Loewen, James W. The Mississippi Chinese: Between Black and
    White. Cambridge, Mass.: Harvard University Press, 1971.

Lowenstein, Edith. The Alien and the Immigration Law. New York:
    Common Council for American Unity, 1957.

Lyman, Stanford. Chinese Americans. New York: Random House,
    1972.

Miller, Stuart Creighton. The Unwelcome Immigrant: The American
    Image of the Chinese, 1785-1882. Los Angeles and Berkeley:
    University of California Press, 1969.

Nee, Victor, and Brett de Bary Nee. Longtime Californ': A Documen-
    tary Study of an American Chinatown. New York: Random
    House, 1972.

Norgren, Paul H., and Samuel E. Hill. Toward Fair Employment.
    New York: Columbia University Press, 1964.

Northrup, Herbert, and Richard L. Rowan, et al. Negro Employment in Basic Industry: A Study of Racial Employment Policies in Six Industries. Philadelphia: Industrial Research Unit, Wharton School of Finance and Commerce, University of Pennsylvania Press, 1970.

Peterson, William. Population. 2nd ed. New York: Macmillan Co., 1969.

Puryear, Alvin, and Charles A. West. Black Enterprise, Inc.: Case Studies of a New Experiment in Black Business Development. New York: Anchor Press/Doubleday, 1973.

Reich, Charles A. The Greening of America. New York: Random House, 1971.

Saxton, Alexander. The Indispensable Enemy: Labor and the Anti-Chinese Movement in California. Los Angeles and Berkeley: University of California Press, 1971.

Smuts, Robert. Women and Work in America. New York: Schocken Books, 1971.

Sovern, Michael. Legal Restraints: On Racial Discrimination in Employment. New York: Twentieth Century Fund, 1966.

Spengler, Joseph J., and Otis Dudley. Demographic Analysis: Selected Readings. Glencoe, Ill.: Free Press, 1956.

Spero, Sterling D., and Abram L. Harris. The Black Worker: The Negro and the Labor Movement. Port Washington, N.Y.: Kennikat Press, 1966, reissue; originally published by Columbia University Press, 1931.

Sung, Betty Lee. Mountain of Gold. New York: Macmillan Co., 1967; reissued as Story of the Chinese in America. New York: Collier Books, 1971.

Terkel, Studs. Working. New York: Pantheon, 1974.

Viewpoints, Red and Yellow, Black and Brown. Minneapolis: Winston Press, 1972.

Waley, Arthur. Three Ways of Thought in Ancient China. Garden City, N.Y.: Doubleday, 1939.

Weiss, Melford S. Valley City: A Chinese Community in America.
Cambridge, Mass.: Schenkman, 1974.

Wolkinson, B. W. Blacks, Unions and the EEOC. Lexington, Mass.:
D. C. Heath, 1973.

Wong, Jade Snow. Fifth Chinese Daughter. New York: Harper Bros.,
1950.

Wu, Cheng-Tsu, ed. "Chink!". New York: World Publishing, 1972.

Yankelovich, Daniel. The Changing Values on Campus. New York:
Washington Square Press, 1972.

_____. The New Morality: A Profile of American Youth in the 70s.
New York: McGraw-Hill Co., 1974.

GOVERNMENT DOCUMENTS

President's Advisory Council on Minority Business Enterprises.
Minority Enterprise and Expanded Ownership Blueprint for the
'70s. June 1971.

United Nations. Department of Economic and Social Affairs. Methods
of Analyzing Census Data on Economic Activities of the Population. Population Studies, no. 43. 1968.

U.S. Civil Rights Commission. The Federal Civil Rights Enforcement Effort—A Reassessment. January 1973.

_____. Hearings and Testimony Presented Before Commission in
New York City. July 12-13, 1974.

U.S. Civil Service Commission. Minority Group Employment in the
Federal Government. 1969-72.

U.S. Department of Commerce. Bureau of the Census. Japanese,
Chinese and Filipinos in the United States. Census of Population, PC(2)1G. 1970.

_____. Marital Status. Census of Population, PC(2)4C. 1970.

_____. The Methods and Materials of Demography. Vols 1 and 2.
1971.

_____. Minority-Owned Businesses: 1969.

_____. Negro Population. Census of Population, PC(2)1B. 1970.

_____. 1970 Census Users' Guide. Pts. 1 and 2. October 1970.

_____. Public Use Samples of Basic Records from the 1970 Census. April 1972.

_____. Social and Economic Status of the Black Population in the United States, 1971. Special Studies, P-23, no. 42.

_____. United States Census of Population, 1960: Non-White Population by Race.

U.S. Department of Health, Education and Welfare. Higher Education Division. Office for Civil Rights. Availability Data, Minorities and Women. June 1973.

_____. Higher Education Division. Office of Special Concerns. A Study of Selected Socio-Economic Characteristics of Ethnic Minorities Based on the 1970 Census. Vol. II: Asian Americans, HEW no. US 75121. Arlington, Va.: Prepared by Urban Associates, July 1974.

_____. Public Health Service. Vital Statistics of the United States. Washington, D.C.: 1946-69.

U.S. Department of Justice, Immigration and Naturalization Service, Annual Reports. 1961-73.

U.S. Department of Labor. Bureau of Labor Statistics. The Economics of Working and Living in New York City. Report no. 29. July 1972.

_____. New York City in Transition: Population, Jobs, Prices and Pay in a Decade of Change. Report no. 34. July 1973.

_____. Occupational Handbook. 1973.

_____. Social, Economic and Labor Force Characteristics of Residents in New York City's Low Income Areas. Report no. 30. September 1972.

U.S. Equal Employment Opportunity Commission. Affirmative Action and Equal Employment: A Guidebook for Employers. Vol. 2. January 1974.

_____. Employment Profiles of Minorities and Women in the SMSAs of 17 Large Cities, 1971. Report no. 41.

_____. Seventh Annual Report, 1972.

U.S. Manpower Administration. Breakthrough for Disadvantaged Youth. 1969.

_____. Immigrants and the American Labor Market. Research Monograph no. 31. 1974.

U.S. Office of Management and Budget. Social Indicators. 1973.

U.S. Office of Minority Business Enterprise. Business Development Program. 1975.

_____. Federal Programs Assisting Minority Enterprise. 1971.

_____. Minority Business Opportunity Committee Handbook. 1974.

_____. Progress of the Minority Business Enterprise Program. 1973.

STATE AND LOCAL GOVERNMENT REPORTS

Boston

Action for Boston Community Development Inc. Planning and Evaluation Department. The Chinese in Boston, 1970.

Harvard Urban Field Service and Action for Boston Community Development. Chinatown Planning Project, 1971.

New York

New York City. Commission on Human Rights. The Employment of Minorities, Women and the Handicapped in City Government. Report of a 1971 Survey. 1971.

New York City. Human Resources Administration. Manpower and Career Development Agency. Chinatown Manpower Project. 1973.

_____. Ethnicity and Poverty in New York City in the Seventies. July 1974.

New York State. Department of Civil Service. Occupations, Job Status and Ethnic Characteristics of Employers in New York State Agencies. 5th Annual Report. 1971.

New York State. Department of Labor. Minority Manpower Statistics with Special Reference to Their Application in Affirmative Action Compliance Programs, 1971.

California

Manpower Planning Council, City and County of San Francisco. Comprehensive Manpower Plan. May 1973.

San Francisco. Department of City Planning. Chinatown 1970 Census: Population and Housing Summary and Analysis. August 1972.

_____. Chinatown 701 Study Staff Report. 1972.

San Francisco Human Rights Commission. Racial and Ethnic Employment Pattern Survey: City and County of San Francisco Employees. December 1971.

State of California. Department of Industrial Relations. Division of Fair Employment Practices. Californians of Japanese, Chinese, and Filipino Ancestry. June 1965.

State of California. Fair Employment Practices Commission. Chinese in San Francisco, 1970.

State of California. Human Resources Development. Area Manpower Review: San Francisco–Oakland SMSA, Annual Outlook and Planning. April 1973.

OTHER DOCUMENTS AND REPORTS

"Asian-America." Bulletin of Concerned Asian Scholars, vol. 4, no. 3 (Fall 1972).

"Asian Women." University of California at Berkeley, 1971.

"Asians in America: A Bibliography of Master's Theses and Doctoral Dissertations." Asian American Research Project, University of California at Davis, March 1970.

"Business and the Development of the Ghetto Enterprise." New York: The Conference Board, Inc., 1971.

Cattell, Stuart. "Health, Welfare and Social Organizations in China-town, New York City." Community Service Society, 1962.

East/West (San Francisco). Weekly paper; various issues.

"The Future of Chinatown." Chinese-American Civic Association, 1972.

"Immigrants and Ethnicity: Ten Years of Changing Thought, 1960–1970." American Immigration and Citizenship Conference, 1972.

Jade Magazine (Los Angeles).

McCue, Andy. "The China Post and the Chinese Language Daily Newspapers of New York City." Columbia University Master's Thesis, 1974.

"National Asian American Studies Conference, II." California State University at San Jose, 1973.

Oei, Kendall. "Black Beans and Shrimp: A Study of the Chinese Cubans of Miami." Harvard University Undergraduate Thesis, 1974.

"Proceedings of the National Conference of Christian Work Among the Chinese in America." Honolulu, 1965.

"Roots: An Asian American Reader." University of California at Los Angeles, Asian Studies Center, 1971.

"San Francisco Chinese Community Citizen's Survey and Fact-Finding Committee Report." 1969.

U.S.-China Business Review (National Council for U.S.-China Trade), January-February 1974.

Wong, John. "Voting Patterns of Inner City Chinese in Boston." Unpublished paper, 1972.

ABOUT THE AUTHOR

BETTY LEE SUNG teaches at City College New York in the Department of Asian Studies, where she initiated a new field of study about Asians in the United States.

Her first book, Mountain of Gold, was published by Macmillan in 1967 and served to heighten ethnic consciousness among the Chinese in the United States. It was republished in paperback under the title, The Story of the Chinese in America, and it has become a standard work for ethnic studies courses. Professor Sung is also the author of two children's books, The Chinese in America (Macmillan, 1971) and Album of Chinese Americans (Franklin Watts, 1976).

The present volume on Chinese-American Manpower and Employment was done for the Manpower Administration of the Department of Labor by Professor Sung under a $68,000 research grant. Another of her publications is "Statistical Profile of the Chinese in the United States, 1970."

Professor Sung is an American-born Chinese who has lived and studied in China and the United States. She is a graduate of the University of Illinois with an M.L.S. degree from Queens College of the CUNY system. She speaks three Chinese dialects, which facilitates her work and research in the Chinese communities.

For many years Professor Sung wrote radio scripts, and she has had considerable editing experience with a number of large publishing firms in New York.

Professor Sung is married to Charles C. M. Chung. Her four children and his four children add up to eight in the family. Her husband works for the United Nations, and the family makes its home in Douglaston, New York.

ETHNICITY AND SUBURBAN LOCAL POLITICS
David J. Schnall

IMMIGRANT PROFESSIONALS IN THE UNITED
STATES: Discrimination in the Scientific Labor
Market
Bradley W. Parlin

POLITICIZING THE POOR: The Legacy of the War
on Poverty in a Mexican-American Community
Biliana C. S. Ambrecht

A SURVEY OF PUERTO RICANS IN THE U.S.
MAINLAND IN THE 1970s
Kal Wagenheim